Selected Essays of Jim W. Corder

Selected Essays of
Jim W. Corder

Pursuing the Personal in Scholarship, Teaching, and Writing

Edited by

JAMES S. BAUMLIN
Southwest Missouri State University

KEITH D. MILLER
Arizona State University

With a foreword by
Wendy Bishop

National Council of Teachers of English
1111 W. Kenyon Road, Urbana, Illinois 61801-1096

Corder's photograph, original art, and materials from unpublished manuscripts are printed with permission of Roberta Corder.

Manuscript Editor: Lee Erwin
Staff Editor: Bonny Graham
Interior Design: Jenny Jensen Greenleaf
Cover Design: Pat Mayer

NCTE Stock Number: 43091

Library of Congress Cataloging-in-Publication Data

Corder, Jim W. (Jim Wayne), 1929–1998
  [Essays. Selections]
  Selected essays of Jim W. Corder : pursuing the personal in scholarship, teaching, and writing / edited by James S. Baumlin and Keith D. Miller ; with a foreword by Wendy Bishop.
      p. cm.
  Includes bibliographical references and index.
  ISBN 0-8141-4309-1 ((pbk))
  1. English language—Rhetoric—Study and teaching—United States.
I. Baumlin, James S. II. Miller, Keith D. III. Title.
  PE1405 . U6C67 2004
  808' .042'071073—dc22
                                                    2004006589

Permissions Acknowledgments

"Aching for a Self," by James W. Corder, unpublished manuscript. Reprinted by permission of Roberta Corder.

"Argument as Emergence, Rhetoric as Love," by James W. Corder, 1985, *Rhetoric Review, 4,* pp. 16–32. Copyright 1985 by Lawrence Erlbaum Associates, Inc. Reprinted with permission.

"Hunting for *Ethos* Where They Say It Can't Be Found," by James W. Corder, 1989, *Rhetoric Review, 7,* pp. 299–316. Copyright 1989 by Lawrence Erlbaum Associates, Inc. Reprinted with permission.

"Hunting Lieutenant Chadbourne: A Search for *Ethos* Whether Real or Pretended," by James W. Corder, in *Ethos: New Essays in Rhetorical and Critical Theory,* edited by James S. Baumlin and Tita French Baumlin, Dallas: Southern Methodist University Press, 1994, pp. 343–65. Reprinted by permission of Southern Methodist University Press.

"I in Mine, You Elsewhere," by James W. Corder, unpublished manuscript. Reprinted by permission of Roberta Corder.

"Late Word from the Provinces," by James W. Corder, *New Mexico Humanities Review* 2 (1979): 24–27.

"A New Introduction to Psychoanalysis, Taken as a Version of Modern Rhetoric," by James W. Corder, *Pre/Text* 5 (1984): 137–69. Published by permission of *Pre/Text.*

"On the Way, Perhaps, to a New Rhetoric, but Not There Yet, and If We Do Get There, There Won't Be There Anymore," by James W. Corder, *College English* 47 (1985): 162–70. Copyright 1985 by the National Council of Teachers of English. Reprinted with permission.

"Places in the Mind," by James W. Corder, unpublished manuscript. Reprinted by permission of Roberta Corder.

"Studying Rhetoric and Teaching School," by James W. Corder, 1982, *Rhetoric Review*, *1*, pp. 4–36. Copyright 1982 by Lawrence Erlbaum Associates, Inc. Reprinted with permission.

"Varieties of Ethical Argument, with Some Account of the Significance of *Ethos* in the Teaching of Composition," by James W. Corder, *Freshman English News* 6 (1978): 1–23. Reprinted with permission of *Composition Studies*.

"What I Learned at School," by James W. Corder, *College Composition and Communication* 26 (1975): 330–34. Copyright 1975 by the National Council of Teachers of English. Reprinted with permission.

CONTENTS

Contents

ILLUSTRATIONS

FOREWORD

Looking for Ethos in All the Right Places

WENDY BISHOP

I am not a writer by any definition that the world would legitimate. I am not known as a writer. Nevertheless, I must confess that I sometimes think of myself as a writer. It's a comforting thing to do on a cold night when wine isn't sufficient. I can safely admit that I have published a few poems and personal essays because I am confident that the journals in which they appeared are so lost to the nation at large as to make my work perfectly secure from pubic scrutiny. . . . I sometimes privately think of myself as a writer—it's a helluva lot better than thinking of yourself as a dean, a court scribe, or a fool.

JIM W. CORDER, "Hunting for Ethos"

Here's the rhetorical situation. I want you to read this book, this writing, this person, Jim Corder. On the one hand, he imagined that you never would, that these essays would long stay safely tucked away in the pages of *Rhetoric Review* or *Freshman English News,* never to achieve the heft and weight of *volume.* Therefore, he could say what he wanted, as he wanted, and to hell with you, imagined reader. On the other hand, he suspected that you would read him and so in his claim to obscurity offers a Corderian "aw shucks," a West Texas deadpan, knowing that maybe, indeed likely, you would be reading him long hereafter. On first or second encounter with the several Jim Corders, whose voices, *ethoi, personae* braid into the rich fabric of this text, you'll realize that no writer cares more fiercely about how he appears, how he sounds, and what he is saying. "The presiding problem I've already mentioned is that all discourse is ethical, revealing speakers' characters by design or by default. Style is the revelation of identity, the syndrome of character, open to diagnosis" ("Studying Rhetoric" 30). And few care more about readers, about making connections with them. By design and by default, not a one is more engaged with the rhetorical condition we call writing, with the image of rhetor that he evokes through his own texts.

So he writes on, scattering textual clues like breadcrumbs, inviting us to follow them. In *Reading as Rhetorical Invention*, Doug Brent reminds us that

> Both the reader and the hearer [. . .] must construct the charac-
> ter of the rhetor. Each must build, from clues in the text, not
> only an evoked meaning but also an evoked writer, a personal-
> ity that lies beyond the text and through the arguments he uses,
> the criteria he demonstrates, and the claims he asserts, projects
> a character that the reader will admire to a lesser or greater
> extent. (67)

By entering this collection, taking this journey, you are agreeing to such a compact with a writer who is eager to meet you at every point of contact.

In "Varieties of Ethical Argument," Jim Corder identifies the tensions that arise when writer and reader travel together with-out really knowing each other (they always hope to, they never can). Since the writer sets out first, arranging words for imagined readers, he is often a nervous package of disclosure and discov-ery. Corder quotes from Georges Gusdorf's *Speaking*: "The more I communicate, the less I express myself; the more I express my-self, the less I communicate" ("Varieties" 3). This seemed to be Jim Corder's lifelong fear, that words would never bring us, truly, to each other. Yet I can't help thinking when reading these pages that, over time, Corder transcended that stylistic conundrum by delivering his rhetorical presence to us, roundly. In his writing, style *becomes* substance and substance delights in its complicated dress. "*Ethos* is generative and fruitful when the time and space stewarded by the speaker give free room for another to live in"

("Varieties" 20), explains Corder in one of his many searches for the meaning of the term.

So we stand here together.

I think this collection is important. I think the work is solid and substantial. I have reasons, three (and more than three): Jim Corder was a writer inventively ahead of his time who also looked back ferociously. He advances, he retreats, he's waves on a shore carving out a coastline. He ranges widely and offers space in his texts for others to enter. He invites co-thinking. Consider the transitions (alone) found in just a single essay (this is one of two "found poems" I'll share):

> I want to . . . . Surely so . . . . This brings me back to . . . . I want to propose . . . . At any rate . . . . In this section . . . . I want to talk . . . . For example . . . . We have assumed . . . . We have accepted . . . . We tolerate . . . . In our teaching . . . . Enough . . . . Which leads me . . . . I did what a scholar should do . . . . This was perfect . . . . You must understand . . . . At any rate . . . . It seems a strange world . . . . Well, at last . . . . The problem is . . . . I'll illustrate by veering aside . . . . Later, I learned . . . . Later still, I learned more . . . . And later still, I discovered . . . . Finally . . . . Perhaps you'll understand . . . . It's hard to find . . . . Must I learn . . . . I began this section . . . . We like to think . . . . Well, enough of that . . . . When I was young . . . . We look ahead . . . . But of course we can't see . . . . Sometimes, everything seems to be coming loose . . . . I don't want to linger indefinitely . . . . If we look . . . . If we look . . . . To be sure . . . . I want to tell . . . . Not far from . . . . My family . . . . As it turned out . . . . For a moment . . . . If you stand . . . . Imagine . . . . Imagine that, if you will . . . . A good teacher . . . . I am trying to say . . . . What are these lessons and hopes? . . . . I'm much interested in mavericks . . . . We are inclined to believe . . . . To the extent that this is true . . . . The trouble is . . . . And worse . . . . I'll take the last first and only briefly . . . . And that brings me back to . . . . I'm not proposing anarchy . . . . First . . . . Second . . . . Third . . . . I started out a while ago . . . . And so we are left in a dilemma . . . . And so we go on . . . .
> ("Studying Rhetoric")

There's something to be said about a writer whose every textual turn works to construct character and exhibit voice (pretty quickly I'll get out of the way and let him speak more fully for himself).

This is *ethos* taken to the *n*th degree, found and pondered wherever it can be found.

Jim Corder offers readers a portrait of a writer as a person, as a text, as a voice, as a character, as a process of learning that exemplifies the generally hidden life of many thinkers and writers. Jim Corder offers a commodious definition of rhetoric and composition, a solid joining of the two, inquisitive, wry, worried. His work is a gift to those in the profession who often feel washed over by the storm waves of many competing voices. If you accept the challenge of reading across this one life in letters, I can pretty much guarantee you'll see ways to better understand your own. And that's the power and the pleasure of reading a "selected works" by any poet or prose author (and Corder was both). There's a geological satisfaction to be found in these pieces. Each builds on the one that precedes, each partakes of that which went before, repeating a theme, melody, subtext, metaphor; a key phrase; a meditative kernel of thought. Yet each essay advances, grows more substantial, just as the layers of pearl grow around grit (to change metaphors yet again).

But claims, appeals, arguments, examples: how effective is *my* rhetoric here? Why should you read? You may suspect that I'm merely performing tricks of the introductory trade, so what else can I do to introduce you to these writings? Perhaps I'll begin with the way I introduced Jim to my husband at the dinner table recently. My husband loves my spaghetti sauce and was dwelling on it. To compete with (or complete) our circle of two, sharing and joking at dinner, I brought along Jim Corder, explaining what I had found in previous days of learning, unlearning, relearning Jim's work by tracking through a messy clutch of manuscript some four-hundred pages long. (This might be one of Jim's phrases: "a messy clutch" would suit him, for he often speaks of himself as metaphorically "doing a jig," and one of his determined strategies is to celebrate the accessible and the colloquial.) Pages spread out on an ottoman before an easy chair (I might investigate the origin of the term "easy chair" as Jim investigated the phrases "well-heeled" and "down at the heel" in one essay). Pages carried along with a pile of books and pillows to the bed where I do much of the nibbling and sampling I call reading.

That is, Jim had been our silent companion for some days now—how to present him at this our dinner assembly?

"It's been wonderful," I said, "to read a collection of someone's work over the years, across the years. To see how it evolves. He was a rhetorician and a writing teacher. A philosopher," I explained, though the sauce still had my husband's greater attention.

"But Corder was also always trying to grapple with social constructionism," I continued, "with the frustrating-to-any-author arguments that there is no author there, really. But he was/is amazingly there in his text, enacting his idea of *ethos*. He grew up in Texas. You know, reading him reminds me of *The Last Picture Show* territory."

We had rewatched that video recently, one of several left behind by my husband's graduate school friend, Kevin, some long years ago. Almost an antique (I found this oxymoron in a newspaper ad recently), the videocassette had been taped off of TV before the entrance of DVDs to the replay scene. The fact that the old technology (which somehow suited the black-and-white movie, interrupted by odd, time-capsule glimpses of 1980s TV commercials) would make me oddly nostalgic was Corderian.

"As a rhetorical philosopher," I continued, "Corder struggled to reconcile rhetorical theory—which requires that you aim to make your presence known, felt, remembered—and contemporary theory—which suggests we're each just a handful of dust blowing across the empty streets of a broken down Texas town.

"Also," I said, "he links talk about rhetoric—ethos and argument—to talk about composition—writing and writers—in a way that makes it useful, contemporary, critical, and crucial. In fact, he was the one whose essay about writing all the essays he assigned his students got me to try the same and changed my teaching profoundly."

My husband was hungry. I didn't really outshine the dinner with my talk. And that's what Jim Corder was worried about. What is the work of our words? And, when we're gone, what remains? Later, I found myself calling to my husband, who was playing guitar in his study: "And he went every Saturday to the public library. Spent the morning there. He tells us so. I love that. It's the best fact."

And for me, it is. Somewhere in this collection you'll find that it is for Corder too. And his quiet habits (pipe smoker, library goer, Las Vegas tourist, teacher, poet, artist, essayist) reveal but don't unduly tidy up a life.

I'm partial to public libraries, having worked in one during high school. Some days I would shelve books furiously fast so I could lose myself at the back of a far stack and read; one week I decided to sample every category in the Dewey decimal system. Hours passed. Libraries aren't what they were. And I could mourn them in a Corderian way, missing the solid *thunk* of card catalog drawers. Mourning them would include doubting the value of the old ways, trying to believe in the benefits of all new, head-turning technologies. Balancing and weighing the past and the future on the fulcrum of the present. But perhaps I shouldn't miss the geeky hunt through microfilm, newspapers wedged into long wooden dowels and hung out for browsers, my own attachment to pulling out art books from the oversized book shelf. After all, I was also an active, impatient adolescent who equally craved release from the library into imagined future lives. Still, I'm unable to put library memories aside, the scent of the date-due stamp's ink pad or the thin, amber, expensive binding glue, because they are the source of the literacy narrative that is me. In fact, I still go happily to the public library for my mystery novels. For 1940s videos. For the free and unexpected collage of texts, images, and data that prime my writer's memory and predict me into new thinking. Give me a public over a university library any day, rich with character and characters.

I resonate to Corder's work, then, because I recognize some of my own rhetorical concerns and moves in his, my own stylistic preferences; but I think that any reader might and most readers should.

In their introduction to this volume, editors Keith D. Miller and James S. Baumlin remind us that "Corder regularly situates his essays in the specifics of time, place, race, gender, history, personal and cultural prejudice, and personal psychology" (15), a psychology marked by continual misremembering and misunderstanding, and that's another element that I admire and set before you. Jim Corder had a manner of constructing character while showing it: "I taught the first course called a rhetoric course at the university where I work. Actually, I called it 'Rhetoric and Chocolate.' In 1966, I didn't think anyone would enroll if I just called it 'rhetoric'" ("Notes" 96).

Like so many writing teachers, I labor in my own way to help writers discover how fully the universal resides in the specific, to share my literature-bred love for the detail-work of writing, the apt phrase; the unexpected metaphor; the rich, narrative aside. I suggest to my students that our texts should have their feet on the ground. If we're writing from a North Florida city, say it's Tallahassee, the thick summer monsoon thunderstorm that sent sheets of rain down the roof—breaking off the large cups of white magnolia blossoms from the tree above and bruising them to the brick walkway, causing me to shut down my computer—should somehow find a way to slightly dampen our discussion. Just so, for Jim Corder: so much depends on explaining that a course called rhetoric would have no takers. So much depends on his readers' understanding that a course called "Rhetoric and Chocolate" could actually go on the books in the 1960s.

Here then, as my final invocation to readers, are just a few of my many favorite Corder lines, offered up in a found pantoum.

Postmodern Pragmatist

Each of us is a narrative.
Each of us lives in a province.
Each of us houses a crowd.
We are always standing somewhere.

Each of us lives in a province.
Sometimes we don't exist.
We are always standing somewhere.
I count myself at the expense of others.

Sometimes we don't exist.
How shall we ever say *love* to each other?
I count myself at the expense of others.
Sometimes I think I am real.

How shall we ever say *love* to each other?
When you write, you are always alone.
Sometimes I think I am real
Though lost and scattered in pieces.

> When you write, you are never alone.
> Each of us is an argument
> Though lost and scattered in pieces.
> Which moment should I have saved?
>
> Each of us is an argument.
> Each of us houses a crowd.
> Which moment should I have saved?
> Each of us is a narrative.

Like a book of poetry, this one should be dipped into. Sampled. Savored. I encourage you to read and rummage around. Quite simply, Jim Corder's writing made me want to write. For myself and to you. I call that a gift. This rhetoric of connection and concern.

Works Cited

Brent, Douglas. *Reading as Rhetorical Invention: Knowledge, Persuasion, and the Teaching of Research-Based Writing.* Urbana, IL: NCTE, 1992.

Corder, Jim. "From Rhetoric to Grace: Propositions 55–81 about Rhetoric, Propositions 1–54 and 82 *et seq.* Being as Yet Unstated; or, Getting from the Classroom to the World." *Rhetoric Society Quarterly* 14 (1984): 15–28.

_____. "Hunting for *Ethos* Where They Say It Can't Be Found." *Rhetoric Review* 7 (1989): 299–316.

_____. "Notes on a Rhetoric of Regret." *Composition Studies/Freshman English News* 25 (1995): 94–105.

_____. "Studying Rhetoric and Teaching School." *Rhetoric Review* 1 (1982): 4–36.

_____. "Varieties of Ethical Argument, with Some Account of the Significance of *Ethos* in the Teaching of Composition." *Freshman English News* 6 (1978): 1–23.

A Note on the Text and Acknowledgments

Through four decades, Jim W. Corder wrote much and published widely, so much so that even his most devoted readers find themselves in occasionally new territory. Along with his better-known essays, we have gathered together pieces that Corder had scattered through a variety of journals, as well as selections from three unpublished book manuscripts. By beginning and ending with personal narratives, our collection makes no ultimate division between Corder's scholarly and his personal, nonfiction prose. How could we do otherwise? While some few of his writings are exclusively academic and some belletristic, the majority refuse to allow any such distinction.

In addition to his published work, we include excerpts from three manuscripts left largely (though not entirely) finished upon Corder's passing. In comparison with his finely polished published work, these remain sketchy and somewhat loose in structure. Weaving together original with previously published materials, they reveal Corder's attempt, rather desperate and finally impossible, to complete a life's work within months: their roughness occasionally shows, in other words. (For example, the works cited lists for these essays contain only those sources we could unquestionably identify.) Still, their experimental, generically hybrid structures and often surprising insights gesture toward where Corder was heading, even if he did not arrive. They are worth our reading.

We have made occasional abridgements to his essays (indicated in each case by ellipses). Throughout his career, Corder continually revisited and revised key passages from previous essays, particularly those passages outlining ideas central to his rhetorical theory. Where we have cut, we have for the most part removed materials summarized or elaborated elsewhere in our collection. Still, readers should prepare to hear arguments and passages echoing and reechoing from one essay to another: such echoing demonstrates the unity and coherence of Corderian thought.

We are aware of the arbitrariness of our selections, which represent a fragment of Corder's life work. We are also aware of the ways that our ordering of materials might restrict a reader's unfolding impression of Corder the stylist, essayist, teacher, scholar. While we bow to convention and present his work in roughly chronological order, we would not at all mind if readers reversed order, turning to the mature Corder first. Read thus, his writings offer a richly ornamented set of lacquered boxes wherein the last, most spacious essay opens to reveal within itself all that the previous essay professed (or thought it knew); this second then opens to reveal its mastery over the next essay's slightly neater contents, and so on to the first, neat essay nestled within the whole. In the end, we believe that order of reading does not much matter and would encourage readers to map out their own itineraries.

We thank the following journals and press for permission to reprint materials. "On the Way, Perhaps, to a New Rhetoric" (47 [1985]: 162–70) first appeared in *College English*. "What I Learned at School" (26 [1975]: 330–34) first appeared in *College Composition and Communication*. "Varieties of Ethical Argument" (6 [1978]: 1–23) first appeared in *Composition Studies* (formerly *Freshman English News*). "Late Word from the Provinces" (2 [1979]: 24–27) first appeared in the *New Mexico Humanities Review*. "A New Introduction to Psychoanalysis, Taken as a Version of Modern Rhetoric" (5 [1984]: 137–69) first appeared in *Pre/Text* (and we thank graphic artist Matt Frauenhoffer for redesigning images originally printed in this essay). Several essays appeared first in *Rhetoric Review*: "Studying Rhetoric and Teaching School" (1 [1982]: 4–36); "Argument as Emergence, Rhetoric as Love" (4 [1985]: 16–32); and "Hunting for *Ethos* Where They Say It Can't Be Found" (7 [1989]: 299–316). "Hunting Lieutenant Chadbourne" first appeared in *Ethos: New Essays in Rhetorical and Critical Theory*, ed. James S. Baumlin and

Tita French Baumlin (Dallas: Southern Methodist UP, 1994 [343–65]).

For their assistance with the bibliography, we thank Kathleen Weinkauf and Ross Chodan.

Corder's photograph, original art, and materials from unpublished manuscripts are printed with permission of Roberta Corder, whose encouragement has sustained us from the beginning of this project.

It grieves us that Wendy Bishop did not live to see this project come to fruition. We thank her husband, Conrad D. Newman, for permission to print her preface to this volume.

CHAPTER ONE

Introduction

KEITH D. MILLER AND JAMES S. BAUMLIN

Beginning "about 1965" (as he writes in the passage below), Jim W. Corder joined some dozen prominent professors— including Edward P. J. Corbett, W. Ross Winterowd, Janice Lauer, James L. Kinneavy, and Frank D'Angelo—in a movement to re- vive the study of rhetoric in departments of English:

> Before 1965 or thereabouts there were all along, I expect, some English teachers who enjoyed the insights, perceptions, and guid- ance of rhetorical study, though they seem for some generations to have done so rather quietly, without widely recommending that study to others [. . .].
>
> By about 1965, however, there began to emerge a genera- tion of English teachers [. . .] who had discovered rhetoric, seen its uses in the teaching of composition and elsewhere, and, more- over, wanted to tell others [. . .]. Most in this first modern genera- tion of rhetoric students were not formally schooled in rhetoric [. . .]. Most had come out of graduate school more or less pre- pared to teach and to study [literature]. At some later moment, then—perhaps because they needed to teach freshman composi- tion and wanted to do so well [. . .]—they found or turned to what others were finding in rhetoric and began to explore its uses and to practice its possibilities. ("Studying Rhetoric and Teaching School" 4; this volume, 102)

Over succeeding decades the many, rich contributions of this "first modern generation" have been pervasively debated and largely absorbed by compositionists. But, even though Corder generated close to one hundred scholarly and professional publications— many in prominent venues—his contributions to the field have seldom been debated and rarely absorbed. Why so?

Some readers may have underestimated him, because his work appeared at times too simple: eschewing jargon, he preferred to mask his complex thought in a colloquial idiom. Some may have dismissed him for the opposite reason, because his work resisted summary and seemed too complicated. And others may have balked at his constant, presumptuous tactic of transgressing the sacrosanct barriers separating disciplines, methods, and genres. Throughout his earlier career (roughly from 1971 to 1988), for example, Corder characteristically blended composition theory with a vastly expanded rendition of Aristotelian rhetoric; existential phenomenology with a neo-Augustinian Judeo-Christianity; and literary analysis (particularly of eighteenth-century poetry) with rhetorical criticism of contemporary magazine advertisements and television. The late Corder (roughly from 1989 until his death in 1998) typically fused autobiographical reminiscences with postmodern or post-postmodern explorations of the failures of memory, history, and identity; rhetorical theory with psychoanalysis; and expressions of a deep longing for success with confessions of loss, failure, and guilt.

Even during the heyday of postmodernism in rhetoric and composition studies (extending from the late 1980s to the early 1990s), Corder anticipated the resurgence of expressivism. While embracing constructionist theory as a necessary and laudable corrective to Western logocentrism and its pervasive—sometimes explicit and sometimes deeply implicit—assumptions about "universal truth," Corder could never fully assent to the postmodern erasure of "personal agency" or, to use Corder's favorite Aristotelian term, *ethos*. As he argues throughout his later writings, the erasure of "the personal" is never complete.

We believe strongly, therefore, that Corder's yet-to-be-absorbed theory and scholarly praxis can and should contribute significantly to current debates in composition studies. As we observe below, part of that contribution lies in his struggle to move beyond the impasse facing social constructionism and expressivism, seeking instead their *rapprochement*.

Corderian *Rapprochement* and the New Preeminence of "the Personal"

In 1999, Wendy Bishop decried the social-constructionist "marginalization" and ultimate "dismissal" of expressivism, wherein "key-expressivists (so called, not self-labeled) are frequently cast as convenient straw-men, as now-aging, no longer composition-ally-hip, and therefore slightly embarrassing advocates of a 1960s touchy-feely pedagogy from which professionals in composition are currently trained to distance themselves" ("Places to Stand" 10). In 2000, Sherrie Gradin complained similarly: "[F]or the past decade we have been trapped in an adversarial relation between expressive [. . .] and social-epistemic theories and their proponents" (403)—during which time, she protested, the latter have become increasingly self-promoting and rigidly doctrinaire. Yet a year later, in the issue of *College English* she guest-edited devoted to "the personal" in academic writing, Jane E. Hindman marked the reemergence of expressivism. She observed: "Any academic even vaguely aware of current trends in scholarship has noted the preeminence of 'the personal' in the last few years" ("Special Focus" 34), during which time such "retrograde," expressivist terms as "self, voice, experience, the personal" (Kameen 100) have become once again "compositionally-hip."[1]

Implicit in this search for rapprochement is a recognition that theories of social constructionism have by now largely completed themselves and, having reached the limits of what they can teach us, stand themselves in need of correction, qualification, and critique: such is the way of all mature theory. Perhaps social constructionism remains the dominant voice in composition studies; still, seeking what lies beyond, scholars are asking what such a perspective has forgotten, ignored, or misunderstood.

At the same time, one can ask whether expressivist rhetoric—whether from 1974 or 2004—enjoys a sufficiently strong foundation in theory to engage constructionism in an equal dialogue. Expressivists, as Alan W. France contends,

> have largely failed "to articulate the theories underlying their practices in any systematic way [. . .] while social construction-ists were working out epistemological positions and promoting theoretical self consciousness [. . .]" (O'Donnell 425). But the inverse is true as well. For their part, social constructionists have not worked out much of a theory of personal agency, failing largely to offer a way out of the "disabling postmodern box of the always already determined subject" (Flannery 707). (148–49)[2]

The claim that expressivists "have largely failed 'to articulate the theories underlying their practices'" has merit; certainly our profession's taste for theory has increased with each succeeding decade, making much pedagogy of the 1970s (representing the high point of American expressivism) seem naïve in comparison.

Yet, beginning in the late 1980s, Corder's "personalized" investigations of poststructuralist and social-constructionist thought enacted the very dialectic that France, Gradin, and others have sought. An amalgam of classical rhetoric, contemporary psychology, and existential phenomenology, Corderian rhetoric offers a complete, coherent, fully articulated "theory of personal agency" capable of standing as an adequate counterpoint and complement to social constructionism.[3]

We do not describe a mere pendulum swing. By asserting Corder's continuing relevance to composition studies, we do not seek to replace the current focus on "the social" with a previous generation's focus on "the writing self." Nor do we wish to resuscitate expressivism per se, which constructionist theory continues to discount: we are content to follow current discussion of "the personal" in scholarship, though we refract its vocabulary through Corderian practice. To revisit Corder's strongest writing is never simply to return to expressivism: as one of the most wide-ranging, original, speculative, and experimental writers of the previous generation, Corder has been waiting for us all, rather, to catch up to him.

An Outline of Corderian Rhetoric

Just as expressivism proves too narrow a term to hold Corderian theory, so classicism falls short as well. Yes, Corder does reinterpret the canons of classical, Aristotelian rhetoric. As he writes in "From Rhetoric into Other Studies" (1993),

> The vocabulary of rhetoric—*invention, structure, style, occasion, audience,* and other terms—is ubiquitous and inevitable and can be used in the discussion of diverse rhetorics: All statements come from somewhere, however knowable or undiscoverable, emerge as structures and styles, however deliberate or accidental, and

occur on some occasion for some audience, however untimely, however small. Any line of inquiry, any field of interest, any subject matter, then, can be taken as a rhetoric or as a set of rhetorics. That, I think, makes it possible to use the vocabulary of rhetoric to discuss any human interest. (95)

The last point above leads to one of Corder's bolder claims: *everything is rhetoric*—a phrase that became, alternatively, a rallying cry among Corder's students and a point of confusion among his critics. This statement means no more (nor less) than that every human perception, thought, or production *can be redescribed within the vocabulary* of the Aristotelian and Ciceronian canons. That is, all human knowledge, all social institutions, all cultural practices, all arts, all sciences, all ideologies, all habits of mind, all thoughts and imaginings must be *invented* (the first canon); ordered and *arranged* (the second); clothed in *style* (the third); recorded and retrievable in *memory*, whether human or artificial (the fourth); and *delivered* (the fifth), put into action or performed.

In Corderian rhetoric, indeed, the Aristotelian vocabulary describes not just the verbal structures of discourse but the cognitive structures and habits of human behavior, which in turn reflect our psychobiological structures. All human activity, all human knowing proceeds by processes of invention, arrangement, style, memory, and delivery. Human beings *live* by such rhetorical-cognitive processes: we invent and arrange or give order to our worlds, we create ourselves out of stylistic habits and preserve our ordered experiences as memories—and, all the while, our actions, thoughts, moods constitute a delivery or performance of self. The human being, in this sense, is a psychobiological system that at the same time organizes and expresses itself as a rhetoric.[4]

Like Edward P. J. Corbett, James L. Kinneavy, and other representatives of what Kathleen Welch has called the "Heritage School" (1) of composition studies, Corder remained a devoted student of classical rhetoric. At the same time—and certainly more than his colleagues aforementioned—Corder sought to pour new wine into the old vessels, radically reinterpreting the classical canons and vocabulary. Whereas Corbett, for example, presented "classical rhetoric as a closed system" fixed in its terminology and "applicable to a relatively narrow range of discourse" (Schnakenberg 164), Corder continually expands its boundaries and capacities. In contrast, thus, with Corbett's "severely limited view of invention" (Schnakenberg 164), Corder treats invention dialectically:

> By its nature, invention asks us to open ourselves to the richness of creation, to plumb its depths, search its expanses, and track its chronologies. But the moment we speak or write, we are no longer open; we have chosen, whether deliberately or not, and so have closed ourselves off from some possibilities. Invention wants openness; structure and style demand closure. We are asked to be perpetually open and always closing. In this sense, rhetoric is a model of the examined life. If we stay open, we cannot speak or act; if we stay closed, we have succumbed to dogma and rigidity. ("From Rhetoric to Grace" 21)

Here and elsewhere, Corderian invention reveals its existentialist roots, in that it arises from (and in some sense constitutes) experience:

> Whenever we use language, some choices have already been made and other choices must be made. Our past accompanies us into our statements and exercises its influence whether or not we are entirely aware of it. Before we speak, we have lived; when we speak, we must continually choose because our mouths will not say two words simultaneously and our hands will not write two words simultaneously. Whether consciously or not, we always station ourselves somewhere when we use language. That means that what rhetoricians call *invention* always occurs. ("From Rhetoric to Grace" 17)

The varied ways that we "station ourselves" in language define not just our modes of invention but, concomitantly, the varied shapes of *ethos*—in effect, our modes of self-invention. Noting that "ethos occurs in more than one [. . .] form," Corder expands the classical-Aristotelian discussion, describing no less than five versions: *dramatic ethos, gratifying ethos, functional ethos, efficient ethos,* and—most important to Corder's existentialist rhetoric—*generative ethos* ("Varieties" 14; this volume, 77–78), whose "self-authenticating language" invites audiences "into a commodious universe" ("From Rhetoric to Grace" 20). In so striving, such a speaker seeks to delay or "shove back," as Corder puts it, the inevitable "closure" of language:

> When we speak, we stand somewhere, and our standing place makes both known and silent claims upon us. We make truth, if at all, out of what is incomplete, or partial [. . .]. Yet language is a closure, for we cannot speak two words simultaneously. Generative language seeks to shove back the restraints of closure, to make in language a commodious universe, to stretch words out beyond our private universes. (20–21)

"Generative *ethos*," thus, proves "always in the process of making itself and of liberating hearers to make themselves. In this form of *ethos* there is always more coming. It is never over, never wholly fenced into the past. It is a speaking out from history into history" (14). For this reason, too, "generative ethos" is "never completely achieved" (21); it is for this same reason that "argument is emergence toward the other, [. . .] a willingness to dramatize one's narrative in progress before the other" ("Argument as Emergence" 26; this volume, 183).

We would like to place the above remarks within a broader outline of Corderian theory. Of first importance is Corder's discovery of multeity within the traditional, European canon. As we have seen, the Aristotelian theory of invention yields to a theory of multiple "inventive worlds" and, further, of multiple rhetorics; similar expansions can be noted within his discussions of arrangement, style, and memory. Second, the structures and processes of rhetoric are shown to mirror the structures and processes of human consciousness. Third, the Corderian/existentialist emphasis upon *ethos*—that is, the responsible "I" that both precedes and is constructed by discourse—provides the essential ethical-intellectual ground of argument. And it is this abiding concern for "generative *ethos*" that turns virtually every essay Corder ever wrote into a *personal* essay. Corderian theory, thus, undergirds his own practice of the "scholarship of the personal."

Corderian theory rests upon the conviction that all discourse proceeds from premises regarding, not simply the nature of language and reality, but also the nature of human consciousness. For this reason, Corder argues, "[W]e may not get a new rhetoric until we get a new kind of creature" ("On the Way" 170; this volume, 201), that is, a new *psychology* or model of the person, upon which a new model of rhetoric in general, and of *ethos* in particular, can be constructed. To this effect, each theorist of rhetoric makes assumptions, explicit or implicit, regarding the structures of the psyche as well as the nature and effects of language, so that changes in psychological theory enable corresponding changes in one's theory of discourse. The history of rhetoric bears out this assertion: witness the Platonic *psychagogia* or leading of the soul by means of speech, the Aristotelian *ēthē* or "group psychologies," the so-called psychological rhetorics of eighteenth-century British tradition, and the numerous modern theories of discourse premised upon the theories of Sigmund Freud, Jacques Lacan, and Carl Rogers, among others. Yet Corder argues more radically, more consistently, and more insistently than anyone else for the adequation of rhetoric and consciousness, going so far as to describe the psyche itself *as a rhetorical system*. And as Corder grows in his understanding of the psyche's complexities—particularly with respect to the workings of memory and the unconscious—his theory of rhetoric grows correspondingly complex.

Though Corder makes occasional use of Freudian concepts, American psychologist Carl Rogers proves the more pervasive (and, perhaps, more salutary) influence, providing a natural extension of Corder's ethic of communication. Rather than maintain a speaker's expertise, power, or superiority over an audience, Rogerian rhetoric affirms the co-presence, equal authority, and mutual responsibility of all participants. In Rogerian rhetoric, the rhetor/therapist practices arts *of listening* and of caring, nonjudgmental response: proceeding from an existentialist "ethic of caring" (Noddings 38–39), Rogerianism teaches therapists and clients alike the tender/risky art of "emergence toward the other," both sides remaining open to the other's inventive world.

Rogers's influence is especially noteworthy in Corder's "Argument as Emergence: Rhetoric as Love" (1985). But Corder remains Rogerian only in his happier moments. In much of his later writing, Corder acknowledges the failure, rather, of such openness and self-invention: *ethos* becomes as much a concealment as a revelation of character; our secrets remain unspoken, and we are as likely to lie about ourselves (to ourselves, as well as to others). In a word, we *disappear* within our texts. Also, Corder's Rogerian rhetoric assumes a capacity for growth and change that the human creature, quite frankly, resists: once formed, old habits die hard. Most rhetoric, however noble, however well intended, falls short of the "talking cure" of which we mortals all stand in such great need.

Still, the problem of identity remains central to Corderian theory, both early and late. Through *ethos* we establish contact with the other, inviting the other into our inventive worlds. Even as he acknowledged the original, Aristotelian definitions, Corder's own theory—most fully articulated in the early essay, "Varieties of Ethical Argument" (1978)—becomes a logical extension of his existentialism. Within the classical discussions of ethical appeal, there is typically no sense of risk on the speaker's part, nor is the audience conceived of as an equally active participant. Yet the "generative *ethos*" that Corder describes is jointly produced— a collaboration between speaker and audience. Hence the success—or failure—of communication remains, quintessentially, an effect of *ethos*, not *logos* or *pathos*.

For Corder, *ethos* is implicated in all aspects of rhetoric: that is, one cannot even speak about invention, or arrangement, or style (or memory, or delivery) without orienting these processes from within the existentialist ethic of the responsible "I." Corder views the Aristotelian *topoi*, too, as so many structures of consciousness. Noting that the *topoi* "were the 'regions,' the 'haunts,' the 'places' where certain categories of arguments resided" ("Learning" 246), Corder radicalizes such spatial, indeed geographical metaphors, redefining topical invention as "places" *in the mind*:

> A place in the mind is a locale where one belongs to an inventive world and can begin to know it and the varieties of thought it provokes and evokes, the locale where an inventive world gains sufficient dimension and quality to promote thought that is useful even if partial [. . .]. (246)

In typical Corderian fashion, Corder presents his theory of multiple invention within a sly narrative of self-analysis and self-discovery. Noting that "I heard myself asking, 'How many places are there in a mind?'" he continues his musings:

In one place in my mind I am a moderately splendid fellow, or at
least pretty all right, *and that allows me to think in some ways.*
In another place I find myself wholly conventional, *and that,
too, allows me to think in certain ways.* [. . .] "How many places
are there in a mind?" I remember thinking. *"Can there be wholly
different inventive worlds swirling inside one head?"* I remember
wondering, and I remember answering, *"Of course there can
be."* (246; emphasis added)

In *Yonder*, Corder goes further, describing not just the workings
of multiple inventions but of the multiple rhetorics—that is, the
"diverse personal rhetorics, cultural rhetorics, folk rhetorics, family rhetorics, emotional rhetorics, physiological rhetorics, and on,
and on" (166) that each of us simultaneously inhabits. Topographical metaphors continue. "Each of us," he writes, "is a gathering place for a host of rhetorical universes":

Some of them we inhabit alone, and some of them we occupy
without knowing that we do so. Each of us is a busy corner
where multiple rhetorical universes intersect. Each of us is a cosmos. All rhetorical universes are still present. The debris of all
our generations is always around us and in us. Sometimes they
cross or try to mix. Sometimes we don't remember them well or
keep order among them. Each of us is a crowd. (165–66)[5]

Corder's typically brief discussions of arrangement (the second
division of traditional rhetorical study) treat it as the dialectical
counterpart of invention: working together in a sort of systole-
diastole movement, arrangement "closes" or delimits what invention "opens up." And such closings remain necessary within
the heartbeat of living discourse. Invention without arrangement
remains a communicative impossibility, yielding mere psycho-
babble.[6] For "structure," Corder writes, "equals meaning"
("From Rhetoric to Grace" 19).

Corderian existentialism discovers "at least two definitions"
(19) of style, the third canon of Western rhetoric. Within the first
version, *"style* signifies something very much like personal identity. In this sense, *style* is a name for the way a person goes about
his or her life, the way a person moves among choices and makes
selections, the way a person bobs, weaves, or plows straight
through his or her own life" (19). Having acknowledged that

"everyone *has* a style in this sense; everyone *is* a style in this sense" (19; emphasis added), Corder offers a second, more generative possibility:

> Sometimes we unwittingly lock ourselves into styles; sometimes we do so out of arrogance or ignorance or dogma. Style understood in this sense need not, however, persist unchanged, for style has another meaning. *Style,* or better, *styles,* is a name for enabling capacities—things we learn that let us do other things, methods we acquire, abilities we acquire. Style understood in this sense can free or enlarge style taken as personal identity. (19)

Corder goes on to note the dangers of inauthenticity: "if a person adopts a style (as enabling capacity) without genuinely making it his or her own, without learning from it, then style in this sense becomes affectation" (19). Not surprisingly, style provides an instrument of "generative *ethos.*"

Corderian psychology—particularly his redescription of topical invention as "places in the mind"—spills into the fourth traditional canon, memory. Whereas "generative *ethos*" remains future-oriented and open to change, it is within memory that our identities are recorded and sustained. Corderian memory mirrors the structures of narrative: expressive (indeed, constitutive) of identity, the stories we tell construct a "home-place for the self." For Corder, what one has become accords with *where one has been:* hence his obsessive attention to place, worked out in a series of unpublished travelogues (to Las Vegas and the Carolinas, among other locales) numbering many hundreds of pages.

More than provide a stable, external reference-point for previous experience, place expresses a quasimagical power in Corder's early writings, involved in the very creation and sustenance of personal identity (see, in this regard, his "Late Word from the Provinces"). While Corder was never directly influenced by Jungian psychology, nonetheless such writing treats place archetypally: that is, as a numinous physical presence capable of bearing witness to one's own living, human presence. To have an identity is to be "at home" in such a place, even when it is rendered as a memory, a "place in the mind."

Yet, as with virtually every element of Corderian rhetoric, memory, too, becomes multidimensional. In his early writings, memory provides the ground—the imaginative topography, as it were—of personal narrative (and, hence, of identity). In his later, often more pessimistic writings, memory fails to anchor identity within a stable, objective history. In the first (existentialist) usage, one inhabits, one *is*, the stories that one tells; in the second (postmodern) usage, one disappears, sinking into the traces of one's texts. Later works, thus, record the narrator's loss of "home-place": of his hometown, Jayton, of the farmhouse of his youth. Though he revisits the scenes of his youthful self making, the "home-places" have all vanished, taking with them his earlier versions of self. In *Yonder*, Corder goes so far as to describe the postmodern "human condition" as a mode of nostalgia—literally, an ache over lost place:

> The text—whether it is a poem, a novel, [. . .] a story told to a friend over coffee at the kitchen table, or a huge history—once it is told, already indeed in being told, may indeed be a home-place for the self, but it also departs into the consciousness, memory, interpretive capacity of the other, and is gone. Gone. Then once again, as Chesterton put it, we are "homesick at home." I will always lack the other's knowledge: I *must* be nostalgic, and so must we all. Nostalgia is a constant human condition.
>
> But nostalgia does not come upon us singly. It is always with us in the presence of other events and forces. Nostalgia is always accompanied by a conflict of tongues, by the failure of memory, and by the threat of personal invisibility. And there is more: we always come into this world educated in the wrong curriculum. (161)

Corderian nostalgia becomes, in effect, a study in the misremembering and misinterpreting of one's "home-places."

While Corder notes the ways that private fantasy, projection, and personal psychology generally falsify our knowing and remembering, his sharper focus falls upon the dangerously delusional effects of popular ideologies—most of which educate us "in the wrong curriculum," as he puts it above. In the late essay, "Lessons Learned, Lessons Lost" (1992), Corder declares, "When you learn strong lessons early, however wrong, no evidence seems to count against them" (15):

How do you remember guilt, disgrace, honorable victory, honorable defeat, and success if the way you first learned them was maybe altogether wrong and certainly altogether mismatched to a world that any soul ever lived in? When persuasive people and daily evidence both testify otherwise, how do you continue to believe—and how wrong you would be if you did—that suffering is noble, that love is always accompanied by chivalric behavior, that the WASP family of 1934 is the appropriate goal of nostalgic dreaming, that true believers will at last be saved? (23)

The "falsified memories" most in need of correction reside in the old narratives of American patriotic, masculinist, fundamentalist ideology, of which (as Corder's later narrator tells us) the youthful Corder proved too willing a consumer.

The above paragraphs hardly do justice to the complexities of Corderian memory, which, clearly, reflect the postmodern "textualization" (one might say, fictionalization) of identity. Unreliable and often delusional, Corderian memory provides the rhetorical site where cultural ideology, lived experience, and language intersect and conflict.[7]

Here (as with other aspects of Corderian theory), we wish to emphasize not just the originality, but the systematic unity and coherence of Corder's thought: just as we speak of a Burkean and a Rogerian rhetoric, we find ourselves fully justified in speaking of a Corderian rhetoric, whose outline we have partly sketched above. Through the rest of this introduction, it is not "Corder the theorist" but "Corder the stylist" or essayist who earns our attention. Through the ensuing paragraphs, we shall explore Corder's experiments in the personal-scholarly essay while seeking out distinctive features of his "ethical style." We shall also give attention to his late meditations upon postmodernism, as these most directly address our profession's reawakened interest in the theory, politics, and stylistics of "personal agency."

Attesting to this renewed interest, Hindman lists several of "the rhetorical moves and genres referred to [as . . .] 'the personal'" in scholarship (38):

a specific, individual positioning of a researcher and/or the subjects of a qualitative study; an instance of "outing" oneself by revealing religious, sexual, ethnic, racial, or economic affiliations; an autobiographical account, a memoir; a hybrid genre of theory and autobiography; an embodied writing that examines the institutional origins of individual affect and taste; a reader's individual decision how to consume and circulate texts. (38)

As we shall see, Corder anticipates current practice in virtually every respect, providing us models for further study, imitation, and critique. In "Tribes and Displaced Persons" (1993), for example, Corder describes the experimental, mixed-genre nature of his personal-scholarly essays, asserting not simply his mistrust of traditional "academic" prose, with its grand claims of objectivity, but also his recognition of the socially constructed nature of such writing:

> I haven't yet learned how to be myself. [. . .] I don't want to learn how to be someone else. I can't be Maynard Mack, whose work I admired so much when I was in graduate school, and I probably won't turn out to be Jacques Derrida. I want to try to think my thoughts, which aren't altogether mine. I don't want to write in the languages of the academic communities I have almost belonged to for years. [. . .] I want to do a scholarly sort of work but to write in a personal sort of way. [. . .] I want to write in my way, which isn't mine, and perhaps even stretch out the possibilities of prose. (281)

Pursuing "a scholarly sort of work [. . .] in a personal sort of way," Corder's mature writing did, in fact, "stretch out the possibilities of prose."[8] The following collection offers ample evidence of this stretching. By writing of "thoughts, which aren't altogether mine," Corder acknowledges the *problem* of personal agency and identity, which remains an abiding theme of his best later work. Indeed, Corder's later writing seeks not simply to theorize but to enact the poststructuralist claims of divided selfhood, alienated language, and authorial absence. As he writes in "Losing Out" (1993):

> I am not a single, unitary, stable personality. I have composed myself and revised myself, always a little nostalgic for that other self I could not compose, the one that sounds like Adrienne Rich, maybe, or Jacques Derrida, but looks like Gregory Peck. I am

provisional and plural. Any writer or speaker is always plural, though the responsible *I* is always singular. (99)

Yet it is important to note, here as elsewhere, that Corder never loses sight of the existentialist ethic of writing: though "plural" by virtue of its participation in various competing social-institutional discourses, the author remains, as a personal agent, a "responsible *I*," which is "always singular."[9]

Corderian Critical Autobiography and Argument by *Epanorthosis*

Describing "critical autobiography" as an experimental "mixed genre," Victor Villanueva writes that "there must be room for elements of autobiography,"

> not as confession and errant self-indulgence, not as the measure on which to assess theory, not as a replacement for rigor, but as a way of knowing our predispositions to see things certain ways, of understanding what it is that guides our intuitions in certain ways. This is the autobiographical as critique. (51)

Hindman writes similarly when outlining an ethics of "qualitative research practices," which demands

> that the researcher reflect on and explain to readers how her own definitive characteristics—such as race, gender, socio-economic background, and so on—as well as those of her subjects influence her findings and the construction of her text. ("Special Focus" 35)

The relevance of such observations to Corderian practice seems patent, since Corder regularly situates his essays in the specifics of time, place, race, gender, history, personal and cultural prejudice, and personal psychology.

Throughout the 1970s and 1980s, Corder continually stirred autobiographical narratives into his academic writing—a tactic rare in composition studies before the 1990s. Blending classical rhetoric and expressivism together along with rhetorical/literary criticism and analysis of pedagogy, his work undercuts the tidy demarcations of composition theory outlined in James Berlin's influential "Contemporary Composition: The Major Pedagogical Theories" (1982). And while he never writes directly about taxonomies of discourse, his insistent practice of genre-bending and genre-breaking subverts the formal categories outlined in James L. Kinneavy's once widely studied *Theory of Discourse* (1971). Indeed, Corder's practice exposes the entire concept of a discursive taxonomy as arbitrary and stultifying. In effect, Corderian rhetoric issues a passport authorizing one to transgress at will the boundaries that have traditionally, albeit artificially, cordoned off autobiography and personal narrative from rhetorical theory, composition studies, and rhetorical/literary criticism.

Even when broadcasting strong views, Corder dismisses his own claims to knowledge; such dismissals, while perhaps paradoxical, describe a conscious, consistent claim to an *ethos* of humility. And such Corderian practice anticipates the latest critical fashion, for, as Candace Spigelman notes, "no truth claims are asserted for autoethnography, personal academic article, or personal scholarly essay"; such writings, rather, "acknowledge and celebrate the ways in which experiential evidence necessarily destabilizes certainty, the ways in which stories encourage contradiction and inconsistency and offer narrative layerings, all open to interpretation" (75).

While scholarly and intellectual in his own right, Corder delicately mocks the pretensions of academic discourse, translating its specialized vocabularies into colloquial, homegrown terms: Lévi-Strauss's *bricolage* thus becomes "jackleg carpentry," the Derridean *trace* a "remaindered text," academic disciplinarity a mode of "tribalism," collaboration in writing a form of "sharecropping." Self-effacement spills into his wry essay titles, including many found in this collection and such others as "On Keeping Posted and Being Nudged" (1973), "You Operationalize—I'll Plug Away" (1980), "Lonesomeness in English Studies" (Corder and Baumlin 1986), "What To Do with Leftovers" (1986), and "Academic Jargon and Soul-Searching Drivel" (1991). In addition, his autobiographical narrator persistently admits to partiality, consistently searching for what he has misremembered or forgotten. Corder's narrator gets enormous rhetorical mileage out of discussing what he *doesn't* know or has gotten wrong.

Corder's ways of disavowing knowledge vary from one work to another. Consider "What I Learned at School"—his 1976 Braddock Award–winning "teaching story," as Kate Ronald ("Review" 256) might put it—an essay whose clichéd title seems to announce a predictably bad undergraduate paper. Explaining that he began the semester as a self-assured professor, Corder's narrator relates his attempts to write each assignment along with his first-year students. Confidence soon vanishes as he finds himself taxed and perplexed by the undertaking—just as his students must have been. The narrator's alleged inexpertise drives the whole essay, whose ironic conclusion offers several randomly numbered "laws" of composition that, upon inspection, hardly prove laws at all.

Consider as well the story that opens "Hunting for *Ethos* Where They Say It Can't Be Found":

> An ancient stone tool holds down a stack of papers on the table in the corner of my office. A rock implement, it is vaguely like the head of a sledgehammer. It is generally cylindrical, about ten inches long, about three inches in diameter at its middle, and comes to a rough, striated point at one end. The other end has a half-circle indentation that cuts through most of the three-inch thickness. [. . .] The indentation at one end creates a reasonably comfortable handhold, and the striations at the other end further suggest that it might have been a grinding tool. My three children [. . .] decided upon other possible uses: Each in turn took the thing to Show-and-Tell at school, lashed with a leather thong to a stout stick, which fit neatly into the indentation. It made a formidable club [. . .].
>
> Then recently a colleague from the Geology Department saw it, said No, it's not a tool, just a funny-shaped rock, wedged for eons against a smaller, harder round rock that eventually wore the indentation. (299; this volume, 202)

As the narrator concedes, the scientist's "alternative view enables the viewer to see things differently [. . .] and deconstructs my rock. The alternative words stop my words, and the reality of the rock changes. The geologist's history appropriates my history" (299; this volume, 202). The story, thus, reveals the narrator's own fallibility. But even while the scientist "knows" enough to dispel Corder's misconception, she, too, reveals a bit of carelessness, if not of ignorance: rather than finally identifying the object under examination, she can only label it a "funny-shaped rock." Here (as on other occasions) Corder asks readers to trust his narrative voice, not because of his expertise, but because he can admit error while hinting that other supposed "experts" might not know much, either.

Throughout Corder's writings, gestures of self-questioning and self-deprecation generate an *ethos* of humility and, hence, of apparent trustworthiness. At the same time, one cannot miss the playfulness of such *ethos*-maneuvers, as in the opening of his essay, "Another Geography Course?" (1989):

> About some things, it seems to me, a fellow should be reticent. Some qualities that we have, or think we have, or wish we had, I think ought to be discovered by others, not proclaimed for oneself, for they may not be as evident as we think they are. [. . .] A fellow probably shouldn't call himself a poet, or a liberal, or a Presbyterian unless others have already done so, and maybe not then.
>
> However, there are some characteristics and behaviors that one might as well go on and announce because they will soon be found out anyway. If you're about to be a dumbass, you might as well say so, for it will become apparent. If you're about to talk about teaching geography and you're not a geographer, you might as well say so. (1)

And, indeed, Corder proceeds heartily to the subject of geography. Despite his strong theoretical convictions and often bold declarations, Corder's modest, often fumbling persona invites readers to join him in puzzling over issues: he challenges us, in effect, to pick up our own sets of ropes and plot our routes as we join him in scaling rhetorical cliffs.

As Bishop notes in her appreciative essay, "Preaching What He Practices," Corder's writing abounds with rhetorical figures (which seem to mark his work as more formal than its homespun *ethos* and colloquial diction might otherwise suggest). In addition to the figures of repetition that Bishop analyzes for their stylistic effects, Corder especially favors a little-studied device that Patrick Hartwell calls the "self-devouring" or "exploding"

sentence (253–54) and that Bernard DuPriez terms *epanorthosis*—
that is, "self-correction."[10] *Epanorthosis* recurs not only in his
texts, but in his titles: *Uses of Rhetoric* thus ends, paradoxically,
with a chapter entitled "Certain Maxims and Questions, with
No Conclusion to Be Found"; note, too, the title "On the Way,
Perhaps, to a New Rhetoric, but Not There Yet, and If We Do
Get There, There Won't Be There Any More" (1985).

In Corder's later writings (particularly those exploring errors
of memory), *epanorthosis* expands from a minor rhetorical figure to a structural principle of argument. Consider, again, his
account of that "ancient stone tool," that "rock implement, [. . .]
vaguely like the head of a sledgehammer." Such descriptions deliberately mislead, as the author writes in full knowledge that
this is *not* a "tool" but merely a "funny-shaped rock," created
by nature, not by human hands. Why, then, begin with the old,
debunked fantasy? For an answer, we must look to the structures
of narrative that map out, chronologically as well as logically,
the author's experience: if readers are to share in the author's
self-correction then they, too, must initially misconstrue the rock-
tool, just as he and his children had misconstrued it and had
urged teachers and classmates to misconstrue the same.

Of course, the story becomes emblematic of his broader subject, which is a critique and self-correction—in effect, a deconstruction—of his previous writing on *ethos*: "Some years ago, I
wrote what I like to think of as a nice, mostly naive, and frequently uninformed paper [. . .]" (299). The narrator then dissects this earlier essay, using the new essay to fashion a
self-correcting intertext with his previous work. In such texts,
Corder elevates *epanorthosis* into a mode of existentialist rhetoric, a rhetoric grounded in self-examination and inquiry rather
than in persuasion: such rhetoric declares itself *always* to be in
process, *always* being created and corrected by a writer and readers—a rhetoric in a perpetual state of becoming.

As we have seen, Corderian argument by *epanorthosis* takes
many forms; and, while we have suggested that such strategies
dominate his later work, habits of self-correction are present from
the beginning. In "What I Learned at School," for example, the
narrator recounts having begun his semester with "coltish vigor,"
only to fret and fumble when writing his own assignments. His

own studentlike bewilderment corrects his original, teacherly confidence. For another variation of *epanorthosis* (and for Corder's probing of expressivist *ethos*), consider the following declarations from "When (Do I/Must I [. . .]" (1988):

> [. . .] I *always* count myself, *always* render judgments, *always* sanctify my judgments, *always* privilege my own way of seeing and thinking. [. . .] I have done so, again and again, by word and deed. (50)

Yet the narrator quickly counters,

> I must learn *never* to count myself, *never* to deny another, *never* to render a judgment against another, *never* to sanctify my judgments, *never* to privilege my own way of seeing and thinking. (50)

The remainder of this essay shoves the second of these views (*never* to count the self) against the first (*always* to count the self), only then to press the first against the second.

While expanding its uses, Corder did not, of course, invent argument by *epanorthosis;* indeed, his master and model was the great English essayist, Samuel Johnson (whose influence is unsurprising, given Corder's doctoral training in eighteenth-century literature). The final chapter of *Uses*, "Certain Maxims and Questions, with No Conclusion to Be Found," thus echoes Johnson's *Rasselas* and its "Conclusion, in Which Nothing Is Concluded" (2711). An especially important model is *Rambler* No. 154—one of Johnson's short, familiar essays, which Corder includes in two early books, *Uses of Rhetoric* (1971) and *Finding a Voice* (1973). In "Ethical Argument and *Rambler* No. 154" (1968), one of his earliest published essays, Corder develops an analysis of Johnson's essay that he would repeat in both *Uses* and "Varieties of Ethical Argument" (1978). Eleven years after "Varieties"—in "Hoping for Essays" (1989)—he appraises *Rambler 154* yet again. On each occasion, Corder spotlights the somersault that Johnson performs in his final three paragraphs, which reverse the assertions of previous paragraphs. After spending most of the essay blasting young people for refusing to study the past, Johnson retreats from his indignation, grandly announcing that "[n]o man ever yet became great by imitation" (89). The section of *Uses* (86–5) that includes and dissects *Rambler 154* serves as a microcosm for the self-correcting structure of Corder's whole book. That is, Corder performs a somersault roughly paralleling Johnson's: having railed at young people for refusing to study the past, he retreats from indignation and offers boldly original proposals.

Despite Corder's continued fascination with *Rambler 154*, much of his rhetorical practice shifted markedly during the mid-1980s, moving from a "heroic" phase (as one of us, elsewhere, has termed it: see Baumlin, "Toward" 27) to a "tragic" phase lasting until his death in 1998. One can ponder whether Corder intended his later musings to supersede (to "correct," if you will)— or merely to complicate and enrich—his earlier, more "heroic" thought. No answer to this question is easy: just as he enacted, rather than explicitly theorized, his rhetoric of *epanorthosis*, so he also enacted, rather than explicitly theorized, his shift from "heroic" to "tragic."

Many titles of Corder's later essays suggest, if not full-blown tragedy, then at least nostalgia, regret, pessimism: "Against a Mournful Wind" (1981); "From an Undisclosed Past into an Unknown Future" (1982); "The Time the Cavalry Didn't Come" (1985); "Lonesomeness in English Studies" (Corder and Baumlin 1986); "The Heroes Have Gone from the Grocery Store" (1987); "Lamentations for—and Hopes against—Authority in Education" (Corder and Baumlin 1988); *Lost in West Texas* (1988); "Lessons Learned, Lessons Lost" (1992); "Losing Out" (1993); "The Tyranny of Inattention" (1993); "Notes on a Rhetoric of Regret" (1995); and *Rhetorics, Remnants, and Regrets* (1997).

During his "heroic" phase, while generating important national publications in composition theory and rhetoric, Corder also produced a stream of familiar essays for regional journals. In "Late Word from the Provinces"—a sweet, engaging short piece about a weather-beaten yet wondrous childhood in West Texas—his narrator recalls the Double Mountains, a pair of inexplicably blue hills where God resides. But, whereas many of Corder's earlier essays were more traditionally academic than strictly personal, the works of his final decade (with a few exceptions) are all, in effect, critical autobiographies. Although he had already written often about his emotionally unsatisfying boyhood during the Great Depression, two later books, *Lost in West Texas* (1989) and *Chronicle of a Small Town* (1989), and several later essays focus on the obscure, windblown corner of West Texas where he lived until age twelve, when he moved with his parents to Fort Worth.

His elegiac "The Heroes Have Gone from the Grocery Store" and more expansive *Chronicle of a Small Town* offer post-postmodern meditations upon *ethos* and its perilous reliance upon memory. Both works explore discrepancies between Corder's recollections of the 1930s and other, reputedly more reliable, "objective" accounts. The narrator of "Heroes Have Gone" tells of an archivist whose research proves that the narrator could never have seen the image of Dizzy Dean, the grand sports hero who, Corder had mistakenly thought, adorned boxes of Cheerios during his boyhood. Though misremembered, the hero's image lingers. The narrator of *Chronicle* shuttles between remembered events of Corder-as-child during the 1930s and a description of Corder-as-researcher during the 1980s, who consults microform copies of *The Jayton Chronicle* (a local newspaper) for reports that definitely jar and, possibly, correct his errant recollections.

In earlier works, the process of self-correction serves as a source of renewal and optimism; but in "Heroes Have Gone" and *Chronicle, epanorthosis* in itself affords little hope. The essay and book share a theme, which we hazard to paraphrase as follows: although self-formation rests on a long skein of remembered experiences, the untrustworthiness of memory threatens to unravel the skein and the self at once. It is only after an enormous struggle against unfounded self-certainty and against cemented, unreliable memories that one can (hope to) begin to (re)constitute the self.

In "Lessons Learned, Lessons Lost" and "World War II on Cleckler Street" (1996), the narrator reflects on his childhood and adolescent immersion in popular culture. After criticizing images of warrior masculinity prevalent in the comic strips, movies, and radio narratives of his younger years, he debunks press coverage that glorified American and British military victories in World War II while sanitizing or erasing American and British atrocities. Interrogating and rejecting widely vaunted athletic and militaristic definitions of manhood, he struggles against his own rising feelings of isolation and disenchantment.

Hunting Lieutenant Chadbourne (1993)—arguably Corder's finest book—and "Hunting Lieutenant Chadbourne" (1994)—one of his finest essays—probe the life of an obscure young soldier who wrote his family no more than a handful of letters before dying in the Mexican War. Corder combines punctilious scholarship on Chadbourne—including a conscientious exploration of a range of possible events suggested by different sources—with reflections on his own sometimes hopeful, sometimes stymied process of research and discovery (or misdiscovery). More important for our scholarly purposes, both the essay and the book serve as post-postmodern musings on reminiscence and historiography. Not only do self-serving partiality, erratic records, and slipshod memories handcuff autobiographers and problematize autobiography; they also shackle historians and confound historiography. Just as vanity and memories cherished, yet inaccurate, warp the self, they also distort historiography and its role in shaping and transmitting culture. Although Corder corrects his initial impressions of Chadbourne, he portrays historiography as a murky process only occasionally punctuated by clarity and the possibility of certitude.

Surely the saddest of Corder's books is *Yonder: Life on the Far Side of Change* (1992), a collage of narratives and prose poems recounting his mental breakdown in 1983 and subsequent hospitalization, electroshock therapy, hospital exit, divorce, and estrangement from his younger daughter. Through lucid shards of nonlinear prose, the narrator reports that, upon leaving the hospital, he failed to discover the solace he sought in cheap white wine, shelled peanuts, and self-pity. In *Yonder*, confession and self-condemnation replace self-correction: in effect, *epanorthosis* has evolved into a mode of self-accusation.

Self-accusation intensifies in the unpublished manuscript *Scrapbook*, which offers some of the last writing that Corder managed to finish. The following passage goes beyond self-correction to a repudiation of the "heroic" rhetoric of his earlier "Varieties":

I spent a good part of my professional life wanting to believe that it is possible to learn each other, to understand a speaker's character or a writer's character if we paid close enough attention to the text the speaker or writer produced. I believed that I was following Aristotle's suggestion regarding the character, or *ethos*, of a speaker [. . .]. I published academic papers testifying that I had learned the character of various speakers and writers—Abraham Lincoln, Samuel Johnson, Shane, the prophet Amos, others.

I was partly right.

I think I did a pretty good job in describing the characters *in the texts that I read*. But of course Abraham Lincoln was somebody apart from his speeches and Samuel Johnson was somebody apart from his *Rambler* essays, and Amos was somebody I couldn't find at all, and even the fictional Shane was somebody outside the story Schaefer tells. What I found and wrote about, I think, does help to account for the appeal of these speakers, but the texts I studied don't *contain* their characters, any more than my scant text contains the self that I imagine that I am or want to be.

And besides, after all these years, I have come to think that my project was suspicious from the outset.

My interest in the project began in the late 1960s, when conflict, commotion, confrontation, and (at least impending) evil seemed to be everywhere. I think I wanted to believe that our wars with each other could be avoided or settled if we could, out of our separate worlds and from our separate rhetorics, learn to hear each other and to understand. I think I wanted to believe that we could notice each other, genuinely acknowledge each other, know each other. I still believe that, as of course most of us do, and as I wrote those academic papers, I wanted to believe that I was studying speakers and writers who had by honest and open means found audiences to listen. I think I was generally right in what I wrote, as far as I went.

But I didn't go far enough.

Gradually, over the years, I began to see that I hadn't sufficiently examined my own motives. To be sure, I did want to learn how speakers and writers had come to be known and to be heard by audiences, and I still do. Ever so slowly, however, I came to see that I didn't first of all want to notice, to acknowledge, to know other speakers and writers—I had come to this study, I finally had to recognize, because I wanted to learn how to get others to notice, to acknowledge, and to know me. I didn't want to die of my own insignificance.

And I didn't go far enough in another respect. I had already begun to learn, of course, that the author was not in his or her text and that readers and hearers kidnapped the text to make of it what they might [. . .].

The passage proceeds to describe Corder's response to the postmodern "death" of the author, the subject to which we now turn.

Corderian Responses to Postmodernism

In such "heroic" essays as "From Rhetoric to Grace" and "Argument as Emergence," Corder seeks to ground his existentialist rhetoric upon a bedrock of progressive Judeo-Christian theology—as if God alone could provide the guarantee of a stable, knowable self and world. While not entirely retreating from faith, Corder's later work confronts the linguistic and epistemological skepticisms of postmodernism, which serve to problematize (rather than lionize) the "heroic" self-in-process. With the possible exception of W. Ross Winterowd, Corder remains the only prominent rhetoric/composition scholar of his generation to acknowledge and actively engage postmodern theory; and crucial to this engagement is his pondering (and, sometimes, apparently embracing) the definitively postmodern insistence that the self is unstable, fragmented, multiple, and ultimately indeterminate. As he declares in "A New Introduction to Psychoanalysis" (159; this volume, 162), "[E]ach of us houses a crowd." Or, as he states elsewhere, "[E]ach of us is a cosmos in which multiple worlds circle, pass, halt, cross, collide, compete" ("From Rhetoric to Grace" 104). Extending over numerous books and essays, the project of problematizing the self deepens his earlier explorations of "generative *ethos*," as well as complicating his rhetorical practice of self-scrutiny and self-correction. Of course, as a personal-scholarly essayist, Corder is never content to theorize about the disappearance or "death" of the textualized authorial self; he explores it, *practices it,* rather, upon his own person. It is not the self in abstract but *his own self*—the reputedly transcendent, "sovereign" individual named Jim W. Corder of Jayton, Texas, Professor of English at Texas Christian University—that Corder subjects to deconstruction.

Did we just note that he was from Jayton, Texas? That his name was Jim W. Corder? Was he? Was it?

As we have observed, topographical metaphors dominate in Corderian self making: to have a self, to *be* a self, one needs a "home-place," wherein one's history and identity can be grounded. In "Losing Out," Corder's narrator fails even in the "simple" task of naming a birthplace:

If you look for me in the public records, you'll find confusion. I may have been born in a small farmhouse just on the west edge of Stonewall County, but the records will not guarantee that. Some time after I started to school in Jayton, over next door in Kent County, I had to fill out a form. One of the things the form wanted to know was where I was born, but the form provided only a little bitty square place for an answer—not room enough to say "in a small farm house just on the west edge of Stonewall County." I wrote down that I was born in Jayton, Texas, where the school was. That fit the square nicely, but it made me uncomfortable, and I expected that the principal would not appreciate my way of composing myself, would instead call me to his office, where I would be punished for lying. I'm still afraid of principals, but I stuck with that account of the place of my birth for a while.

Then, years later, I was drafted, and the United States Army wanted to know where I was born. I was pretty sure that I couldn't mess around with the United States Army. This time, in the interest of somewhat greater accuracy, I composed myself in another way. I wrote down that I was born in Stonewall County, where the little farmhouse may have been. That bothered me, too; for one thing, it was a little presumptuous, I thought, to claim a whole county for the place of my birth.

Then, a little later, I got married, and the county clerk wanted to know where I was born. I was still a little interested in accuracy, so I wrote down that I was born in Aspermont, in Stonewall County. That's the county seat, you see, and I thought surely that I must somehow be recorded there. But I had never lived in Aspermont. At the time, I had only passed through Aspermont, but there it is, on the record.

In due time, our first child was born, and to record that properly, someone insisted on knowing where I was born. This time, in sheer bravado and in my pride at being a father, I wrote down Spur, Texas. I never lived in Spur, up in Dickens County, but it seemed like more people on the outside would have heard of it. Spur had a rodeo once, and a concrete swimming pool. It was a kind of status symbol, you see, and I had sold out, hoping to compose significance for myself.

That's how it began, how I began to be lost. I expect my parents could have told the truth about where I was born, but they're both dead now, and I haven't discussed the matter with anyone else recently. (97–98)

More dire than the loss of birthplace is the shifting history of his name—the very token and guarantee, one might assume, of one's stable, public identity. In "I in Mine, You Elsewhere" (a chapter-excerpt from the unpublished manuscript, *Rhetorics, Remnants, and Regrets*), the narrator—named "Jimmie Wayne" at birth—recounts the offhand action of a first-grade teacher, who records him (in effect, renames him) as "Jim," which he would later tweak into an official pen name, "Jim W." Imagining that he had gotten the name right, a university president once cheerily handed him a plaque, inscribed "Jimmie W. Corder," while press editors bestowed dignity by preferring "James"—their own invention, obviously. Such name-changing, the author concludes, necessarily destabilizes identity: "Perhaps, after all, I am not here. Perhaps I am here under another name" (304; this volume, 245).

In "Notes on a Rhetoric of Regret," Corder shoves the standard expressivist view of writing-as-self-disclosure against Roland Barthes's poststructuralist assertion of the author's death-in-writing. As long as notions of authorship survive in writing classes, surely—as the narrator asserts—the authorial self must still live, even if hospitalized and on a respirator. Holding the expressivist and poststructuralist positions in suspension and allowing neither to triumph, Corder (who was not a Burkean) investigates what Burke calls "not terms that avoid ambiguity, but *terms that clearly reveal the strategic spots at which ambiguities necessarily arise*" (xviii; emphasis in original).

An earlier (but seemingly more conclusive) piece, puckishly titled "At Last Report I Was Still Here," abuts the same two positions (writing as self-disclosure *vs.* authorial absence) while providing a different ending. Even as the authorial self shrinks to a textual construction supplied by readers, the author nonetheless persists, ethically as well as pragmatically: "If I lie in what I write," Corder observes, "the social group that constructed me won't sit beside me to share the judgment against me. I'll be alone, and I'll be held accountable" (265). Here and in other late works, Corder moves beyond postmodernism and social construction-ism, resisting claims that an authorial self is constructed by read-ers and that the everyday self is constructed by culture. In effect, such later investigations gesture toward a sort of post-Burkean, post-postmodern pragmatism.

The hard-shell Baptist theology of Corder's childhood warned against illusions of self-sufficiency, of egotism created and propped by vanity and sin. Joining the attack, postmodern criticism might have unmasked the self's pretensions to sovereignty and unity, reducing selfhood to a mere verbal tissue or social agglomera-tion. Despite assaults from the right and left—that is, from com-peting fundamentalist and postmodern rhetorics—tantalizing traces of childhood flood the narrator's mind, even when misre-membered. In writings both early and late, Corder's narrator observes the uniqueness and quirkiness—the "blessed particu-lars" ("Aching for a Self" 8; this volume, 268), as he might put it—of family members, each of whom, despite the Depression-era poverty that they shared with millions, belong only on their little postage stamp of soil below the Texas Panhandle, never in Vermont or Louisiana. Never are the subjects of Corderian nar-rative reduced to mere character types, whether sociologically or archetypally defined. And Corder's narrator evokes other indi-vidual, specific, not-quite-erased signs. One is the cement grave marker of a boy who died in 1935, a marker embedded with the marbles that he once rolled in the dirt ("Learning" 243). For the narrator, clinging to such traces, such "blessed particulars," surely matters.

Unlike memories of one's family, some reminiscences belong to an entire generation that heard Toscanini on the radio, gazed at issues of *Life* magazine, and devoured comic books ("Lessons," "World War II"). Although memories of popular culture are, by definition, shared, people still recall and misrecall differently. For Corder's narrator, the visage of Dizzy Dean lingers on a cereal box, where it never in fact appeared. While erroneous memories expose one's illusions, they also reveal such illusions as vastly nuanced and highly variegated—that is, as imaginative expres-sions capable of sustaining identity. Paradoxically, Corder teaches us to respect, as well as to correct, the ineluctably stubborn individuality of our errant memories, for such provides the ground and inventive resources for further self making.

Yet an illusion is, in the end, an illusion. Each of us houses a crowd, the author disappears within his or her text, we are each socially constructed, identity remains indeterminate, and memory fails. The acids of deconstruction bite deep. Though held accountable by courts of law, the Corderian self is never a self-sufficient, unified, finished entity but, rather, a dynamic process of perpetual interrogation and (re)constitution, whose verbal/imaginative recomposition proceeds (that is, is enabled by) recognitions and confessions both large and small: Dizzy's image never adorned a cereal box; male athleticism does not equal masculinity.

Recall the narrator whose self-assurance dissolves when attempting the "easy" task of tackling his students' writing assignments; then compare the narrator whose self-assurance dissolves when a geologist renames his "ancient stone tool." Treating the latter as an allegory of Corderian rhetoric, it would seem that learning, unlearning, and relearning the odd rock resembles learning, unlearning, and relearning how to write. Although composition textbooks typically aim to reduce students' uncertainties, learning to write—by Corderian implication—means not reducing uncertainties but, rather, multiplying them. Corder implies that, when one writes, floors move, walls shift, and doorways slide, unpredictably.

Recall the narrator who maintains that, "at its best, rhetoric has never been static and fixed and stable and finished." Yes, rhetorical conceptions forever spill, collide, buckle, smash, melt, crystallize, sink, and resurface. Returning to our allegory, perhaps Corder implies that learning, unlearning, and relearning the rock resembles learning, unlearning, and relearning rhetorical theory— whether Aristotelian, Derridean, or (early- or late-) Corderian.

Consider Corder's later, postmodern project of problematizing the self. Perhaps relearning and reconstituting the rock resembles processes of relearning and reconstituting identity. Perhaps, after dissolving the "ancient stone tool" together, a geologist and an English professor can unite in re-forming the rock—and themselves. The work of rhetoric is long, though life is short. So Corder would wish to remind us.

Mundus est Fabula.

We have not written enough about Corderian rhetoric, though we have written too much already. Let us end, therefore, with a brief meditation upon the narrativity of human knowing, as encapsulated in René Descartes's personal motto, "[T]he world is a fable." We agree, though we resist (and, in his less pessimistic moments, Corder too would resist) Macbeth's more dire version, that "life is a tale told by an idiot, / Full of sound and fury, signifying nothing." Following Corderian practice, life *is* a tale—no more, no less. If our aim is to become our stories, to grow into our structures and styles and to emerge toward others, then, ethically, it would seem that we are obliged to tell the most generative stories we can imagine—even when these recount how we got our earlier stories wrong. In any case, the stories themselves matter, as they contain our own "blessed particulars." They are all we have: they are all that we can hope, or fear, to become.

Notes

1. In a recent review-essay of books by Thomas Newkirk, Donna Qualley, Kathleen Blake Yancey, and Christian Knoeller, Kameen writes,

> . . . all of these books and others like them—books that value, even valorize, a set of terms that on first take seem retrograde (*self, voice, experience, the personal*: all bulwark terms of '70s expressivism)—are coming out now in such a flurry. One way of reading them is, of course, as atavistic—attempts to resuscitate an epistemology that never really got that well established in our disciplinary research before the twin juggernauts of poststructuralism (in English studies) and process research (in composition) overran things. [. . .] Another approach is to see them as a stage in the evolutionary development of our discipline: a recursion to, and reconceptualization of, that same set of terms in light of more up-to-date—mostly social-constructionist—theories of language. (100–101)

Ultimately, Kameen embraces the latter: "I believe the books of the sort I'm writing about here are beginning to make that turn toward what might be 'next and new' in our profession" (102).

2. France (who was, by the way, a student of Corder's) quotes from Thomas O'Donnell's "Politics and Ordinary Language" and Kathryn Flannery's "Composing and the Question of Agency."

3. Whereas recent histories trace the roots of expressivist rhetoric to American Romanticism, a more vital influence proceeds from existential phenomenology. This should not surprise, given that existentialism defined postwar intellectual culture and remained a dominant philosophical movement from the late 1940s through the early 1970s (only then to be eclipsed by social constructionism). Inspired by Jean-Paul Sartre's *What Is Literature?* (1947), "Why Write?" (1949), and other Sartrean reflections upon writing, an existential phenomenology of language was developed in such seminal works as Georges Gusdorf's *Speaking* (1965) and Maurice Merleau-Ponty's *Prose of the World* (1973); even our current use of the terms "expressivism" and "expressionism" may originate in these authors' emphasis upon language-as-expression. As Gusdorf argues, personal expression is always "present as a coefficient of speech" (70), so that "the whole of human experience in its militant sense may be understood as a striving for expression" (73). Though the great urgency of humankind is to establish interpersonal relationship, nonetheless one's "relation to others is only meaningful insofar as it reveals that personal reality within the person who is himself speaking. To communicate, man *ex-presses* himself, i.e. he actualizes himself, he creates from his own substance [. . .]" (69).

For a fuller discussion of the existentialist influences upon American Expressivism, see Baumlin, "Toward a Corderian Theory."

4. Indeed, Corder sought to apply the vocabulary of rhetoric even to the human biological organism: arguably, such psychophysiological aberrations as schizophrenia and cancer result from competing "inventive worlds," the schizophrenic suffering from a disordering of one site of invention by another, the cancer cell literally (and direly) reinventing itself oncogenetically, out of cells once healthy. As Corder explains in "From Rhetoric to Grace,"

> Some forms of schizophrenia [. . .] may be seen as the consequence of a crossover from one inventive world into a structure and style that belong to another inventive world. The presence of the oncogene in every cell suggests another analog: hidden features of an inventive world will sometimes force their way out into the structures and styles of our lives. (27)

See also his essay "On Cancer and Freshman Composition" (1982).

5. Earlier in this same chapter, Corder offered specific examples of the presence and workings of multiple rhetorics:

The notion of multiple rhetorics should not be alien to us. They are all around us and inside us. The Left will not talk as the Right talks. The Baptist will not make the same speech that the Catholic makes. The woman will probably not talk as the man talks. The conscious mind and the subconscious will shape experience differently. The man who believes he was born in sin and continuously damned thereafter will not use language in the same way that a woman will who believes she was born innocent or good with every possibility of better yet to come. The first can at best only use words to try *to recover* from his own limitations. The second, however, may be free to use words *to reveal* her own present character. (*Yonder* 164)

6. Indeed, Corder describes schizophrenia as a breakdown in the normal relations between one's "inventive worlds" and their enabling structures. One inventive world can collide with and invade a second; a third inventive world can cross over into an alien structure. For a detailed account of such breakdowns and crossings, see his "New Introduction to Psychoanalysis."

7. In his unpublished *Places in the Mind* (1997), Corder was working toward a book-length summation of these many aspects of his mature theory. We quote from the introduction:

All that we see and think and say is in a continuing history. History occurs in places. Our itinerary from place to place and our way of inhabiting places form our rhetorics—that is, our way of seeing, thinking, and speaking in a particular space. While some of us, I suppose, will stay rooted to one place, therefore to one rhetoric, most of us live in diverse places, therefore in diverse rhetorics. These multiple rhetorics sometimes coexist harmoniously enough; sometimes they compete with one another for dominance. I mean to suggest that *rhetoric* and *place* are affiliated, coexistent, coterminous, isomorphic. Rhetoric does not exist except in place; place does not exist except in rhetoric. Place generates rhetoric; rhetoric creates place. If place changes, rhetoric changes [. . .]. Some, I expect, might call this marriage by another name and say that we are always ideologically situated, but I hope it may be found that some advantages accrue through the association of rhetoric and place, the latter taken as both figurative and geographical.

This association will help to account for the loss, mourning, regret, nostalgia that will always, in one way or another, accompany our speaking. We cannot keep rhetoric and place, however tightly we grasp and cling. Sooner or later, in one way or another,

we go on. We lose place and rhetoric, rhetoric and place, and as
we do, we lose the other, including the self as other, for the other
is always in a different place. (7–8; this volume, 275)

8. Corder's introduction to *Places in the Mind* claims that the entire
manuscript aims "to join the personal to the academic":

> The book that follows does not have the appearance of an aca-
> demic, scholarly work, though I believe that it is sufficiently
> founded in study. I have chosen not to depend upon the appara-
> tus or the manner of what some think is conventional academic
> writing. I wanted to join the personal to the academic here: I
> know I live in the first; perhaps I have visited the second. I hoped
> the two would come together so that I could be, you might say,
> in a new place. I wanted this work to be, as nearly as possible,
> cumulative and exploratory, and not thesis-driven. For that rea-
> son, the chapters that follow will not seem to follow each other
> inexorably. They are varied, and I have made no special effort to
> stitch them neatly into a seamless fabric. I wanted to try to be in
> different places and rhetorics so that I might think about differ-
> ent rhetorics and places. (8)

9. For further illustration, we quote at length from the late essay, "At
Last Report I Was Still Here" (1993):

> When you write, you're always alone and with someone. Every-
> thing anyone ever wrote intrudes upon, alters, blesses, and damns
> anything anyone writes. The language doesn't belong to me.
>
> Still, I think I'm here, though I'm a little uncertain. I think
> I'm here and I think the language does belong to me. I think you
> may be here. I think composition students may be here. A little
> while back, I said that ". . . I'm obliged to listen to writers of our
> time who tell me I've been wrong." I'm obliged because they
> compel me. They pull at me. They are real.
>
> If they are real, there's a chance that I may be, too, some day.
>
> And there's one other thing I remember.
>
> I can hold them accountable for what they say. They can
> hold me accountable for what I say. If I slander someone in what
> I write, interpreting readers won't go with me to court and sit
> beside me as co-defendants. I'll be alone, and I'll be held account-
> able. If I lie in what I write, the social group that constructed me
> won't sit beside me to share the judgment against me. I'll be alone,
> and I'll be held accountable. I am responsible for what I write.
> No one else is. Just me. (265)

10. First named and defined within Greek rhetorical tradition, *epanorthosis* has been known alternatively as *metanoia* (in Latin, *correctio*). The Elizabethan poet-rhetor, George Puttenham, offers the first extensive description in English, translating *metanoia* as "the Penitent." "Sometimes," as Puttenham writes, "we speake and be sorry for it,"

> [. . .] as if we had not well spoken, so that we seeme to call in our word againe, and to put in another fitter for the purpose: for which respects the Greekes called this manner of speech the figure of repentance: then for that upon repentance commonly follows amendment, the Latins called it the figure of correction, in that the speaker seemeth to reforme that which was said amiss. (223–24)

Though quaint (and, given Corder's modernism, anachronistic), Puttenham's description marvelously anticipates Corderian practice, whose habit of self-correction transforms *metanoia/epanorthosis* into a mode of verbal "repentance."

Having declared *epanorthosis* a "little-studied" device, we should call attention to Priscilla Perkins's recent essay, "A Radical Conversion of the Mind" (2001), which explores the metanoic resources of personal essay and "scholarship of the personal." While Perkins argues that conservative Christian notions of metanoia as "repentance" have "no place [. . .] in a progressive writing pedagogy" (597), nonetheless she notes a "more forward-looking definition":

> every time we ask students—Christian and otherwise—to read something new, we hope they will approach their work in the spirit of *metanoia*: willing to risk a "conversion of the mind." As Qualley has shown, such reading practices must be taught; regardless of our students' backgrounds, very few of them know intuitively how to approach a text "openly, tentatively, dialogically, and reflexively" ([*Turns of Thought*] 6). (597)

Such "conversion of the mind" is, in fact, modeled by Corderian argument by *epanorthosis*.

Works Cited

Banks, William P. "Written through the Body: Disruptions and 'Personal' Writing." *College English* 66 (2003): 21–40.

Barthes, Roland. "The Death of the Author." *The Rustle of Language.* Trans. Richard Howard. New York: Hill, 1986. 49–55.

Baumlin, James S. "Toward a Corderian Theory of Rhetoric." Enos and Miller 25–57.

Berlin, James A. "Contemporary Composition: The Major Pedagogical Theories." *College English* 44 (1982): 765–77.

Bishop, Wendy. "Places to Stand: The Reflective Writer-Teacher-Writer in Composition." *CCC* 51 (1999): 9–31.

———. "Preaching What He Practices: Jim Corder's Irascible and Articulate Oeuvre." Enos and Miller 89–101.

———. *Teaching Lives: Essays and Stories.* Logan: Utah State UP, 1997.

Brandt, Deborah, Ellen Cushman, Anne Ruggles Gere, et al. "The Politics of the Personal: Storying Our Lives against the Grain." *College English* 64 (2001): 41–62.

Burke, Kenneth. *A Grammar of Motives.* Berkeley: U of California P, 1969.

Corbett, Edward P. J. *Classical Rhetoric for the Modern Student.* New York: Oxford UP, 1965.

Corder, Jim W. "Academic Jargon and Soul-Searching Drivel." *Rhetoric Review* 9 (1991): 314–26.

———. "Against a Mournful Wind." *New Mexico Humanities Review* 4 (1981): 13–17.

———. "Another Geography Course?" *Perspectives* 19 (1989): 1–7.

———. "Argument as Emergence, Rhetoric as Love." *Rhetoric Review* 4 (1985): 16–32.

———. "Asking for a Text and Trying to Learn It." *Encountering Student Texts.* Ed. Bruce Lawson, Susan Sterr Ryan, and W. Ross Winterowd. Urbana, IL: NCTE, 1989. 89–98.

———. "At Last Report I Was Still Here." *The Subject Is Writing: Essays by Teachers and Students.* Ed. Wendy Bishop. Portsmouth, NH: Boynton/Cook, 1993. 261–65.

———. *Chronicle of a Small Town.* College Station: Texas A&M UP, 1989.

_____. "Collaboration and Autonomy, Owning and Sharecropping." *Freshman English News* 19 (Spring 1991): 11–12.

_____. "Ethical Argument and *Rambler* No. 154." *Quarterly Journal of Speech* 54 (1968): 352–56.

_____. "From an Undisclosed Past into an Unknown Future." *Liberal Education* 68 (1982): 75–78.

_____. "From Rhetoric into Other Studies." *Defining the New Rhetorics.* Ed. Theresa Enos and Stuart C. Brown. Newbury Park: Sage, 1993. 95–108.

_____. "From Rhetoric to Grace: Propositions 55–81 about Rhetoric, Propositions 1–54 and 82 *et seq.* Being as Yet Unstated; or, Getting from the Classroom to the World." *Rhetoric Society Quarterly* 14 (1984): 15–28.

_____. "The Heroes Have Gone from the Grocery Store." *Arete: The Journal of Sports Literature* 5 (1987): 73–78.

_____. "Hoping for Essays." *Literary Nonfiction: Theory, Criticism, Pedagogy.* Ed. Chris Anderson. Carbondale: Southern Illinois UP, 1989. 301–14.

_____. "Hunting for *Ethos* Where They Say It Can't Be Found." *Rhetoric Review* 7 (1989): 299–316.

_____. *Hunting Lieutenant Chadbourne.* Athens: U of Georgia P, 1993.

_____. "Hunting Lieutenant Chadbourne: A Search for *Ethos* whether Real or Pretended." *Ethos: New Essays in Rhetorical and Critical Theory.* Ed. James S. Baumlin and Tita French Baumlin. Dallas: Southern Methodist UP, 1994. 343–65.

_____. "Late Word from the Provinces." *New Mexico Humanities Review* 2 (1979): 24–27.

_____. "Learning the Text: Little Notes about Interpretation, Harold Bloom, the *Topoi,* and the *Oratio.*" *College English* 48 (Mar. 1986): 243–48.

_____. "Lessons Learned, Lessons Lost." *Georgia Review* 46 (1992): 15–28.

_____. "Losing Out." *Diversity: A Journal of Multicultural Issues* 1 (1993): 97–100.

_____. *Lost in West Texas.* College Station: Texas A&M UP, 1988.

_____. "A New Introduction to Psychoanalysis, Taken as a Version of Modern Rhetoric." *Pre/Text* 5 (1984): 137–69.

_____. "Notes on a Rhetoric of Regret." *Composition Studies/Freshman English News* 23 (1995): 94–105.

_____. "On Cancer and Freshman Composition, or the Use of Rhetorical Language in the Description of Oncogenetic Behavior." *CEA Critic* 45 (1982): 1–9.

_____. "On Keeping Posted and Being Nudged: Some Problems in the Continuing Education of Practicing Teachers." *English in Texas* 4 (1973): 32–34.

_____. "On the Way, Perhaps, to a New Rhetoric, but Not There Yet, and If We Get There, There Won't Be There Anymore." *College English* 47 (1985): 162–70.

_____. *Places in the Mind: Essays on Rhetorical Sites*. Unpublished ms. 1997.

_____. *Rhetorics, Remnants, and Regrets: An Essay on Shifting and Competing Rhetorics*. Unpublished ms. 1997.

_____. *Scrapbook*. Unpublished ms. 1997.

_____. "Studying Rhetoric and Teaching School." *Rhetoric Review* 1 (1982): 4–36.

_____. "The Time the Cavalry Didn't Come, or the Quest for a Saving Authority in Recent Studies of Higher Education." *Liberal Education* 71 (1985): 305–19.

_____. "Tribes and Displaced Persons: Some Observations on Collaboration." *Theory and Practice in the Teaching of Writing: Rethinking the Discipline*. Ed. Lee Odell. Carbondale: Southern Illinois UP, 1993. 271–88.

_____. "The Tyranny of Inattention." *Journal of Higher Education* 64 (1993): 594–99.

_____. *Uses of Rhetoric*. New York: Lippincott, 1971.

_____. "Varieties of Ethical Argument, with Some Account of the Significance of *Ethos* in the Teaching of Composition." *Freshman English News* 6 (1978): 1–23.

_____. "What I Learned at School." *College Composition and Communication* 26 (1975): 330–34.

_____. "What to Do with Leftovers." *Bulletin of the American Association for Higher Education* 38 (1986): 9–13.

_____. "When (Do I/Shall I/May I/Must I/Is It Appropriate for Me to) (Say No to/Deny/ Resist/Repudiate/Attack/Alter) Any (Poem/ Poet/ Other/Piece of the World) for My Sake?" *Rhetoric Society Quarterly* 18 (1988): 49–68.

_____. "World War II on Cleckler Street." *Collective Heart: Texans in World War II.* Ed. Joyce Gibson Roach. Austin, TX: Eakin, 1996.

_____. *Yonder: Life on the Far Side of Change.* Athens: U of Georgia P, 1992.

_____. "You Operationalize—I'll Plug Away." *Liberal Education* 66 (1980): 440–45.

Corder, Jim W., ed. *Finding a Voice.* Glenview, IL: Scott Foresman, 1973.

Corder, Jim W., and James S. Baumlin. "Lamentations for—and Hopes against—Authority in Education." *Educational Theory* 38 (1988): 11–26.

_____. "Lonesomeness in English Studies." *ADE Bulletin* 85 (1986): 36–39.

Cracken, H. Thomas, Richard L. Larson, and Judith Entes, eds. *Teaching College English and English Education: Reflective Stories.* Urbana IL: NCTE, 1998.

DuPriez, Bernard. *A Dictionary of Literary Devices.* Toronto: U of Toronto P, 1991.

Enos, Theresa, and Keith D. Miller, eds. *Beyond Postprocess and Postmodernism: Essays on the Spaciousness of Rhetoric.* Mahwah, NJ: Erlbaum, 2003.

Flannery, Kathryn T. "Review: Composing and the Question of Agency." *College English* 53 (1991): 701–13.

France, Alan W. "Dialectics of Self: Structure and Agency as the Subject of English." *College English* 63 (2000): 145–65.

Goldthwaite, Melissa A. "Confessionals." *College English* 66 (2003): 55–73.

Gradin, Sherrie. "Revitalizing Romantics, Pragmatics, and Possibilities for Teaching." *College English* 62 (2000): 403–7.

Gusdorf, Georges. *Speaking (La Parole)*. Trans. Paul T. Brockelman. Northwestern Studies in Phenomenology and Existential Philosophy. Evanston, IL: Northwestern UP, 1965.

Hartwell, Patrick, with Robert Bentley. *Open to Language*. New York: Oxford UP, 1982.

Hindman, Jane E. "Making Writing Matter: Using 'the Personal' to Recover[y] and Essential[ist] Tension in Academic Discourse." *College English* 64 (2001): 88–108.

_____. "Special Focus: Personal Writing." *College English* 64 (2001): 34–40.

_____. "Thoughts on Reading 'the Personal': Toward a Discursive Ethics of Professional Critical Literacy." *College English* 66 (2003): 9–20.

Holland, Norman N. "The Inevitability of the Personal." *PMLA* 111 (1996): 1146–47.

Johnson, Samuel. *The History of Rasselas, Prince of Abyssinia. The Norton Anthology of English Literature*. 7th ed. Vol. 1. Ed. M. H. Abrams. New York: Norton, 2000. 2679–712.

_____. *Rambler* No. 154. Corder, *Uses* 86–89.

Kameen, Paul. "Review: 'Re-Covering the Self in Composition.'" *College English* 62 (1999): 100–113.

Kinneavy, James L. *A Theory of Discourse: The Aims of Discourse*. New York: Norton, 1971.

Knoeller, Christian. *Voicing Ourselves: Whose Words We Use When We Talk about Books*. Albany: SUNY P, 1998.

Merleau-Ponty, Maurice. *The Prose of the World*. Ed. Claude Lefort. Trans. John O'Neill. Northwestern University Studies in Phenomenology and Existential Philosophy. Evanston, IL: Northwestern UP, 1973.

Miller, Keith D. "Jim Corder's Radical, Feminist Rhetoric." Enos and Miller 59–77.

Newkirk, Thomas. *The Performance of Self in Student Writing*. Portsmouth, NH: Boynton/Cook, 1997.

Noddings, Nel. *Caring: A Feminine Approach to Ethics and Moral Education*. Berkeley: U of California P, 1984.

O'Donnell, Thomas G. "Politics and Ordinary Language: A Defense of Expressivist Rhetorics." *College English* 58 (1996): 423–39.

Perkins, Priscilla. "'A Radical Conversion of the Mind': Fundamentalism, Hermeneutics, and the Metanoic Classroom." *College English* 63 (2001): 585–611.

Puttenham, George. *The Arte of English Poesie.* 1589. Ed. Edward Arber. London: A. Constable, 1906. Rpt. Kent, OH: Kent State UP, 1970.

Qualley, Donna J. *Turns of Thought: Teaching Composition as Reflexive Inquiry.* Portsmouth, NH: Boynton/Cook, 1997.

Ronald, Kate. "Review: How to Tell a True Teaching Story." *College English* 62 (1999): 255–64.

Roskelly, Hephzibah, and Kate Ronald. *Reason to Believe: Romanticism, Pragmatism, and the Possibility of Teaching.* Albany: SUNY P, 1998.

Sartre, Jean-Paul. *Being and Nothingness: An Essay on Phenomenological Ontology.* Trans. Hazel E. Barnes. New York: Washington Square, 1953.

———. *What Is Literature?* 1947. Trans. Bernard Frechtman. New York: Philosophical Library, 1949.

———. "Why Write?" *Critical Theory since Plato.* Ed. Hazard Adams. New York: Harcourt, 1971. 1058–68.

Schnakenberg, Karen Rossi. "Classical Rhetoric in American Writing Textbooks, 1950–1965." *Inventing a Discipline: Rhetoric Scholarship in Honor of Richard E. Young.* Ed. Maureen Daly Goggin. Urbana, IL: NCTE, 2000. 146–72.

Spigelman, Candace. "Argument and Evidence in the Case of the Personal." *College English* 64 (2001): 63–87.

Sullivan, Patricia A. "Composing Culture: A Place for the Personal." *College English* 66 (2003): 41–54.

Trimbur, John. "Agency and the Death of the Author: A Partial Defense of Modernism." *JAC* 20 (2000): 283–98.

Trimmer, Joseph F. *Narration as Knowledge: Tales of the Teaching Life.* Portsmouth, NH: Boynton/Cook, 1997.

Villanueva, Victor. "The Personal." *College English* 64 (2001): 50–52.

Welch, Kathleen E. *The Contemporary Reception of Classical Rhetoric: Appropriations of Ancient Discourse.* Hillsdale, NJ: Lawrence Erlbaum, 1990.

Yancey, Kathleen Blake. *Reflection in the Writing Classroom.* Logan: Utah State UP, 1998.

ESSAYS SCHOLARLY AND PERSONAL

CHAPTER TWO

Late Word from the Provinces

I f you could go from Fort Worth straight as the crow flies, just a little to the north of west, you'd be there after about 180 miles, though I don't know, actually, that I've ever seen a crow fly straight. The way there by the wavering, bending route that people take is longer by a little—maybe 195 miles.

The road, though a little crooked, is chiefly west, as are most of the roads I take. I've been by and have glanced at those easterly and southerly stretches of Texas, but I find myself feeling choked and edgy there, the air too low and heavy, the trees too near and copious. The road I've mentioned goes into the lonesome middle of country that just barely begins along a line that lies generally north and south down from the Red River through Fort Worth and on to Austin before it angles off southeastward toward the Rio Grande.

Texas has been split along that axis before: Anglo-Americans moved across the territory as far as that Fort Worth–Austin line as early as the 1830s, and they were still stalled there in the 1870s because they knew that out beyond that line the lonesome country was chancy and the Comanches were lords. The census of 1870 shows that only thirty-three towns and cities in the state were able to report a population, and all thirty-three were east of the line down across the state through Fort Worth and Austin.

But I was saying that if you go from Fort Worth—better, I expect, by the crooked road than by the crow's path—just a little north of west, you'll be there after about 180, or maybe 195, miles. You'll understand that I don't mean the main western road that goes through Abilene to Big Spring and on to El Paso, nor do I mean the other major road that goes through Wichita Falls

First published in *New Mexico Humanities Review* 2 (1979): 24–27.

and into the Panhandle and Amarillo. I mean a quieter road in between.

This road takes you from Fort Worth through Weatherford and onto Mineral Wells. Out of Mineral Wells it runs down through the rough Brazos country and across the Brazos, and then you're in the long, mostly straight, and generally uncluttered stretch to Breckenridge.

I remember riding that road, much rougher then, in 1941 with my aunt. She was young then, and frisky, though she's not now. It was an early summer night, and the moon was big, and its light was bright and clean and lovely, and she decided that the world was so clear with moonlight she could drive without the headlights, and she did, and we drove for miles, enthralled.

Albany is next. Just at the near edge of Albany a farm road splits off to the north that will take you to the ruins of Fort Griffin, a staging ground for the last campaigns against the Comanches, and the jumping-off place for the hunters who slaughtered the last of the buffalo in the late 1870s.

On the yonder side of Albany the road splits and the northwesterly branch takes you to Lenders. I don't know much about Lenders, but I do remember a loud and bawdy song that the older boys once brought back from a church camp there—and on to Stamford. Out of Stamford the road goes past Sagerton to Aspermont.

When you get to Aspermont, you're there. "There" is just around a long curve on the other side of town. "There," off to the left in the blue distance, blue above the broken plain surrounding them—the Double Mountains.

If you're acquainted with mountains, the Double Mountains would look to you like two hills. They rise to an elevation of maybe 1,700 feet, always blue—I never saw them otherwise—on the horizon of my youth, always present, the markers of that province.

I have come this long way to the Double Mountains for a particular reason. God lives on top of the Double Mountains.

This may be startling news to some of my theologically disposed colleagues who are still searching for God, whether on high, or out there, or in here, and to some of my philosophically disposed colleagues, who haven't yet commenced the search, wanting first to complete their inquiries into his-slash-her nature. Startling though it may be, it is nevertheless true. God abides on top of the Double Mountains.

And that's not all. The Double Mountains are not only the dwelling-place of God, but also, as the markers of my province, they are the first boundary of the cosmos.

The cosmos, as I am able to apprehend it, stretches from the Double Mountains northwestward some forty miles to the Big Rock Candy Mountain just south of Spur, the other, outer boundary of the cosmos. I can't tell you how to find the Big Rock Candy Mountain. On up that road from Aspermont, through Swenson, through Jayton, where my family lived, past Girard, I'd see it after a while off to the left. But you wouldn't see it. It's not there any more.

The Big Rock Candy Mountain was more an outcropping than a hill, I guess, and mostly rock. My father worked for the State Highway Department in 1937, while they made gravel for the new highway out of the mountain. We moved for the short term to a two-room house not far away. From the edge of the mesquite-strewn pasture that was our back yard, I could see the mountain and see the chunks chewed out of it as they ground the world to gravel. I remember my father coming home, his eyes red from the dust, his body still jumping and jerking from the jackhammer. He made two dollars a day.

One day we looked, and the machines had eaten all of the Big Rock Candy Mountain. It was gone. I would see it if I drove that way, but I can't tell you how to find it. You wouldn't see it.

But it is the other end of the cosmos. Cosmos stretched from the Double Mountains to that gone hill. In between lay Swenson and Jayton (where my family returned) and Girard and Spur. Most importantly, in between lay the Croton Breaks, my own wondrous middle earth. In these years since, I have left this cosmos. I have ignored it. I have, I do believe, lived awhile elsewhere. But it is still my province—my cosmos—still there just over the horizon. I can almost see it when my wife and I sit on the front porch.

A year or so ago an elderly lady wearing a red tam spent several weeks evangelizing among students and others on the campus. Almost every morning she would take her place on the sidewalk that runs along the east side of University Drive. She would stand sort of between the old Science Building and the library so that she was in the main line of student traffic between classes. When I first encountered her, I didn't know it, but her opening to all she stopped was, "Where do you expect to go when you die?"

I had been to the library and was headed back, angling out of the way a little, thinking I'd go by the post office before I went back to the office. That's how I fell to meet her—it came from angling out of the way a little.

"Where do you expect to go when you die?" she asked me.

Now I'm not too good with answers, even when I've practiced, and hers wasn't the kind of question that you get too many chances to practice on in an ordinary day. I didn't know what to say. To claim that I had a ticket to heaven seemed unrealistic. But then to declare that hell's my destination seemed a vain and prideful thing to do. So I told her that if it was all the same to her and to all concerned, I believed that I'd just go to the Croton Breaks.

I suppose that most folks would just as soon not retake that trip. And there may be some who'd say that going to the Croton Breaks is going to hell. I can see their way of thinking—one's no improvement over the other as far as annual rainfall is concerned. But anyway, that's what I told her.

The Croton Breaks make the middle of the cosmos I have sketched. You won't find them marked on some maps, but all maps will show a great empty space, a rough square using up parts of four counties, marked at four vague corners by Aspermont on the southeast, Jayton on the southwest, Spur on the northwest, and Guthrie on the northeast, where the Four Sixes Ranch falls into the bad country. Mr. J. W. Williams, in his book, *The Big Ranch Country*, offers first prize to the Croton Breaks for bad country in Texas, and tells of a roundup on the Matador Ranch in 1936 when cattlemen finally flushed out of the Breaks an old cow wearing a brand that hadn't been used in seventeen years.

No towns lie in the Breaks. They stretch thirty to forty miles in most any direction. Winding through the South is the Salt Fork of the Brazos River, and mostly dry and winding through all over is Croton Creek. An old reconnaissance soil survey says the soil is Vernon, very fine sandy loam, passing at about two feet into a reddish-yellow loam that carries considerable grayish calcareous material.

The Breaks are an eroded plain, a network of shallow gullies, deep gullies, deep mysterious canyons, dry stream courses with steep, sometimes vertical walls. They have their name from Colonel Randolph Marcy, who crossed the area in 1849, tending goldrushers on their way west, and marking out spots for cavalry forts on his return trip. He thought the waters of the creek he came to, of high mineral content and highly antithetical to constipation, were reminiscent of similarly curative waters from Croton Springs in New York. So it came to be Croton Creek, and the area came to be Croton Breaks.

But when I lived in Jayton, along its southwest edge, as I did until I was twelve or so, I didn't even know the name. I knew the stretch of country only as "the canyons." The first falling-off place was about ten yards from our back door, and I knew my corner of the canyons in a way not told by reconnaissance soil surveys, from days and hours alone, poking here and there, naming a dry waterfall in one place, marking the way to a special "lost canyon" in another, marveling at a dry water course just the width, at its bottom, of my foot from some rivulet an eon ago. It was the center of my cosmology, then, when I thought the top of a windmill was high, and the Double Mountains near Aspermont were the southerly end of the earth, and the Big Rock Candy Mountain was the other end of everything.

So when I said that I would just as soon go to the Croton Breaks, I intended no flippancy to the lady in the red tam. I meant her no disrespect. For quiet, I couldn't find a better place, and maybe, for knowing; the earth opens itself up in layers there, and each rock that falls after an age's pushing from the side of a gully reveals another surprise. But only if you go slow, and are willing to wait and watch, hunkered.

This is my province, though I think I have at least squatter's rights in others. Its outer dimensions, you may conclude, are narrow, but I will reply that its middle is wide and varied. This is my province. I am a provincial.

And I'm undisturbed about being provincial.

Each of us lives in a province. Not all are measured in the same way. Some are spatial. Some are temporal. Some are familial. Some are urban. Some are rural. Some are measured by information, some perhaps by insight. Some are walled by bigotry and ignorance. Size has little to do with province. Some people can make a province out of a hemisphere or out of a skin color. Each of us lives in a province, and we measure the world's dimensions by our own. Some people can move from one province to another and be at home. Others must visit, and then return. Some, if they're lucky, can stretch their province wider. Schools, if they're good, map a host of provinces and show you the roadways in and out. But each of us lives in a province.

We cannot be in all provinces at once, nor hear all melodies at once, nor say all words at once, and there is no final sadness in that. A province need not be a prison. Your primary metaphor, it is the place you stand to sense and measure your experience.

A province is only a prison if you live in it ignorant of nature. A province is only a prison if you do not know that it is a province. I pray that you know your province, wherever it lies, that you know it is a province, that you know it abuts and overlaps and entwines with all others, that it overlies and is overlain by all the provinces that ever were or will be.

The Double Mountains are sisters to the mountains that rise beyond South Fork in Colorado. The waters of the Neckar River that flow beneath the bridge at Heidelberg once trickled down the wash behind our house. The waters that lap at the pier in Rotterdam once lapped at the sides of the Double Mountains. Tomorrow's cosmos is visible in today's—if we look. And though an age has passed since it vanished, the Big Rock Candy Mountain still stands plain against the sky, off to the left of the road that runs northwestward through my cosmos.

CHAPTER THREE

What I Learned at School

When fall comes and the school year begins, I'm sometimes plagued by a temporary friskiness that tends to cause me some trouble before it subsides. This friskiness, I think, rises from two sources: part of it is left over from the summer when for a moment or two I'm led to think that I can really be a teacher, chiefly because there are not any committee meetings in the summer; part of it is left over from old times when I thought September 1 was New Year's Day because soon school would start and the Sears Roebuck catalogue would come.

At any rate, I am sometimes troubled by this coltish vigor before it wanes to be replaced by the decrepitude that is my more normal wont. This year, it led me to make a special mess of things. In an excess of zeal during the first meeting of my freshman composition class, I vowed that I would write an essay every time they did and that I would turn my essays over to them as they turned theirs in to me. Once I had said that, I was led by fear, desperation, and a smidgin of honor to do what I had said I would do. Now, nine essays and some short written exercises later, the term has ended, and I am blurred and fuzzy around the edges. Still, I want to do two things: I want to report what I think I learned while I was writing essays with my students, and I want to exhibit the last of these essays as one way of thinking about a composition class.

When I try to tally the things I learned while writing essays, the total is not impressive, but what's there is sufficiently troublesome, perplexing, confusing, instructive, and vexatious to bring me up short and to cast doubt upon certain assumptions about freshman composition.

First published in *College Composition and Communication* 26 (1975): 330–34.

1. I learned that writing out one's own assignments is a marvelous corrective to any tendency one might have for using merely habitual assignments or for witlessly making thoughtless or stupid assignments.

2. With some of the arguments and assumptions that undergird freshman composition I am familiar. I know that "the ability to write a literate essay is the hallmark of the educated person." I know that "a competent student ought to be able to produce a decent piece of writing on call." But I also learned that to write nine essays in a semester of fourteen weeks (I'm leaving out holiday weeks and the like) is a task very nearly not doable. I thought for a while that I would have to give myself an "I" for the course. I'll return to this item a bit later.

3. I learned that I often did precisely what I urged my students not to do: I hurried; I waited until the last moment, because that was the only moment there was; I accepted available subjects that came easily to mind; I wrote some "nice" essays and some "acceptable" essays; once or twice I turned in rough drafts as if they were finished papers. Perhaps I should add that I did usually get semicolons in the right place.

4. I need to say more about items 2 and 3 in order to tell what I really learned, to tell why writing nine essays is a task very nearly not doable. Perhaps what I really learned is that I have not learned enough. Or perhaps what I really learned is that part of what I know *about* writing (though right enough in its way) is not germane or immediate or companionable when one is *doing* the writing. Perhaps I shall be thought merely naïve, but as I was writing the nine essays I found myself being shocked and surprised and stunned. (I'd not want anyone to think I was in a state of heightened sensibilities all of the time—a good part of the time I was simply stuporous.) The things that kept disturbing me can be suggested best, I think, under two headings: problems in the inventive capacities given by a semester, and problems in establishing occasions for writing.

I know some of the hopes and goals associated with invention or "prewriting" and some of the methods developed to foster rich and generative invention. But a term has markedly little time in it. Last semester when I was writing the nine essays, I was busy (and I'd like to stop and sing a sad song or two about that), but that's no great matter: every person's life is usually busy to the level that can be tolerated. Students in the class, who also had to write nine essays, were in this sense as busy as I was. A semester affords precious little time for genuine invention, exploration, and discovery. I found that I frequently was unable to do what I often advised my students to do in searching out subjects and finding ways to be with the subject and an audience in a paper. Actually, in class I was pretty reckless in recommending ways of thinking into subjects: I proposed that my students use journals and write existential sentences; we tackled the topics; I recommended the series of exploratory questions offered by Richard E. Larson (in *College English,* October, 1968); we practiced using problem-solving systems for locating the materials of a paper; we hungered after various heuristic models for discovery; we looked at this, that, and the other thing as particles, waves, and fields. We even tried the TUTO rhythmic method (and I'll be glad to answer letters inquiring after the TUTO mysteries).

But the sorry truth is that, whatever the students were able to do as they were writing, I was almost never able to think a paper out ahead of time; I was never able to write a draft and let it alone awhile before I revised it for final copy; I was never able to try portions of the essays from different perspectives and in different styles. I was never able to take a possible subject, hold it in my hand, look at it in this way and that way, and scout its possibilities. What I actually did was to cash in ideas I *already* had for writing, threshing around among scraps of paper, notebooks, and lists of things to do that were piled on my desk, finding subjects and sketched designs for writing that I wanted to do some time. A dark thought struck me one night: What if I didn't have these notions collected to cash in? That dark thought was followed by another: What if I were not in the habit of writing, of expecting to write, of saving notes against the time when I would write? In other words, I finally thought, what if I were in the same fix that most of the students in my class were in?

But the perturbation I felt went further. I found myself continually troubled by the character of what I'll call the occasions for writing. I remember sitting at my desk one evening when I *had* to get an essay written to give to my students the next morning. I remember the moment clearly. I was sitting there looking at the assignment I had given to my students, when another dark thought came: "I *know* how to write this thing," I remember saying to myself, "but why in hell would anybody *want* to?"

What I am trying to get at here is that the occasion is wrong. The occasion contains no immediacy; it offers no genuine need that must be genuinely answered. I mean to suggest that even some of our best assignments—imaginative and thoughtful as they may be—do not elicit a driving need to write. I mean to suggest that some of our best assignments do not elicit the students' investment of themselves in the work.

Perhaps I should learn not to worry. Perhaps I should learn to accept the freshman composition course as a place for the acquisition of tools and for practice in using them skillfully in finger exercises. There'd be no shame in that—indeed, nothing but good. But I think I won't learn that, because I keep learning something else at school, every term. I can best begin to say what that is, I believe, by exhibiting the last essay I wrote with the students in my class.

Half Thoughts on a Whole Semester

I was ruminating last night over certain features of English 1203, sensing a weight that some of its parts carry. Ruminating, I should say, is an activity, better still a condition, I assign high priority to. Given the choice, I'll ruminate any time rather than turn the compost pile or paint the dining room or grade papers or fix the shelf that's been waiting for five and a half years or work on the manuscript that's due March 1. At any rate, I was ruminating, turning the semester's topics this way and that to see how they looked from the underside and what consequence they had.

But I can only speak of consequence in certain ways. I'd not presume to declare that topics of my devising had this, that, or the other specific consequence for students. I'm generally inclined to think that all courses are failures: there's always more to be said than can be said in a given moment, way more reaches of thought to be in than one can be in at a given moment. So if I speak of consequences, I am not speaking of consequences of the course, but of consequences, weights, significances carried by the topics of concern themselves. The topics, the issues, the practices carry meaning, I think, even if it is not presently realized in us. The subject makes its own assertions, to which we're seldom equal.

On the first day of the term, I remember remarking that I wanted to conceive of the work we might do not as the work of a single term, but as the work of a two-term, nine-month period. I said then, I recall, that as I was presently able to understand the work before us, it could be seen in three stages: the practice of *invention,* the shaping of *structure,* and the tuning of *styles.* As I recollect the occasion, I noted that I expected the end of the fall term to come between the second and third of these.

Since that day much has happened, though often without notice. Miss Puckitt has always come early, usually followed by Miss Ramsey. Miss Daniel and Miss Cesarotti have always been punctual—two minutes late. Miss Pugh and Miss FitzSimmon have walked down the hall together. Mr. Ragsdale has written an essay about toothpaste. Mr. White has been quiet in the back, though his essays are not quiet alone but forceful. Miss Steinberg has seen to it that I remembered to be humble. Miss Stamper has found sonata form in Stegner's essay. Miss Westbrook has meditated on epistolary ills. Mr. Spleth from a "Bad Beginning" has surged toward who knows what ending. Miss Fouch has found a way to talk about intravenous tubes and cats in the same essay. Mr. Haney has embarked upon a series of essays that may come at last to seventeen volumes and be studied by freshmen. Miss Bachman has told a strange Thanksgiving narrative in which much depended on a word heard out of context. Mr. Hayes has vowed his distaste for hickory nuts. Mr. Posselt, lately arrived from the north, has encountered a street evangelist. Mr. Sherwood has found in empathy a way of distinguishing among teachers. Miss Lawson has almost learned to be decisive. Mr. Whitney has celebrated his hometown's virtues, though we both hope that the actual text of the celebration is not to be published abroad in Tyler. And Mr. Steimel has slept as well as could be reasonably expected, though of late he has taken to staying awake and disturbing the class.

Meanwhile, with various fanfares, flourishes, and fallings-down, I like to imagine that I have been talking about *invention* and *structure*. What I think I said (as distinct from what you may have heard, distracted by 372 pipe lightings) arranged itself in something like this order:

INVENTION (the exploration that precedes and leads to writing)

—where you find subjects if you don't have one, or what to do with a subject that someone else hands you

—taking a subject over, making it into something of your own

—seeing the fullness of a subject, learning its potential

—ways of thinking through subjects

—relationships among writer, subject, and audience, and the distances between them

—using the resources that you need to deal with a subject

—logical development and emotional appeals

—learning to be real with an audience

STRUCTURE (design, organization, shape in writing)

—some practice in describing structures

—some talk about structural transfers from one medium or art form to another

—using structures that others use

—some talk about the relation of structure and meaning

A little earlier, you may recall, I was talking about the consequences such topics have, trying to establish that the consequences I am talking about are not those of the course, but the weights, values, meanings the topics themselves carry. I can illustrate what I mean, I think, by referring to the list just above. For example, we talked at various times about using the resources that are available to you, including research, and about taking over and using a structure that other writers have used. Those two notions, whether I managed to say it fully or not, whether you managed to hear it fully or not, can carry an import in their own right, an import and significance not limited to freshman composition. They give us a way of knowing that we are, after all, together with each other, that we are in community if we wish to be, that others have striven and learned, and that we may learn from them with less strife, that we are not alone, though we can be if we wish. In some way or another, I think each of the items arranged above carries such meaning.

But I have been thinking from the start not about the signification of each topic raised, but about the meaning carried by invention itself, by structure itself, and by the order in which they appeared. Such meaning—and it is of course not complete—stretches out, it seems to me, from English composition to everything, but can at the moment best be expressed in the context and language of a composition class, as I have tried to do below. I herewith advance to you certain propositions intended to suggest what is learnable from composition study and practice (though it's also nice if you learn where to put semicolons). If you find the numbering system below a bit strange, you will understand from it, I think, that there are yet other propositions I have not found.

Ninth law of composition: Everything comes from somewhere and goes some place. You touch other people, and they enter your world, coming from another. You read a book and capture its author into your world. Both come from somewhere and move elsewhere, into your thoughts, giving texture to the universe you live in, becoming finally the words you speak.

Eleventh law of composition: Some things precede other things. Invention precedes structure. Thinking and feeling and being precede writing. Structures made without invention are false or superficial. There probably is a fit sequencing of things, even if we don't always see it.

Eighteenth law of composition: You are always standing somewhere when you say something. You are in a world, you have thoughts, you've made choices (whether or not consciously) any time you say anything. If you are in a position whenever you say anything, it's probably best to know what the position is.

Twenty-fifth law of composition: Invention is an invitation to openness. It asks of you that you open yourself to the ways other people think, to the knowledge that already exists, to the intricacies and whims of your own being. It asks of you that you therefore be tentative a while, consider alternatives a while, be in process a while.

Twenty-sixth law of composition: But structure is a closure. You can't organize an essay or a sonata unless you have ruled out other organizations. When structure begins to be made, you are no longer open: you have made choices.

Twenty-seventh law of composition: Invention and structure, then, represent a way of being in the world. They exert certain demands upon you, and they afford you certain pleasures. Invention invites you to be open to a creation filled with copious wonders, trivialities, sorrows, and amazements. Structure requires that you close. You are asked to be open and always closing.

Thirty-second law of composition: What follows feeds, enlarges, and enriches what precedes. Invention precedes and is open. Structure follows and closes. That may seem a narrowing disappointment, a ruling out of possibilities. It needn't be. Every choice, every decision, every structure has the potential of being another entry in the inventive world you live in, modifying it, punching it in here, pooching it out there, giving color to it yonder. Invention precedes, structure follows, but invention does not cease thereby. The structure we make today may give grace to tomorrow's invention. That means that if today we fail to be wise and generous and good, tomorrow we may succeed, and if not, we may fail at a higher level.

I should report, in closing, that when the students in my class examined my papers, as I examined theirs, they concluded that I was given to rambling.

CHAPTER FOUR

Varieties of Ethical Argument, with Some Account of the Significance of Ethos in the Teaching of Composition

Much of what follows may seem remote from the customary interests and uses of *Freshman English News.* To be sure, there is some risk that in the end all of what follows will both seem and be distant from the journal's usual concerns. I hope otherwise, of course, but do concede that I have begun far off from composition. Briefly, what I want to do is to examine what *ethos* means in a rhetorical context, then to propose a way of differentiating among different forms of *ethos,* and then at the last to explore what all of this means for the teaching of composition.

But since the route is twisty and since I am asking to be tolerated, I should be more specific in forecasting what is to follow. In the first section, I want to try to account for what brings me to *ethos* as a subject. The second section will record a minor exploration of other approaches to the nature of *ethos* and of ethical argument. The third section introduces a primary problem: since all discourse may be taken as ethical discourse, then talking about *ethos* and ethical argument means taking on the hopeless task of talking about all discourse without any means of differentiation. The section closes with particular instances of *ethos* which suggest that differentiation is possible. Section 4, then, proposes a scheme of classification and explores some examples. Section 5 amplifies the discussion of one kind of *ethos* and uses that discussion as a base for suggesting a model for communication and

First published in *Freshman English News* 6 (1978): 1–23.

for outlining a conception of commodious speech. At the last, Section 6 wants to show what bearing all this has upon the teaching of composition.

The manifestation of character or *ethos* in discourse, together with the origin, nature, and consequence of this process, compels attention for many reasons, both private and public. I cannot account in any single or simple way for focusing on this particular feature of rhetorical study. I can give some partial explanations.

Lemuel Gulliver provides a place to start. When I was young, I read *Gulliver's Travels,* and I believed what Lemuel Gulliver said. Now I still believe in Lemuel Gulliver, but I don't accept everything he says. Sometimes he gets things wrong. Sometimes his way of looking at things is peculiar. He reports his perceptions accurately enough, but his report also gives us evidence enough to question his perceptions. In all of this there is much that continues to interest me. Why did I believe all that Gulliver says when I first read him? Why do I respond differently now? What happens in the text to elicit first the one response and then the other?

In the second place, a general interest in argument and its outcomes can always arise easily enough from disguised or open megalomania. I sometimes think that I know the truth about things. Apparently other people sometimes think that they know the truth. Yet each of us knows that we are sometimes unable to say the truth we fully know to another so that he or she may hear it as truth. Sometimes we make splendid arguments and no one listens. Sometimes other people listen and then disregard and repudiate what we say. I want to know—I think I *need* to know, and I expect others in their way also need to know—why apparently good arguments sometimes eventuate in nothing. We have all seen sweet, clear logic disavowed, and we have all seen decent, honorable emotional appeals denied. I'm interested in the nature of *ethos* and ethical appeal, then, on the possibility that understanding this feature of discourse will explain accords and rebuttals where knowledge of logical arguments and emotional appeals will not.

In the third place, Aristotle's brief early remark (*Rhetoric* 1356A) is compelling:

Ethical proof is wrought when the speech is so spoken as to make the speaker credible; for we trust good men more and sooner, as a rule, about everything; while, about things which do not admit of precision, but only of guess-work, we trust them absolutely. Now this trust, too, ought to be produced by means of the speech,—not by a previous conviction that the speaker is this or that sort of man. It is not true, as some of the technical writers assume in their systems, that the moral worth of the speaker contributes nothing to his persuasiveness; nay, it might be said that almost the most authoritative of proofs is that supplied by character.

Although the skepticism we sometimes seem to have learned from our age may lead us to wonder whether the absolute trust suggested above ever occurs, Aristotle's judgment that character affords "almost the most authoritative of proofs" demands attention.

And the passage suggests a fourth reason for focusing on *ethos* and inquiring about the nature of ethical proof. The preoccupation with *credibility* on all sides during these last ten years or so indicates that we have been involved in fact in learning about *ethos* whether we knew it or not. We are already interested in the process by which words are used to constitute a view of the speaker's self, and we have had many occasions to learn that words are sometimes used to create a self that replaces or masks the speaker's real self. During the Watergate hearings we heard speakers use language apparently intended to cleanse their characters and thereby to promote credibility: when a motive or an action is located "at that point in time," it is, one presumes, liberated from its antecedents and consequences so that the speaker is purified for a given moment. But we learned that this kind of purification may work in many ways. "Failure to call dirty business by its "rightful name," according to a 1975 interim report of the Senate Intelligence Committee, "may have increased the risk of dirty business being done."[1] It has sometimes seemed, as Christopher Lasch puts it, that "[t]he very distinction between truth and falsehood has receded into obscurity. In politics, as in advertising, truth has given way to credibility, facts to statements that sound authoritative without conveying any authoritative information" (24).

The subject requires attention, I think, for a fifth reason, or rather I should say, a related and messy set of reasons. Along with everyone else, I notice that people often don't listen to each other even when they're making sense. I'd like to know why. Along with everyone else, I notice that we have the habit of diminishing each other's words. When another person speaks, we're likely to register and accept only those words that fit a discourse that we have already in our minds. I'd like to know why this is so. We have to wonder whether the truth will ever get heard. Supposing someone should learn the truth and want to announce it to others? What will cause people to listen to the truth? And if we *cause* people to listen, have we already disturbed the truth? What is it that transpires when one person speaks and another truly listens?

> In *The Presentation of Self in Everyday Life* (1959), the first of his books, Goffman argued that we are all essentially performers. [. . .] "A correctly staged and performed scene," he writes in *The Presentation of Self,* "leads the audience to impute a self to a performed character, but this imputation—this self—is a product of a scene that comes off, and is not a cause of it." When a performance "comes off," he adds, "the firm self accorded each performed character will appear to emanate intrinsically from its performer." What Goffman seems to be denying, then, is the possibility of precisely the sort of authenticity our society values most highly. A being is authentic, Lionel Trilling tells us in *Sincerity and Authenticity,* "by reason of its entire self-definition: it is understood to exist wholly by laws of its own being." Conversely, inauthenticity is a condition to which we fall when "the sentiment of individual being depends upon other people." If, then, in Goffman's world the self is no more than an optical illusion which merely "appears" to emanate from the actor—if the self is, as Goffman says, an "imputation"—the notion of personal authenticity can hardly be more than an arrogant conceit. "In this enterprise of presenting the self, of putting ourselves on the social stage, sincerity itself plays a curiously compromised part," Trilling observes. "Society requires of us that we present ourselves as being sincere, and the most efficacious way of satisfying this demand is to see to it that we really are sincere, that we actually are what we want our community to know we are. In short, we play the role of being ourselves, we sincerely act the part of the sincere person, with the result that a judgment can be passed upon our sincerity that it is not authentic." (Rosenberg 21)

Sixth, I come to this subject, I think, partly because of what Kenneth Burke taught us. We are, after all, apart from each other, and it may be, as Burke said, that the only thing we have in common is our separateness. Distances open between us. We keep trying to tell ourselves to others across the way. We keep trying to enter their world or bring them into ours. Often we fail, but we keep trying. The trouble is that our speaking-forth—the primary need and issue of any age—is complex, confused, and messy, and often creates as many problems as it solves. Language is our way of composing ourselves. It is our first and last line of defense, and we are vulnerable on each line.

A seventh reason for coming to this study is that, quite simply, nothing else seems so important right now as the questions generating and generated by such study. Can we learn how to say the truth? If we learn how to say the truth, can we say it to another? Whom will we listen to? Who will listen to us? Can we sing the Lord's song in a strange land? Will we recognize it if we hear another sing it? Somehow or other, everything depends on our speaking-forth. In a recent essay on the relation of rhetoric to poetic, Stanley Plumly remarks that "[r]hetoric, whatever the year, and whatever the aesthetic, establishes credentials, establishes voice" (21). A little later, he adds, "What pulls us into the good book, the whole book, what keeps our attention, from poem to poem, part to part, is the accumulating strength and complexity and interest and full character of the speaking voice" (28). Plumly's remarks are useful reminders of that clue from Aristotle. We can learn from rhetoric, at least, where to look—to character as it emerges in language. But while rhetoric may tell us where to look, traditional forms of rhetorical study won't tell us all we need to know. S. M. Halloran has explained why the study of *ethos* has become so crucial and why traditional rhetorical wisdom won't suffice. He points out that while classical rhetoric rested on the assumption that wisdom is open and publicly available, in the modern world the speaker can scarcely know where to begin. No commonly accepted process of invention is available to us. There is no widely accepted set of common values that he or she can assume. There are no universally accepted *topoi* that he or she may use as places of argument. Modern man, Halloran suggests, has been denied the possibility of achieving knowledge on which to base his life. Assumptions about knowledge, Halloran goes on to say, are no longer tenable—external reality is paradoxical, and the effort to know something alters what we seek to know. Modern rhetoricians, Halloran says, face the fundamental problem of discovering why the speaker's world and a hearer's world is so broad and learning how one might bridge it successfully. When a speaker and a hearer inhabit the same world, it is enough, commonly, that both attend to the argument. But when a speaker and an audience inhabit different worlds, the audience may never be able to hear what the speaker is saying.[2] When speakers are deprived of a given world, Halloran concludes, they are deprived, too, of a given rhetoric. They must create their own *topoi*, their own schemes and tropes, their own way of inventing. They must constitute their own world and themselves by their language. They must create their own rhetoric. Rhetoric, then, won't tell us all we need to know, but we can learn from rhetoric where to look—at the ways character emerges in language, at the ways worlds are constituted in individual discourses.

And finally, there is an eighth reason for coming to this study. There's always that ominous curse: "Let us go down and there confound their language, that they may not understand one another's speech." It both is and isn't a curse, of course. Great gaps open between us because we speak different tongues, and we face the extraordinary dilemma described by Georges Gusdorf in *Speaking:*

> It seems that the use of speech obliges us to choose between two opposite forms of alienation. On the one hand, like the madman or the mystic, we can speak as no one else speaks. On the other hand, like the practitioner of a "basic" language, we can speak as everyone else does. In both cases the very meaning of personality is done away with. The more I communicate, the less I express myself; the more I express myself, the less I communicate. It is necessary to choose between incomprehensibility and inauthenticity—between excommunication and self-denial. (52)

But because we do speak different tongues we can be different and say different things. And since we do speak different tongues, we still face intriguing questions: Whom will we listen to? Who will listen to us? What transpires between us? How do we sing the Lord's song in a strange land?

To be sure, no study will answer all the questions, or locate and solve all the problems, but surely there are reasons enough to study *ethos* and ethical argument.

2

The passage from Aristotle cited a little earlier suggests strongly that ethical argument is central in human discourse. Halloran proposed that *ethos* is all we are left with, the chancy capacity to constitute a world and compose ourselves with language. If they are right, then the questions that Richard E. Vatz poses ought surely to be a focus of study among rhetoricians: "What *ethos* creates salience?" and "Who has the *ethos* to infuse meaning?" (68). Many have examined the nature of *ethos*, of course, but as often as not their studies have been incomplete, or they have left us where we do not want and cannot bear to be.

Certain obvious qualities might be expected to account for the incidence of authentic speech, the ethical appeal that binds a revealed character and an audience, but they do not. We might expect a compelling *ethos* to emerge where lofty learning and a thoughtful personality converge at some grand occasion, but we look through our history and find unlearned speakers and erratic personalities gaining hearers on trivial occasions.

The standard sources that we rely on for so much else in rhetorical studies don't tell us enough, or they tell us a great deal that does not turn out to be useful. Aristotle, having already proposed that "almost the most authoritative of proofs is that supplied by character," says that three things make a character trustworthy—intelligence, virtue, and goodwill. That is difficult to dispute, and it is needless to do so, but we still know that intelligent, virtuous, and benevolently disposed speakers have failed to win hearings. Quintilian gives a just and appropriate account of the truly virtuous speaker:

> For however we strive to conceal it, insincerity will always betray itself, and there was never in any man so great eloquence as

would not begin to stumble and hesitate so soon as his words ran counter to his inmost thoughts. Now a bad man cannot help speaking things other than he feels. On the other hand, the good will never be at a loss for honourable words or fail to find matter full of virtue for utterance, since among his virtues practical wisdom will be one. (*Institutio Oratoria* I.i.)

But we know that speakers only perceived as good seem never "at a loss for honourable words," and we know that bad men have won audiences who thought they heard virtue speaking.

Compounding our difficulty with some traditional discussions of *ethos* is that, despite best intentions, they seem so easily convertible to artifice and calculation, as in this passage from Cicero:

A potent factor in success, then, is for the characters, principles, conduct and course of life, both of those who are to plead cases and of their clients, to be approved, and conversely those of their opponents condemned; and for the feelings of the tribunal to be won over, as far as possible, to goodwill towards the advocate and the advocate's client as well. Now feelings are won over by a man's merit, achievements or reputable life, qualifications easier to embellish, if only they are real, than to fabricate where nonexistent. But attributes useful in an advocate are a mild tone, a countenance expressive of modesty, gentle language, and the faculty of seeming to be dealing reluctantly and under compulsion with something you are really anxious to prove. It is very helpful to display the tokens of good-nature, kindness, calmness, loyalty and a disposition that is pleasing and not grasping or covetous, and all the qualities belonging to men who are upright, unassuming and not given to haste, stubbornness, strife or harshness, are powerful in winning goodwill, while the want of them estranges it from such as do not possess them; accordingly the very opposites of these qualities must be ascribed to our opponents. (*De Oratore* II.xliii.182)

If a speaker sets out on purpose to win a hearing by displaying his or her "mild tone," or "countenance expressive of modesty," or by demonstrating intelligence, virtue, and goodwill, then we shouldn't be too surprised if what we get, at times, is a contrived image and a staged virtue.

A little earlier, I suggested that some studies of *ethos* leave us where we do not want and cannot bear to be. What if it turns out that our reasons for listening to another person are selfish and ignoble? What if it turns out that we respond to a speaker as a trustworthy *ethos* only if we have something at stake in what he or she says? "The trinity of Aristotle," Otis M. Walter says, "cannot explain many whose styles of thought, styles of living, and styles of hair-do are cherished and imitated. Aristotle's analysis may be a good statement of whom we *ought* to believe, but it is inadequate to account for the many in whom we *do* believe" (37). Walter suggests that the speaker having a trustworthy *ethos* for us fulfills a strong need that we perceive as worthy or moral but are unable to fulfill ourselves, the speaker having some sort of exclusive ability to fulfill the need: "*Ethos* arises only when there is a strong need, only when the need can best be gratified by another, and only when such needs are perceived to be (correctly or incorrectly) worthy" (43). Perelman's concept of presence admits a similar possibility. Things may exist, Perelman says, and we may perceive them, without accepting them into consciousness: "[I]t is not enough indeed that a thing should exist for a person to feel its presence" (43). A thing has presence for us only when we are aware of it; we are aware of a thing only if it has meaning for us, and it has meaning for us only if it satisfies a need we have.[3] The circumstances that determine presence, Perelman says, are time, place, relation, and self-interest. When a speaker proposes change, for example, he or she is asking the hearer to change, to risk self, to engage self in the discourse. Presence is essential in argumentation, Mader says, "not only because it compels one to attend to a problem but also because it compels one to recognize his own significance in relation to reality" (381). If a thing is to enter our consciousness, engage us, Perelman (117–18) says that it must be overestimated, that is, isolated from all else in the hearer's mind. "Basically, then," Mader adds, "the argumentation must be of such a nature that on the one hand it focuses the hearer's attention on the attitude to be adopted or the action to be performed, while on the other hand, it *distracts* the hearer from taking into account other matters that might impede the adoption of the attitude or the performance of the action" (37).

Perhaps in the end that's all there is. Perhaps we have to acknowledge that we will listen to a speaker only when gratification is possible or when self-interest is at stake. I don't think so.

I do know, however, that good ideas sometimes don't get a hearing, and it may be that they don't because they have not yet been spoken into existence in such a way as to engage our self-interest. Most arguments on energy conservation and development, for example, have apparently not yet become present to us.

We are alone, separate from each other, trying to define ourselves to each other, trying to bring others into our world, ourselves into the worlds of others. It is difficult to face the possibility that we can only be heard if we offer gratification, or if we manipulate others so that they think they need what we offer.

3

If that is the way we are, we plainly need to know. We need to know why we are sometimes frightened or self-seeking in our relations with others, why we are sometimes so exclusive in our convictions about who is a friend and companion, who is a stranger and perhaps an enemy. Understanding the nature of *ethos* will not, to be sure, end wars and alarms. It may help us to understand better.

Accepting for the moment Aristotle's classification of the persuasive modes, we know or should know that *pathos* does not account for all accords that occur between speakers and hearers and, indeed, seems curiously ineffectual at critical moments. The prospects of thermonuclear disaster or of complete energy shutdown seem to offer bases for ultimate emotional arguments, yet speakers addressing those subjects have not yet persuaded us to study war no more or to discover new skills. In all likelihood, as Halloran says, *logos* generates accord only when speaker and hearer inhabit the same universe of language and value. If neither emotional argument nor logical argument can account for all discursive accords, we must turn back to ethical argument and inquire how the presentation of one self to another creates acceptance or agreement, or fails to do so.

About this it is difficult to learn how to talk. Conventional discussions of ethical argument focus on its demand for the speaker to demonstrate his or her good sense, good character, and benevolent disposition. Yet the moment we tell a potential speaker that he or she must be certain to demonstrate good sense, good character, and easy disposition, we are, as I have already suggested, close to advising artifice and the exercise of calculated design upon an audience. We have already more than we need of good images and designed credibility. It is, perhaps, more important for us to ask just *how* character is revealed in language, or just what qualities of character in particular reveal good sense, good character, and goodwill and so elicit accord, or just how we are to discriminate among ethical appeals. But since ethical argument appears to be contingent upon a presence emerging in discourse, the real voice of a genuine personality, it may be that the mode cannot be defined or described for general purposes and that we must content ourselves with observation of its particular manifestations.

Certainly a host of problems stands in the way of learning about ethical argument, whether we wish to describe the mode generically or seek only to describe the operation of *ethos* in a single discourse. One presiding problem is that all discourse is ethical, revealing speakers' characters by design or by default. Style is the revelation of identity, the syndrome of character, open to diagnosis. If all discourse is ethical, then talking about ethical discourse means talking about the whole range of human discourse. One who sets out to talk about emotional argument, for example, can probably exclude a number of discourses that are not emotional in mode and thereby focus attention upon the residue. But if one sets out to talk about ethical argument, nothing can be excluded. And that generates another major problem: if all discourse is ethical, how shall we distinguish among discourses, or mark the fruitful and the perverse?

Both worthy and unworthy discourses have won hearings in their own time or after the passage of time has brought new versions of truth, new audiences with new needs. Many have found ethical appeal in and believed pathological speakers. Indeed, *ethos* may win us for insufficient or bad reasons, and the perverse, neurotic voice may exercise for some the same appeal that the virtuous voice generates. Walter's account of *ethos*, cited earlier, suggests that *ethos* always operates in the same way, regardless of associated virtue or vice: "*Ethos* arises only when there is a strong need, only when the need can best be gratified by another, and only when such needs are perceived to be (correctly or incorrectly) worthy" (43).[4]

The first problem posed above, that no discourse can be excluded in the study of *ethos,* cannot be solved. But we can be in the process of solving it as we examine individual discourses, facing the issue of our presentation to each other and learning ways of talking about *ethos.* The second problem, that we have no means of discriminating among forms of *ethos,* can at least be considered, if not solved.

One way to approach this second problem is, for the moment at least, to abandon the rhetorical monism that we find in Walter's work and elsewhere and thereby discard the notion that *ethos* always works in the same way. Clearly, there are different forms of *ethos,* and it may be possible to discern not just individual instances, but also reasonable groupings.

To begin with, I want to suggest two forms of *ethos,* neither of which can be satisfactorily explained by a monistic insistence on, for example, "presence" or gratification.

The first is literary. *Ethos* does not belong to argument alone. *Ethos is* character, particularly as it may emerge during the process of a discourse. An *ethos* emerges in any literary work in which a fictive character becomes believable. Characterization creates *ethos.* The *ethos* of the speaker in "My Last Duchess" emerges pretty plainly to us while at the same time the speaker aims a different *ethos* at the hearer in the poem. An *ethos* forms as Ulysses speaks in Tennyson's "Ulysses," and in fact Ulysses makes an interesting, though largely inadvertent, ethical argument in favor of his own abdication. We know the characters in *As I Lay Dying* as separate entities. Any well-realized literary character is well-realized by virtue of his or her language. This form of *ethos* does not appear to depend upon "presence," or upon need-gratification, or upon intelligence, virtue, and goodwill.

A second form of *ethos* occurs that does not appear to be explicable by monistic standards. To show what I mean, I must turn for a moment to some other features of rhetorical study and then, at somewhat greater length, to Jack Schaefer's novel *Shane.*

Inventio, by its nature, calls for openness to the accumulated resources of the world a speaker lives in, to its landscapes, its information, its ways of thinking and feeling. *Dispositio* and *elocutio,* by their nature, are closures. When speech emerges as structure and style, choices have already been made, consciously or otherwise, and the speaker is no longer in a state of openness. (I'd not presume to say that we all open ourselves freely to the possibilities of our inventive world before we speak, only that the nature of invention is such as to invite openness.)

It is reasonable to say, then, that characteristically *inventio* is larger than *dispositio* and *elocutio.* It holds more. There is always more to be said than can be said in a given discourse. *Inventio is* the world the speaker lives in. Whatever its dimensions, it is normally larger than any structure the speaker can make or any style he can command. *Inventio is* greater than *dispositio* and *elocutio.*

That is at least "normally" true. In certain circumstances, it is not true.

At least in a certain kind of hero it does not appear to be true. In this hero there is a perfect economical balance. *Inventio* is equal to *dispositio* and *elocutio; dispositio* and *elocutio* are equal to *inventio.* This hero appropriates and owns all that is in his inventive world, and he can make all the structures and styles that his inventive world will generate. He uses his world fully. His invention makes fully possible a range of structures and styles; his structures and styles use up his invention. He is master of his world, and its model. He owns all its resources, uses all of its structures, all of its styles, and he is not tied to or limited by any one of them. Beowulf, I think, is such a hero. Shane is another.

Shane's inventive world stretches far, and he commands it all. His world reaches in time from a deep past to a distant future. Back of the events of *Shane,* he has a past "fenced as tightly as our pasture" (11). In a scene with the boy-narrator he tells and then shows the boy how to draw and point his gun, the demonstration causing him to slip back into his past:

> As the words came, he was doing it. The old gun was bearing on some target over by the corral and the hammer was clicking at the empty cylinder. Then the hand around the gun whitened and the fingers slowly opened and the gun fell to the ground. The hand sank to his side, stiff and awkward. He raised his head and

the mouth was a bitter gash in his face. His eyes were fastened on
the mountains climbing in the distance.

"Shane! Shane! What's the matter?"

He did not hear me. He was back somewhere along the dark
trail of the past. (79)

In a discussion of the screen western, Peter Homans says that the
hero is characteristically

> [. . .] a transcendent figure, originating beyond the town. Classi-
> cally, he rides into town from nowhere; even if he is the marshal,
> his identity is in some way dissociated from the people he must
> save. We know nothing of any past activities, relationships, fu-
> ture plans, or ambitions. Indeed, the hero is himself quite am-
> biguous about these. (77)

But if we do not know the details of Shane's life outside the context given in the novel, we do know that his capacities stretch
not only out along "the dark trail of the past," but also far into
the future. Shane was, the boy says, "one of us, unchangeable
and always" (102). Later the boy remarks, "[H]e came to us and
you knew that the spirit in him would sustain him thus alone for
the farthest distance and forever" (137). And the boy comes to
know that even though Shane has gone, "He was there. He was
there in our place and in us. Whenever I needed him, he was
there" (212).

But the range of Shane's inventive world is best revealed by
the variety of structures and styles he commands. He can do all
there is in his world to be done. He knows how to bow over
Marian's hand when they are introduced (10), and he knows how
to dissemble when they try to draw him out (11). By contrast, he
holds violence and knows its ways. At first, he evokes in the boy
a "sudden chill terror," and there "were sharp hidden hardnesses
in him. But these were not for us. He was dangerous as mother
had said. But not to us as father too had said" (30). At the same
time, he masters simple, if demanding, chores. As Shane settles in
to work on the tree stump, the boy is impressed by "the easy way
the power in him poured smoothly into each stroke. The man
and the axe seemed to be partners in the work" (32). Whenever
a need arises, whenever "a call came,"

[. . .] there would be a concentration in him, a singleness of dedication to the instant need, that seemed to me at once wonderful
and disturbing. (62)

He commands a variety of styles—all that his inventive world
generates. His manner is potent from the start. "Anything he
does," Joe Starrett says, "will be done right" (59). Even at the
first and from afar, he is seen to be decisive and durable (2–3).
He is "nice and polite and sort of gentle"; at the same time, "he's
dangerous all right" (15). He handles six runaway steers "neat
as pie" (72), yet becomes "the full sum of the integrate force that
was Shane" only when he buckles on his gun belt (181). The
consummate gunfighter, he also has the gentleness to hear and to
reassure the boy following the climactic gunfight:

> "I don't care," I said, the tears starting. "I don't care if he was the
> fastest that ever was.
>
> He'd never have been able to shoot you, would he? You'd
> have got him straight, wouldn't you—if you had been in prac-
> tice?"
>
> He hesitated a moment. He gazed down at me and into me
> and he knew. He knew what goes on in a boy's mind and what
> can help him stay clean inside through the muddled, dirtied years
> of growing up.
>
> "Sure. Sure, Bob. He'd never even have cleared the holster."
> (202)

Shane owns the styles that will let him speak to men in various
contexts—to farmers, ranchers, to the young cowboy he beats
and then gently tends—to a woman, Marian Starrett, and to the
boy who is narrator of the book.

Shane's mastery of his world is apparent from the start, though
at the outset observers respond only to his depth since they have
not seen him in action. He is clearly special: the first people in the
valley to see him up close, two cowhands, "stop and stare after
him with curious intentness" (1). The boy-narrator is immediately struck by the "impact of the man himself" (3). The boy
senses early on the power and depth in Shane. Potent in him, the
boy knows, is "a burst of indescribable deadliness" (28), and in
his eyes there is reflected "some pain deep within him" (29). By
the time of his systematic beating of Chris, the young cowboy,

Gerald Haslam remarks, "The full capabilities of Shane's mysterious potency are now unmistakable" (16). Shane is efficient at
everything he undertakes; the breadth of his inventive world is
revealed by the variety of structures and styles he masters.

Broad and deep and various as Shane's world is, however, it
hasn't size enough for the other world that is waiting. "The open
range can't last forever," Joe Starrett tells Shane, and he continues:

> "The fence lines are closing in. Running cattle in big lots is good
> business only for the top ranchers and it's really a poor business
> at that. Poor in terms of the resources going into it. Too much
> space for too little results. It's certain to be crowded out."
> "Well, now," said Shane, "that's mighty interesting. I've been
> hearing the same quite a lot lately and from men with pretty
> clear heads. Maybe there's something to it." (12)

Shane recognizes the interface of the two worlds when he learns
that Fletcher, the big rancher, is crowding Starrett and the other
farmers:

> He moved his head to look out the window over the valley to the
> mountains marching along the horizon. "It's always the same,"
> he murmured. He was sort of talking to himself. "The old ways
> die hard." (57)

The old ways are Shane's ways. Bob recognizes that Shane "was
not a farmer and never really could be":

> He never shirked the meanest task. He was ever ready to take the
> hard end of any chore. Yet you always felt in some indefinable
> fashion that he was a man apart. (60)

"A man is what he is," he tells the boy, "and there's no breaking
the mold" (203).

Being what he is, Shane won't go into that new world. He
departs, and "no word or thought could hold him" (203). He is
different from the people of this new world; he is "in the past
fenced off so securely" (74), "far off and unapproachable at times
even when he was right there with you" (54). He cannot go into

the new world without forfeiting himself. "As soon as the hero identifies himself entirely with a community his nature changes" (Calder 191).

Learning why this is so provides a way back to the second problem I mentioned a little earlier, the need to find a way of discriminating among different kinds of *ethos*.

While the study of *ethos* needs no defending, it justifies itself, I think, as central to rhetoric and vital to our hopes for generous and perceptive human relationships. "Language is always a dis-closure—more or less deliberate, profound, and honest—of the one who speaks, of his personal view of the world," Halloran says. "The concept of *ethos* is crucial to rhetoric," he continues, "because the object of rhetoric is *man speaking*" (631). And if we are to learn more about *ethos*, it seems clear, we must learn more about how to distinguish among different kinds of *ethos*, and refrain from supposing that *ethos* always emerges to us in the same way.

Shane is a particular kind of hero, and he presents a particu-lar kind of *ethos*. He is a master of his world, but he is fenced off from the new world of the Starretts. The new world will not hold all of the structural and stylistic possibilities that could be real-ized from Shane's inventive world. To live in the new world, then, Shane would have to close off a part of his inventive world, and he would have to accept the structures and styles that the new world offers. This, incidentally, is precisely what the Virginian does in Owen Wister's novel: he comes out of the old world and settles into a particular structure and style given by the new world, thereby surrendering his old inventive world and accepting a new one. This Shane cannot do. At the end of the book, he rides away, preserving his identity, keeping—for a little while at least—the balance between his inventive resources and his structural and stylistic powers.

This balance is a clue to the identification of one kind of *ethos*. Shane is what I shall call an "efficient *ethos*." He fully uses his world, without waste. All that is in his inventive realm realizes itself in an array of structures and styles so varied that some of them reach over into use in another world. Invention in Shane's world equals structure and style. The same thing, I think, might be said of Beowulf and of Robin Hood and of many of our heroes. The perfect economy of invention, structure, and style makes them heroic realities to us, and makes Shane a presence to the boy. But this kind of *ethos* is self-completing—hence Shane's departure at the end. It is not self-renewing. Shane will be a memory, not a model for behavior. Neither Shane nor Robin Hood can live in a world devised by others.

This self-completing *ethos* is not the same as the *ethos* described by Walter, Perelman, and others. Clearly *ethos* occurs in more than one kind of form.

4

Five general groupings seem possible. I understand that the form and manner in which any single *ethos* emerges in discourse has to be determined by examination of the discourse and its necessary contexts. But I believe that it is urgent for us to understand the incidence of *ethos*—we must learn over and over again, after all, how to compose ourselves and our world—and I believe that we can be aided in our understanding if we can learn to make some general and unbinding distinctions. At any rate, I propose five general groupings. I have already mentioned some of them directly or indirectly.

Dramatic ethos. In this category are literary characters, who are clearly created by their language, and the fictive creations that appear, for example, in "public service" advertisements where advertisers create an image of concerned public virtue for themselves.

Gratifying ethos. Otis Walter's account of the operation of *ethos* clearly seems to be an accurate explanation of the large majority of ethical connections. I include here politicians, public leaders, television personalities and other entertainers, and various popular figures, all of whom seem characteristically to satisfy Walter's conditions: we do have a need; we judge the need to be worthy; the figure in question is uniquely fitted to fulfill the need.

Functional ethos. Some forms of discourse seem to create an *ethos* that, instead of providing gratification, serves as a mark of recognition. Some brand names represent an *ethos* in this sense, and some entertainers project such an *ethos*.

Efficient ethos. I have already, in the discussion of *Shane* above, suggested what I mean by this term. I judge this to be a relatively rare form, developed for example in certain heroes and archetypal figures.

Generative ethos: This, I think, is a form of *ethos* that we need both to hear in others and to make ourselves. Unlike the "efficient *ethos*" of Shane, which, heroic as it is, is tied to a particular inventive-structural-stylistic set and completes itself, this "generative *ethos*" is always in the process of making itself and of liberating hearers to make themselves. In this form of *ethos* there is always more coming. It is never over, never wholly fenced into the past. It is a speaking out from history into history.[5]

The first four categories I have suggested above are, it seems to me, fairly well, if simply, defined, though I certainly don't assume instant acceptance of either the categories I have suggested or the names I have proposed. The last category, what I have called "generative *ethos*," is more troublesome, and more important. I want to try to explain what I mean for this fifth category, first by looking at some discourses that seem to belong in this grouping, and then in the following section by exploring further the compelling possibilities of this ethical form. No doubt there are many qualities that constitute what I call a "generative *ethos*." Perhaps in each discourse there is a web of qualities indistinguishable from the discourse. Still, I think it is possible to isolate some attributes of "generative *ethos*" by looking at particular texts.

Richard Weaver's discussion of the Gettysburg Address provides a useful starting place. It suggests a transcendent capacity, an *ethos* torn by the tragedy of a particular time and place, yet awake to the great reaches of time and space beyond the moment and compelled to stewardship of the future:

"Fourscore and seven years ago our fathers brought forth on this continent a new nation, conceived in liberty and dedicated to the proposition that all men are created equal." Again tremendous perspective, suggesting almost that Lincoln was looking at the little act from some ultimate point in space and time. "Fourscore and seven years ago" carries the listener back to the beginning of the nation. "This continent" again takes the whole world into purview. "Our fathers" is an auxiliary suggestion of the continuum of time. The phrase following defines American political philosophy in the most general terms possible. The entire opening sentence, with its sustained detachment, sounds like an account of the action to be rendered at Judgment Day. It is not Abe Lincoln who is speaking the utterance, but the voice of mankind, as it were, to whom the American Civil War is but the passing vexation of a generation. As for the "brave men, living and dead, who struggled here," it takes two to make a struggle, and is there anything to indicate that the men in gray are excluded? There is nothing explicit, and therefore we may say that Lincoln looked as far ahead as he looked behind in commemorating the event of Gettysburg. (109)

The form of *ethos* I am trying to describe no doubt occurs in many ways. Lincoln's speech opens wide space for all of us; it embraces us. Time past is in his speech, and hope for time future begins to take shape in his call for dedication. [. . .]

Stewardship of a kind similar to Lincoln's may be seen in Goldsmith's "The Deserted Village." A sense of the speaker's range is established early in the poem. Lines 76–96 make it clear that he has wandered widely across the earth; his experience (call it his range in space) enables him to see and to understand the contrast between the peace of the past and the desolation of the present, between the innocence and health of former times and present grief, between the frugality and vigor of old and modern luxury and corruption. Even if it does nothing else, his experience abroad distances him from the village so that he can see its alteration. His range in space is apparent in other ways. He lives in space large enough to house contradictions, knowing that the changes he sees bring "increase of our luxuries," but understanding at the same time that the same changes that bring good also bring evil. Out of this range grows a command of time, particularly its extension into the future: he has looked and seen and knows that present actions thrust themselves into the future, which he can know (and we can testify to the accuracy of his predictions by looking around). In old time, man and seasonal change set the tempo of life:

> Sweet Auburn! loveliest village of the plain,
> Where health and plenty cheered the laboring swain,
> Where smiling spring its earliest visit paid,
> And parting summers lingering blooms delayed;
> Dear lovely bowers of innocence and ease,
> Seats of my youth, when every sport could please,
> How often have I loitered o'er thy green,
> Where humble happiness endeared each scene! [. . .]
> How often have I blessed the coming day,
> When toil remitting lent its turn to play,
> And all the village train, from labor free,
> Led up their sports beneath the spreading tree;
> While many a pastime circled in the shade,
> The young contending as the old surveyed;
> And many a gambol frolicked o'er the ground,
> And sleights of art and feats of strength went round;
> And still, as each repeated pleasure tired,
> Succeeding sports the mirthful band inspired; [. . .]
> These were thy charms—but all these charms are fled.
> (ll. 1–34)

But in the new world coming there will be a new tempo, set by things, and it will be hurried, crowding life:

> If to the city sped—What waits him there?
> To see profusion that he must not share;
> To see ten thousand baneful arts combined
> To pamper luxury, and thin mankind;
> To see those joys the sons of pleasure know
> Extorted from his fellow-creature's woe. [. . .]
> Here, richly decked, admits the gorgeous train;
> Tumultuous grandeur crowds the blazing square;
> The rattling chariots clash, the torches glare.
> (ll. 309–22)

In Johnson's *Rambler* No. 154 the speaker is transformed in the course of the essay; the process of speaking extends the *ethos*.[6] It is important to remember the essay as a transforming process, for at its opening, the speaker is not singularly endowed, except in a special way with learning. Johnson calls on Virgil and his translator, Dryden, for epigraph, not solely to cause his audience to know that he is learned, but to introduce immediately the sense of sequentiality so important to the essay. He will "treat of arts disclos'd in ancient days," and "[o]nce more unlock for thee the sacred spring." The early citation of Virgil and Dryden and, in the first paragraph, of Aristotle, establishes briefly the speaker's learning, to be sure, but more importantly his capacity for bringing learning to bear on issues at hand; he can bring Aristotle's injunction on politics to his use in discussing "any other part of knowledge." Thus Aristotle is not simply an authority, though he is that: "The direction of Aristotle to those that study politicks, is, first to examine and understand what has been written by the ancients upon government; then to cast their eyes round upon the world, and consider by what causes the prosperity of communities is visibly influenced, and why some are worse, and others better administered." Aristotle is also the means for moving into Johnson's real subject; the passage cited above is the entire first paragraph. The opening sentence of the second paragraph moves us from Aristotle's to Johnson's subject: "The same method must be pursued by him who hopes to become eminent in any other part of knowledge."

The rest of the second paragraph (it has only three sentences) suggests by stylistic means a quality of *ethos* that will grow with the essay. The effect of the paragraph, as its opening sentence, quoted above, indicates, is to transfer Aristotle's direction from politics in Paragraph 1 to sequential education in Paragraph 3. To get to this effect Johnson restates Aristotle's direction generally, as it applies to all parts of knowledge, in the second sentence, "The first task is to search books, the next to contemplate nature." He then restates the direction again in the third sentence, this time amplifying: "He must first possess himself of the intellectual treasures which the diligence of former ages has accumulated, and then endeavour to increase them by his own collections." What is important to the ethical argument here is that neither sentence is exclusive; by means of coordinate constructions in both sentences, the speaker is able to include both study *and* original effort, but he states the sequences clearly—*first* study, *then* original work. This is an early specimen of the contribution, not fully examined here, of stylistic excellence to the writer's ethical image.

With the opening of the third paragraph the speaker appears to move to the attack, castigating those who violate the sequence established with Aristotle. Having seated Aristotle's dictum generally in Paragraph 2, he can now move to the matter of immediate concern, the violation of sequence: "The mental disease of the present generation is impatience of study, contempt of the great masters of ancient wisdom, and a disposition to rely wholly upon unassisted genius and natural sagacity." While this sentence has the force of an attacking proposition, the later development of the ethical argument modifies the statement. Again in the third paragraph certain qualities emerge in the character speaking, not yet *ethos,* but under transformation. First, in the sentence just quoted there is a thoroughness, an inclusiveness in the attack. The antagonists are guilty of, first, impatience, then contempt, finally, of "a disposition to rely wholly upon unassisted genius"; that is to say, we are conducted in one sentence through a catalog, from mere folly (impatience) to sin (pride). Second, despite the sharp attack in this sentence, there is in the long second sentence that concludes the paragraph no marked vindictiveness. The speaker accepts his antagonists' terms (they are the "wits of these happy days") and expands his attack by restating their error in such a way as to give it with each restatement a wider range: "The wits of these happy days have discovered a way to fame, which the dull caution of our laborious ancestors durst never attempt; they cut the knots of sophistry which it was formerly the business of years to untie, solve difficulties by sudden irradiations of intelligence, and comprehend long processes of argument by immediate intuition."

An ethical character, not yet fully formed, begins to emerge in these opening paragraphs. The speaker uses learning wisely, he is inclusive both in his attack and in his willingness to accept options *(first* study, *then* original work), and he is relatively free of vindictiveness even in the midst of attack.

The fourth paragraph restates and reinforces the speaker's attack, describing men "who have flattered themselves into this opinion of their own abilities," and who thus condemn study.

The fifth paragraph advances the attack with Johnson's deflating reversal of the flattering opinion men have of themselves: "It is however certain that no estimate is more in danger of erroneous calculations than those by which a man computes the force of his own genius." This paragraph also introduces some further qualities of the *ethos* addressing us. The deadly deflation in the sentence just quoted is accomplished not with a sudden brutal thrust, but rather through the slow accumulation of the loose construction. Then in the long sentence that completes the paragraph Johnson accepts his share in the fault with the self-condemning first person: "It generally happens at our entrance into the world, that by the natural attraction of similitude, we associate with men like ourselves young, sprightly, and ignorant, and rate our accomplishments by comparison with theirs; when we have once obtained an acknowledged superiority over our acquaintances, imagination and desire easily extend it over the rest of mankind, and if no accident forces us into new emulations, we grow old, and die in admiration of ourselves."

This vanity is made to appear more pervasive in the sixth paragraph. A great breadth of experience is pulled into the long coordinate constructions of the third sentence: "He then listens with eagerness to the wild objections which folly has raised against the common means of improvement; talks of the dark chaos of indigested knowledge; describes the mischievous effects of heterogeneous sciences fermenting in the mind; relates the blunders of lettered ignorance; expatiates on the heroic merit of those who deviate from prescription, or shake off authority; and gives vent to the inflations of his heart by declaring that he owes nothing to pedants and universities." Through the sequence of verbs, Johnson telescopes a life of prideful folly into one sentence; his antagonist "listens," then "talks," then "describes," then "relates," then "expatiates," and finally "gives vent" in a rhetorical history of the development of youth to maturity.

The tentative summation of the seventh paragraph is unassumingly assertive, the attack moderated by "very often": "All these pretensions, however confident, are very often vain." His series of charges brought in this way to a preliminary conclusion, Johnson turns temporarily in the eighth paragraph in another direction to accept his antagonist's argument that ground may be naturally fertile: "But though the contemner of books had neither been deceived by others nor himself, and was really born with a genius surpassing the ordinary abilities of mankind; yet surely such gifts of providence may be more properly urged as incitements to labour, than encouragements to negligence. He that neglects the culture of ground, naturally fertile, is more shamefully culpable than he whose field would scarcely recompence his husbandry." Johnson uses even his recognition of natural endowment as a means of rejecting the pride he has been attacking—the gift is from providence.

To this recognition in Paragraph 8 Johnson has developed, after his introduction and the preliminary proposition in Paragraph 3, what is essentially a *confutatio*. Following Paragraph 8, he develops an expanding *confirmatio,* moving toward the enlarged proposition in the last paragraph of the essay. Beginning with Paragraph 9 he renews his charges, but with a difference, for the *ethos* undergoes further transformation in the six-paragraph sequence, paragraphs 9 through 14.

In the ninth paragraph, as in his opening, Johnson uses an authority at a key transition point. Cicero's advice in the first sentence is restated simply in the second sentence, amplified in the third, then narrowed to the specific in the last sentence:

> Cicero remarks, that not to know what has been transacted in former times is to continue always a child. If no use is made of the labours of past ages, the world must remain always in the infancy of knowledge. The discoveries of every man must terminate in his own advantage, and the studies of every age be employed on questions which the past generation had discussed and determined. We may with as little reproach borrow science as manufactures from our ancestors; and it is as rational to live in caves till our own hands have erected a palace, as to reject all knowledge of architecture, which our understanding will not supply.

Paragraphs 10 and 11 suggest that Johnson is now moving to affirmation rather than attack. Reminding his audience in Paragraph 10 that "it is far easier to learn than to invent," he gains sufficient comprehensiveness in Paragraph 11 both to admit the happy consequences of natural insight and to reiterate the need for study. "Sometimes," he says, "unexpected flashes of instruction were struck out by the fortuitous collision of happy incidents, or an involuntary concurrence of ideas [. . .]." But, as the modifier-noun combinations in this passage suggest, these insights are beyond men's power: "The happiness of these casual illuminations no man can promise to himself [. . .]." Consequently, Johnson says in Paragraph 12, we are obliged to study: "The man whose genius qualifies him for great undertakings, must at least be content to learn from books the present state of human knowledge; that he may not ascribe to himself the invention of arts generally known; weary his attention with experiments of which the event has been long registered; and waste, in attempts which have already succeeded or miscarried, that time which might have been spent with usefulness and honour upon new undertakings."

But now the *ethos* has become greater than it was in the beginning. Natural endowment and a man's own toil, mentioned in Paragraph 8 and recognized in Paragraphs 10 and 11, are now fully accepted in Paragraphs 13 and 14 as a part of Johnson's argument: "But though the study of books is necessary, it is not sufficient to constitute literary eminence." A man must add, Johnson says, "by his own toil to the acquisitions of his ancestors," for "[n]o man ever yet became great by imitation."

This brings Johnson to the affirmation of the final paragraph. Unlike the attacking proposition of Paragraph 3, it is an affirmation that rests on demonstrated capacities of the arguer, his openness and comprehensiveness, on his capacity to acknowledge good in his adversary without slacking his own thrust. Where in the early paragraphs (all before Paragraph 8, but especially 2 and 3) Johnson insists on study first, then exercise of man's natural endowments, he now reverses the order of the terms, placing endowment first, following it with reinforcing study: "Fame cannot spread wide or endure long that is not rooted in nature, and manured by art."

The ethical argument in *Rambler* No. 154 begins with an attacking proposition that is sustained by the *confutatio* attacking vanity. Breaking his argument at Paragraph 8 with the recognition *of* natural (unlearned) capacities, Johnson moves into an expanding *confirmatio* attacking pride even as he acknowledges good in contrary positions. When he comes at last to the restated proposition in the last paragraph, it is a proposition enlarged and enriched by the convergence of views expressed by a transformed voice that seeks identification without sacrificing conviction. "Identification is compensatory to division," Kenneth Burke tells us in *A Rhetoric of Motives*: "If men were not apart from one another, there would be no need for the rhetorician to proclaim their unity. If men were wholly and truly of one substance, absolute communication would be of man's very essence."

Amos offers another opportunity to get at the kind of *ethos* I am trying to describe. In a strange land a man sings the Lord's song; in a smooth season a man preaches hard words—and continues to be heard. Why has he been heard, even if not always by multitudes? What is there specifically in his words that has commanded audiences? What makes his words worth listening to?

The book of Amos is an ethical argument. What the speaker *is* emerges in what he says and in the way he says it, and what we hear arouses a response in us (not always articulated) for certain observable qualities.

Before I try to identify some of these qualities, I should try to explain why *Amos* is an ethical argument. To put the matter simply, it is an ethical argument because neither logical argument nor emotional argument is functional in such an instance. It would be, at the very best, difficult to get an audience to respond emotionally in any very fruitful way to the news of its own doom. Logical argument, on the other hand, seems to function best—perhaps solely—when speaker and hearer abide in the same universe. There is an important sense, I believe, in which Amos and his hearers do not occupy the same referential sphere, cannot share or mutually accept premises, therefore cannot share the arguments tracking from these premises. Rather, an *ethos* functions here, because, I think, the *ethos* may be seen to acquire strength and wisdom in the act of speaking.

If a man respects his own thoughts, he may feel a responsibility to share them. If he sets out to share them with others, he takes on certain obligations—obligations, I hasten to add again, that cannot be once and for all prescribed for our easy instruction, but must rather be seen at work in this, that, or the other specific instance as each *ethos* becomes itself. We learn if we listen to Amos that he discovers, defines, and fulfills particular obligations in the course of his argument. He is, first, specific, thorough, painstaking, and appropriate in his linguistic grasp of the experiences he gathers into discourse. Second, he owns and guarantees what he is talking about. Third, he extends certain necessary ministries to us.

He is specific, thorough, painstaking, and appropriate in his linguistic embrace of the situation, exerting his freedom through the precision of his words. We prize our freedom of speech, and abuse it mightily. "You're not free to move unless you've learned to walk," Northrop Frye remarks in *The Educated Imagination,* "and not free to play the piano unless you practice. Nobody is capable of free speech unless he knows how to use the language [. . .]." But Amos qualifies. He is specific, not general, in his charges. Before he mentions Israel, he has charged seven specific peoples with specific crimes against specific peoples: brutal conquest, enslavement, selling men into slavery, violation of familial and filial bonds, murder, desecration of tombs, violation of commandments. His mode of address is particular and specific. Approximately 75 percent of the nouns in the book are either proper nouns or common nouns with a high level of specificity. A count in 2:6–11 shows 78 percent of the nouns to be proper names and therefore clearly delimiting and specific or common nouns given specificity by the context. In the same passage (2:6–11) a sequence of specific, active verbs not only specifies particular actions but also in their sequence chronicles in a downward, then upward cycle the diminution of the Israelites into sin and the ascending level of the Lord's punishment: *sold, pant, turn aside, lay [themselves] down, drink*—actions attributed to the Israelites—*destroyed, brought, led, raised,* in the consequent response of the Lord.

Such precision—scarcely hinted at here—is a function of his thorough, painstaking care, which manifests itself in two ways. First, he is thorough in the sense that he is unrelenting. The catalog of the nations and their sins is not abstract, but quite specific, and the greatest detail comes in his indictment of Israel, which, once begun, he never ceases. Israel is indicted in 2:6–16, and her sins are explored again in 4:1–13; again in 5:10–13 he counts her transgressions, and yet again in 8:4–14. Persistently, again and again, he lays her sins before Israel, forcing them upon the consciousness. Yet this relentless catalog is not solely for the sake of a dramatic, hammering repetition, for Amos is thorough in another sense. He does not, as is our common practice today, simply shout his primary assertion at his audience, expecting that the vigor of his shouting will demonstrate the truth of his assertion. Instead, he sets out, painstakingly, to make himself clear, to make himself known. He brings his history to his argument; he has been in the past, and has explored it—he knows and can name the specific sins of the peoples—and he takes his audience with him from his observations to his conclusions. He speaks with great care to be understood.

His care is apparent, too, in the appropriateness of the language he uses. It is not only specific, as I have already suggested, but also peculiarly fitting to his argument. I will linger here to cite only one example, but it is a particularly striking example. In the fifth chapter, after he has again warned Israel about the nature and effect of her transgressions, Amos speaks of the Lord's judgment:

> 21 I hate, I despise your feast days, and I will not smell in your solemn assemblies.
> 22 Though ye offer me burnt offerings and your meat offerings, I will not accept them: neither will I regard the peace offerings of your fat beasts.
> 23 Take thou away from me the noise of thy songs; for I will not hear the melody of thy viols.
> 24 But let judgment run down as waters, and righteousness as a mighty stream.

The naturalness of his language, particularly in the twenty-fourth verse, is uniquely felicitous to his argument. He has been attacking, among other things, vain piety and false ritual. Here ("let judgment run down as waters, and righteousness as a mighty stream") he uses similes that show us the nature of his argument. Justice and righteousness, rightly understood, are integral parts of a rich creation, natural and fit as the running waters, not to be artificially realized. It is the best conceivable repudiation of the hollow, insincere, artificial worship, pitting natural fidelity and plenitude against artificial piety and ritual. We learn of Amos, I would say again, that he is specific, thorough, painstaking, and appropriate in his linguistic grasp of experience.

A little earlier I attributed a second major quality to Amos: that he owns and guarantees what he is talking about. We know from the start, I think, that there is an audacity in Amos. So far as I am able to know as a layman, there was little, if anything, to presage what was to happen. So far as I know, there was no prophetic development that led naturally to Amos, no record of written prophecy before Amos. He was not, by his own words, the product of any school. Yet there he is, in Bethel, at the temple, speaking. And we know from the start that he is willing: "The lion hath roared, who will not fear? the Lord God hath spoken, who can but prophesy?" He has received and accepted the call, and he *goes*. But audacity and willingness are not enough; these qualities do not inevitably inform a voice and strengthen an argument. Were they sufficient, one supposes, any man who found himself simultaneously sincere and energetic could move multitudes. But to his audacity and willingness, Amos brings this new quality: he owns and guarantees what he says. To own and guarantee one's words, I take it, means to be fastidiously and meticulously aware of their background, keenly thoughtful of their consequence and future; it entails giving one's words the backing of such a history of search and thinking as will stand scrutiny.[7] What guarantees the words of Amos is the moving, commanding capacity to catch the moment and get outside the moment; he is caught and compelled by the moment, to be sure, but he sees elsewhere as clearly as he sees here, and he can see as far ahead as he can see behind.

Amos has his authority given, we know: "The Lord God hath spoken, who can but prophesy?" But the point I wish to make is that his discourse *creates* its own authority; his words are self-authenticating. Here, particularly, I wish to suggest that he gains his authority and his audience by a space-full and time-full argument. A space-full argument, it looks *there* as well as *here*. He has seen and recorded the sins of others, and he sees the sins of Israel. When he concludes his first catalog of the peoples with Israel, the effect is not just to include Israel, not just to save Israel for last, not just to admit sins close to home in a gesture of false humility. He has looked abroad, rather, and seen men's folly. Israel is not free of sin, nor is she uniquely guilty. All are subject to the same judgments, for the Lord is no tribal god; neither is righteousness a national principle.

Space is gathered in the argument of Amos, and the words are full of time. He has seen the past, but he also has a keen and compelling sense of futurity. The acts he condemns are in the past, but they do not stay in the past: they have consequence; nothing is lost. When he knows that, as he plainly does, Amos knows that the sins of Israel and the sins of all the people will have their consequence, too. All the sins he condemns are acts of dehumanization. The dehumanizer must eventually be dehumanized. He is doomed. His own acts wreak their consequences upon him: "Seek the Lord, and ye shall live; lest he break out like fire in the house of Joseph, and devour it, and there be none to quench it in Bethel."

The book of Amos ends with a series of visions. It might be argued that they are evidence of his granted authority: the Lord has spoken to him, and he has, therefore, the unspeakable weight of ultimate authority. I think, however, that this is not the actual effect of the visions. They are visions of acts that lead to judgment and to consequence. Nothing is lost; the past does move into the present and into the future. The visions are, I believe, the last clear evidence of Amos' sense of futurity. He has seen abroad to the far borders; he has seen back to beginnings; and he has seen forward to endings.

I understand that there is some evidence to indicate that the last verses of the book do not belong to Amos. I am limited to the written, Englished version and to the kind of knowledge of the book as scripture that a layman can have, and so, in my limited frame of reference, the last verses also belong. In point of fact, they do make an appropriate ending, the fruition of his sense of judgment and futurity. Over against the past and the present, for which man must be condemned, there is a future. Over against the artificiality and the dehumanizing exploitation in the sins of men, there is a fulfillment. The last verses picture a natural reciprocity working out the fullness of creation, one thing answering to the other, one thing fulfilling the other, one thing creating the other:

13 Behold, the days come, with the Lord, that the plowman shall overtake the reaper, and the treader of grapes him that soweth

seed; and the mountains shall drop sweet wine, and all the hills shall melt.

14 And I will bring again the captivity of my people of Israel, and they shall build the waste cities, and inhabit them; and they shall plant vineyards, and drink the wine thereof; they shall also make gardens, and eat the fruit of them.

15 And I will plant them upon their land, and they shall no more be pulled up out of their land which I have given them, saith the Lord thy God.

Acts do have consequence, and we are condemned. But while we are caught in the grief and tragedy and vexation of the moment, Amos sees a richly space-filled and time-filled creation, still full of promise.

What is it that we learn from the ethical presence that is Amos? Amos is specific, thorough, painstaking, and appropriate—and so may we be. Amos owns and guarantees his words—and so may we. But I also mentioned a third quality in Amos: he extends certain ministries to us, such ministries as Bonhoeffer described in *Life Together*. We know from the specific nature of his charges and his care in chronicling them that he has, first of all, *listened*, thereby extending what Bonhoeffer calls the first great ministry one owes to another. He is *patient*, patient to learn, and patient to speak, knowing that he will sometimes be misunderstood, or not heard, yet patient to keep talking. He has learned to *think little* of himself. "And the Lord took me as I followed the flock, and the Lord said unto me, Go, prophesy unto my people Israel." He is willing to go and to be alone, to speak when he must, to insist, *to proclaim:* "The Lord God hath spoken, who can but prophesy?" And so we learn finally from Amos that if, when we speak, our words issue from a spirit of forbearing, care, and patience, then even if our words appear only to pronounce doom on our brothers, they can yet, as in the paradigm of Amos, be healing and liberating words.[8]

5

Ethos is singular, and can only be described as it appears in a discourse. Even so, particular forms of *ethos* seem to hold sufficient qualities in common to justify some groupings. Of the groups I have suggested, the last, or "generative *ethos*," most deserves attention.

Good discourse is always moving toward completeness. What complicates and intensifies the process is that discourse is a closure, a stoppage, hence in itself an incompleteness. We do not speak *these* words unless we have already chosen or unless we have already been directed not to speak *those*. The act of speaking eliminates possibilities for speaking; when something is named, it is not named otherwise. There is always more to be said than can be said. The language of the generative *ethos* moves toward completeness, beyond closure, reaching somehow beyond its synecdochic nature.

One way this begins to become apparent in the discourses cited in the preceding section is in their demonstrable extension in space and time. The *ethos* in each in one way or another opens the borders of the discourse to hold extraordinary space and time. The speaker in the Gettysburg Address makes space enough for all to come into the future he is summoning them to create. The speaker in "The Deserted Village" distances himself from the village, largely ridding himself of self-interest, and as he does so begins to see the village so well that he can also see its future—so accurately, I might add, that two hundred years later we are still trying to correct problems he identified. [. . .] The speaker in *Rambler* No. 154 grows as he speaks. As Walker Percy puts it, "[A] sentence entails a world for both utterer and receiver" (174), and the *Rambler* speaker creates a world spacious enough to house his antagonists, modifying his own world and future in the process. The speaker in *Amos* makes a world full of time and space, getting far beyond tribal boundaries and seeing what consequence looks like as it works itself out in the future. Each of them is a steward, not an owner, of space and time.

This incipient understanding of "generative *ethos*" creates some dissatisfaction with the still common conception of communication as the clear acceptance by a *receiver* of a *message* effectively transmitted by a *sender*. This radio model of communication has, to be sure, figured centrally in many provocative studies of language; the sender-message-receiver (encoder-message-decoder) model gives an enabling language that has made it possible for students to explore communication in successful ways, as readers of Kinneavy's *A Theory of Discourse,* for example, will know. But the model has severe limitations. It does not provide a useful means of understanding ethical appeal. It is, though useful, an inaccurate description of the language process. Implicit in the model is the notion that the message is separate from the speaker, that it leaves the speaker and reaches a hearer. But Walter Ong argues that "all words projected from a speaker remain, as has been seen, somehow interior to him, being an invitation to another person, another interior, to share the speaker's interior, an invitation to enter in, not to regard from the outside" (1162). Our words never leave us; the message is not separate from the speaker. When I speak, I must use words that are in the public domain. The jangly meaning accumulations of others reverberate in the words, though I may fail to hear them, and if I hear them I may fail to use them or choose not to use them, and if I hear them and use them my audience may fail to hear them or choose not to hear them. A speaker manifests his universe in his words; his words are his universe, and its shape is in the words whether or not he understands and controls, whether or not we listen and see. "To say that we speak in order to communicate," Paul van Buren writes, "is to abstract a tiny section of the use of words and call that the whole" (49). With language, he continues, we "fashion (or accept from others) the world about us. The only world we have is the one we can speak of. The world is ours, therefore, *as* we speak of it" (57).

To consider communication, then, not as a radio system but as an *invitation* gives us what may be a better conception and, not coincidentally, a better accounting of what "generative *ethos*" does: communication seen as invitation brings a hearer (guest) into a world that he or she can live in, that has living space and time.

What frequently stands in the way of communication is some violation of space or time or both. We believe that the flood of language around us often blocks human correspondence; if that is so, it is not just because language at floodtide is all too often careless and sometimes corrupt, but also because the volume crowds our living space and our time, sometimes generating frenetic speed, sometimes a paralysis. We understand, too, that communication is often blocked because, as Geoffrey Wagner has mentioned, "[W]e are, in short, our own enchained listeners" (218). We may hear ourselves, not another; the other's words may act only as a trigger to release our own, unlocking not the other's meaning, but one we already possessed. When this happens, we are bound in space, caught tightly in our own province. Specialized languages—slang, cult tongues, professional jargons, and the like—stand in the way of communication because they bind space; the specialized language of the speaker prohibiting entry by a hearer into the speaker's discursive universe. Forms of utterance that I might call Pavlov language—clichés, some cultural commonplaces, conversational forms that we use instead of thinking—are the speaker's violation of his or her own space and time, evidence of failure to explore and to know his or her own world. The languages of television and other mass media crowd our time and hurry our responses, or stop our responses entirely. The languages of confrontation set space against space, universe against universe, and cannot wait for meditation time. Many episodes of failed communication and many instances of communication never attempted are consequences of some violation of space or time or both.

Ethos is generative and fruitful when the time and space stewarded by the speaker give free room for another to live in. (What I earlier called "gratifying *ethos*," for example, while it may at a particular moment be compelling and satisfying, is at last restrictive and binding.)

"Generative *ethos*" is commodious. The self-authenticating language of such an *ethos* issues an invitation into a commodious universe. What makes that possible is its extension in space and time. Argument is partial; when a speaker argues a proposition or develops a theme or makes an assertion, he or she has knowingly or not chosen one proposition, one theme, one assertion from all available. When we speak, we stand somewhere, and our standing place makes both known and silent claims upon us. We make truth, if at all, out of what is incomplete, or partial. "An individual utterance," Bonhoeffer said, "is always part of a total reality which seeks expression in this utterance" (129). Yet language is a closure, for we cannot speak two words simultaneously. Generative language seeks to shove back the restraints of closure, to make in language a commodious universe, to stretch words out beyond our private universes. Extension in time and space seems to be one effort that makes this possible. [. . .]

6

What has all this to do with freshman composition? Must I now, having come this far in this direction, break off, stop, and whiz off in another direction to find some way of connecting myself with composition? I don't think so, though I do remember and prize Graham Martin's remark: "The only thing that is totally certain is that one may be mistaken. The only valid ideology is an anti-ideology" (3).

Everything is connected with freshman composition. The course is not a service course to other disciplines in the university. All other disciplines in the university provide service courses to freshman composition. All other courses are inventive resources; structural arrangements, or stylistic displays of varying uses in the central human activity, language-making.

But there are more specific connections, I think, between the study of *ethos* and the teaching of composition. Some are important for localized and practical purposes. Others, I believe, have a continuing importance. And I hope there are values in the study of *ethos* for the teaching of composition that I have not had wit enough to see.

A. The study of *ethos* and the forms of ethical appeal is valuable in any course of study because it requires close attention to the text of a discourse.

B. The study of *ethos* provides a mode of criticism that students may practice, a potential means of distinguishing among the voices they hear, and a possible defense against the seductive voices of the seller, the image-maker, and the tyrant.

C. The study of *ethos* suggests, quite simply, some interesting and useful writing for students to do—the creation of *dramatic ethos*, for example, and the imitation of the language of an *ethos* not their own. One form this latter exercise might take, for instance, is for students to write what some actual or fictional personage would say in some new context. What would Johnny Carson say if he were interviewing inhabitants of a shelter for battered wives? What would J. Alfred Prufrock say if he were visiting a sick friend in the hospital? How would Howard Cosell talk about pornography? To do this kind of exercise students would have to pay close attention to the voice they were to imitate, and that would never, I think, be a loss. It would also direct attention to the way character and language create and reveal each other, and that would be an extraordinary gain in any composition class.

D. The study of *ethos,* and particularly of the notion of "generative *ethos,*" provides a way of explaining why flaws in writing are flaws. We can declaim against the euphemism and the cliché and red-pencil their occurrence until a month from Tuesday, and the effect we have will be less than if we explain *why* a cliché, for example, works against the writer. When we accept someone's cliché into our writing, we are binding ourselves with another's language and another's thought, substituting another's language and thought for our own. If students can learn that—and we can teach them—then we will no longer have to red-pencil their clichés, for they will have a reason to edit them out on their own.

E. In *Speaking,* Georges Gusdorf remarks that "each audience orients us in a world which, moreover, is not given as such, once and for all, but appears to be constructed word by word" (37). A little later, he continues, "[L]iving speech acknowledges the requirement of the spiritual life in travail—not at all a closed system achieved once and for all—but an effort of constant regeneration" (45). If we remember that, and if we can learn from the study of *ethos* that the creation of a "generative *ethos*" can never be wholly done, then we may remember to approach our students' papers as editors, and not as policemen.

F. The study of *ethos,* and particularly of the forms of *ethos* I have mentioned, may help us find a way to cope with which language a student can or should use, which language the student has a right to. We may be able to learn that students can with honor and honesty use different languages, and that they must be free to make their own character however they will. For functional or gratifying purposes, students may adopt languages of the marketplace or languages of the dominant class, but the study of "generative *ethos*" may help them to know that they must speak their own way, embracing us if it is possible, but going it alone if they must.

G. The study of the forms of *ethos* I have mentioned might one day remind us to look at ourselves as teachers of composition and to examine the kind of *ethos* we present to our students. Sometimes we create a dramatic *ethos*. Sometimes we present a gratifying *ethos*, and promise, for example, that success follows literacy and the well-placed comma. Often, I think, we present forms of efficient *ethos* and emerge to our students as capable, knowledgeable, but forever separate from them.[9]

H. Perhaps the conception of "generative *ethos*" will in some way remind us to bring to our students all that is at stake in composition. Style, Winston Weathers has said, is "the proof of a human being's individuality"; it is "a revelation of himself" and "a gesture of personal freedom against inflexible states of mind" (144). Everything is at stake. "Once again let us make clear that words witness to being," Gusdorf says, "for what is being played out in the world of speech is the very destiny of human souls" (98).

I. And finally, perhaps the notion of "generative *ethos*" may help us to remember that we can both speak ourselves into existence and be with another in language:

> True communication is the realization of a unity, i.e. a piece of common labor. It is the unity of each with the other, but at the same time the unifying of each with himself, the rearrangement of personal life in the encounter with others. I cannot communicate as long as I do not try to bring to the other the profound sense of my being. The communion of love, which represents one of the most complete modes of understanding between two persons, can't be achieved without a recall of personality, each discovering himself in the contact with the other. (Gusdorf 57)

Last spring I went to a concert at our daughter's high school. From where we sat, we could just see our daughter with her violin. Fathers being what they are, she being lovely and the music sweet, I found myself welling over. Among other things, I thought, "How can any other outside the family know her and love her so, not being joint members as we are of her whole history?" I wanted to answer, "No one can." But then I remembered that there is such a thing as love between a young woman and a young man who did not participate in her whole history. And that let me think that it is possible for any of us—if the stars are right and we work to make ourselves human—to *enfold* another whose history we have not shared. In this act of enfolding, the speaker becomes through speech; the speaker's identity is always to be saved, to emerge as an *ethos* to the other, whose identity is also to be cherished. Then they may speak, each holding the other wholly in mind.

Notes

1. Reported in Anthony Lewis, "The Honorable, Murderous Gentlemen of a Secret World" (1).

2. R. R. McGuire, in "Speech Acts" (30–45), makes an interesting distinction between communication, which occurs "against a background of mutually assumed validity claims," and discourse, which occurs when one or more of the claims is challenged.

3. See also Thomas F. Mader, "On Presence in Rhetoric."

4. Having made this claim, Walter saw that we need defenses against certain forms of *ethos*:

> If *ethos* arises in seeming hopeless situations where needs are desperate, then one defense must be to *reduce the needs* that pave the road down which the man on horseback rides. One strong defense against *ethos* is to reduce starvation, hopelessness, and degradation. In a word, we must prevent the uniform frustration of a whole people. When needs are too strong, people may abandon democratic problem-solving and turn to the father-figure. The process can be stymied by seeing that no single

need provides enough fertilizer to nourish the malignant growth of the single 'savior.' [. . .] When needs are relatively well satisfied we have a defense against the social pathology of *ethos*. Secondly, we may help a society develop immunity to pathological *ethos* by the educational process of *developing sophistication about which needs are worthy and which are superficial or neurotic*. To whatever extent the human being can refine his own needs, criticize them, suppress some and develop others, to this extent he can existentially create himself and help determine the kinds of people he will admire. One great objective of education should be to create people who will not be subject to neurotic needs. A second defense against the pathology of *ethos* lies in creating people with a conscious and sophisticated sense of value. A third defense is that societies must produce *many men who can meet the needs of people. Ethos* does not become strong unless the agent possessing it seems to have some sort of exclusive power to gratify needs. [. . .] This third defense, that of producing many men who are sensitive to human need and who search for ways of meeting needs, is partly, again, a matter of education. (44)

5. The discussion *of Shane* and efficient *ethos,* including a first attempt to define "generative *ethos,*" appeared in slightly different form in "Efficient *Ethos* in *Shane.*"

6. The discussion *of Rambler* No. 154 first appeared in slightly different form in "Ethical Argument in *Rambler* No. 154."

7. See Harry H. Crosby and George F. Estey, *College Writing* (18–19).

8. The discussion of *Amos* first appeared in slightly different form in "Ethical Argument in Amos."

9. See Kenneth R. Johnston, "Reforming English," and Leon C. Petrus, "Word and World."

Works Cited

Aristotle, *Rhetoric.*

Bonhoeffer, Dietrich. *Ethics: On Being Responsible,* ed. James M. Gustafson and James T. Laney. New York: Harper and Row, 1968.

Calder, Jenni. *There Must Be a Lone Ranger.* New York: Taplinger, 1974.

Cicero, *De Oratore.*

Corder, Jim W. "Efficient *Ethos* in *Shane,* with a Proposal for Discriminating among Kinds of *Ethos.*" *Communication Quarterly* 25 (Fall 1977): 28–31.

———. "Ethical Argument in Amos." *Cresset* 35 (Mar. 1972): 6–9.

———. "Ethical Argument in *Rambler* No. 154." *Quarterly Journal of Speech* 54 (Dec. 1968): 352–56.

Crosby, Harry H., and George F. Estey. *College Writing: The Rhetorical Imperative.* New York: Harper and Row, 1968.

Gusdorf, Georges. *Speaking.* Evanston: Northwestern UP, 1965.

Halloran, S. M. "On the End of Rhetoric, Classical and Modern." *College English* 36 (Feb. 1975): 621–31.

Haslam, Gerald. *Jack Schaefer.* Boise State University Western Writer Series No. 20. Boise, ID: Boise State UP, 1975.

Homans, Peter. "Puritanism Revisited: An Analysis of the Contemporary Screen-Image Western." *Studies in Public Communication* 3 (Summer, 1961).

Johnston, Kenneth R. "Reforming English: Aesthetic Personae in the Profession." *College English* 36 (Apr. 1975): 853–76.

Lasch, Christopher. Review of *Nightmare, the Underside of the Nixon Years,* by J. Anthony Lukas. *New York Times Book Review,* 25 Jan. 1976: 24.

Lewis, Anthony. "The Honorable, Murderous Gentlemen of a Secret World." *New York Times* 23 Nov. 1975: Sect. 4, p. 1.

Mader, Thomas F. "On Presence in Rhetoric." *College Composition and Communication* 24 (Dec. 1973): 375–81.

Martin, Graham Dunstan. *Language, Truth, and Poetry.* Edinburgh: U of Edinburgh P, 1975.

McGuire, R. R. "Speech Acts, Communicative Competence, and the Paradox of Authority." *Philosophy and Rhetoric* 10 (Winter 1977): 30–45.

Ong, Walter J., S.J. "A Dialectic of Aural and Objective Correlatives." *Critical Theory since Plato,* ed. Hazard Adams. New York: Harcourt, 1971.

Percy, Walker. *The Message in the Bottle*. New York: Farrar, Straus and Giroux, 1975.

Perelman, Chaim, and L. Olbrechts-Tyteca. *The New Rhetoric: A Treatise on Argumentation*. South Bend: U of Notre Dame P, 1969.

Petrus, Leon C. "Word and World—Crisis in the Classroom." *College English* 32 (Feb. 1971): 590–604.

Plumly, Stanley. "Chapter and Verse." *American Poetry Review* Jan./ Feb. 1978: 21–28.

Quintilian, *Institutio Oratoria*.

Rosenberg, Phillip. Review of *Frame Analysis, an Essay on the Organization of Experience*, by Erving Goffman. *New York Times Book Review* 16 Feb. 1975: 21.

Schaefer, Jack. *Shane*. Boston: Houghton Mifflin, 1949.

van Buren, Paul. *The Edges of Language*. New York: Macmillan, 1972.

Vatz, Richard E. Letter to the Editor. *Philosophy and Rhetoric* 8 (Winter 1975): 68.

Wagner, Geoffrey. *On the Wisdom of Words*. Princeton, NJ: Van Nostrand, 1968.

Walter, Otis M. "Toward an Analysis of *Ethos.*" *Pennsylvania Speech Annual* 21 (1964).

Weathers, Winston. "Teaching Style: A Possible Anatomy." *College Composition and Communication* 21 (May 1970): 144–48.

Weaver, Richard. *The Ethics of Rhetoric*. Chicago: Henry Regnery, 1953.

CHAPTER FIVE

Studying Rhetoric and Teaching School

Before 1965 or thereabouts there were all along, I expect, some English teachers who enjoyed the insights, perceptions, and guidance of rhetorical study, though they seem for some generations to have done so rather quietly, without widely recommending that study to others. Many speech teachers kept rhetoric close by, to be sure, but some don't seem to have minded too precisely what got done with it or in its name.

By about 1965, however, there began to emerge a generation of English teachers (I am remembering Richard Weaver and other earlier exceptions) who had discovered rhetoric, seen its uses in the teaching of composition and elsewhere, and, moreover, wanted to tell others—sometimes including innocent bystanders—the values of rhetorical study. Most in this first modern generation of rhetoric students were not formally schooled in rhetoric, that is to say, had taken no courses, pursued no program, carried about no mimeographed bibliographies for the study of rhetoric. Most had come out of graduate school more or less prepared to teach and to study the literature of some epoch, nationality, or genre. At some later moment, then—perhaps because they needed to teach freshman composition and wanted to do so well, perhaps because they were as interested in writing as they were in writing already done by others—they found or turned to what others were finding in rhetoric and began to explore its uses and to practice its possibilities.

Because I am, however peripherally, a part of that generation, I am particularly interested not just in rhetoric, though that's enough, but also in how studying rhetoric changes a student who

First published in *Rhetoric Review* 1 (1982): 4–36.

had started off in another direction. To that end, at other times and in other places, I have tried to work my way toward answers to various questions about possible effects of studying rhetoric. What happens, for example, if you come upon rhetoric and take it as a subject matter in its own right without regard for its uses? What happens if you look for the consequences of rhetorical study in the teaching of composition and in the design and style of composition courses? What happens if by some madness you connect the study of rhetoric to the study of literature? What happens if you see rhetoric as a guide for curriculum planning and design within departments and across the university? What happens if you see rhetoric as a portal of entry into other fields?

Now I want to try to address another question: Does studying rhetoric change us as schoolteachers? I don't for a moment even want to ask whether or not studying rhetoric changes all who do so as schoolteachers, nor do I want to inquire whether or not studying rhetoric might change all in the same way—it surely wouldn't. What I want to ask, rather, is this: Does studying rhetoric have the potency to change us as schoolteachers, and, if so, in what directions might it move us?

I have not come this far in order to tell people what to be. I do believe, however, that thinking through rhetoric—being in rhetoric—tends to change those who find that way to think and be, and that includes schoolteachers.

But I owe some previous explanation, I believe. Asking whether the study of rhetoric can change us as schoolteachers seems to presuppose that we may need to change. The best of us probably change some all of the time anyway. Some of us probably don't change much from year to year. Some of us probably change by fits and starts. I'm inclined to think that teaching must change, or it becomes only the display of memory, and that teachers must change, or they become only antiquarians. The trouble is that change is not easy. Some don't see the need for change. Some don't see the hope in change. Some, since they already possess the sacred texts, see change as barbaric. We have to see the need, the hope, the potential blessing in change, and then inquire about rhetoric as an agent for change. Because I think I owe some previous explanation about the need and hope for change before I talk about rhetorical study as a means of change among schoolteachers, the sections that follow—while they are of course clear and obvious to me in their sequencing—may seem to meander on their way to proposing an evolutionary conception of teaching with rhetoric as its informing spirit. Part 1 explores the hope that may wait in change. Part 2, gone dismal and sour, is an account of certain kinds of stasis, stagnation, and despair among teachers that ought to be, but aren't necessarily, the breeding grounds for change. Part 3 examines some of the reasons that despair among schoolteachers may seem, but need not be, inevitable. Finally, Part 4 turns to some of the lessons and hopes that await when rhetoric moves us as schoolteachers.

1

In years past I have taken some modest pleasure in mowing the lawn. The ritualistic nature of the process offered some simple comforts. In the green season there is teeming, squirming life among the blades, the grass seems to grow behind the mower, and the copiousness of life twined secretly in the grass seems to promise birth and re-birth. Always before, I felt I could lace my fingers in the thick mat of the lawn and feel the tremors and stirrings of growth in my hands and up along my arms.

It's a little harder to do so now. The lawn mower has grown heavier. The yard is wider than it was, and its slopes are higher. Weights real or imagined sometimes encumber my hands and arms. Woes real or imagined sometimes interrupt the current of hope I thought I felt rising through the grass. Sometimes, just as I sag behind the lawn mower, the world seems to sag as well, and I think I am not alone in these sorry circumstances.

Sometimes we all sag. For some years—perhaps the possibility is always there—our energy has slackened. For some years we have seen and have been taught a host of alarms, perils, and fears. At times we suffer, as Norman Cousins put it, from a sense of helplessness that derives from a collective perception of imminent defeat, from the imperfection of human organizations, from onrushing depersonalization, from the dread of loneliness (*Saturday Review,* December 4, 1973). Robert Heilbroner wrote with frightening assurance in *An Inquiry into the Human Prospect* that "[t]he answer to whether we can conceive of the future other than as a continuation of the darkness, cruelty, and disorder of the past seems to me to be no; and to the question of whether worse impends, yes." Norman Borlaugh, called "the father of the green revolution" for his development of high-yield cereal grains, predicted some time ago, in June, 1974, the early possibility of famine and an attendant epidemic of ten to fifty million deaths. The National Center for Atmospheric Research announced as early as November 1975 that a catastrophic drought is overdue for the Great Plains. Any news medium on any day will add accounts of war, poverty, and violations of both the flesh and the spirit. A single section of a single issue of almost any newspaper is likely to raise our anxiety with accounts of assassination plots, of our impending desperation for energy resources, of war in the Middle East and in the South Atlantic, of the Social Security system's demise, and of the possibility that both coffee and bacon may be cancer-inducing. Susan Sontag, writing in the *New York Times* for February 8, 1976, said, "This civilization, already so far overtaken by barbarism, is at an end, and nothing we do will put it back together again." We were advised early on by *Saturday Review* that "the traditional program of liberal arts in undergraduate education has crumbled" (July 22, 1974) and that "America is in headlong retreat from its commitment to education" (March 20, 1976). Teachers doubt what they're to hand down to the next generation and wonder if anyone will take it if it is handed. Disciplines of learning that we have cherished seem in peril of extinction. Job markets shift, and while good people called to vocation are abandoned, others thrive who seem to have no vocation except to manipulate their fellow beings. We are already almost entombed in mounds of paper, files, forms, and printouts, and we are always being deluded, not by grandeur, but by triviality. If we can't find ailments enough outside, we can bore ourselves to death. Meanwhile, some turn to apathy, not as a passive retreat, but as a conscious revolt against complexities that can no longer be handled. The metaphor for our age may someday be found in some hellish landscape such as that at Verdun, where for a year men fought over and over again for the same few inches of ground, paying half a million lives neither to gain nor to lose. We are sometimes afraid of all our sorrows, present and yet to come. Sometimes we're pretty sure everything is going to clog up or wear out.

The items on a list of lamentations might be multiplied again and again. Indeed, I'm moved to question the judgment of anyone who is not occasionally disturbed, confused, alarmed. I don't think about such things all of the time, but hearing about them does make the mower heavier and the mowing harder. It does make the life in the grass seem empty of hope. Truly, as Maynard Mack has remarked, "to the wretched, all weather is wintry."

And yet, failure and woe need not be ultimate facts of life. Our past, even if it sometimes seems to have brought us to a sorry, woeful condition, has held dear and precious things—good houses full of sweet people, some long since gone; good coffee, though now we'll have to learn to plant a better crop; good country, much of it now paved; good music, dimly heard in the cacophony of change.

Besides, we were not promised that earth would come of age in us. We were not promised that change would cease when it reached our house. We were not promised that evolution would end at our belly button. All of creation may yet groan and lurch up out of itself, and we can go into a new world clasping to our memories what was dear in the old. Strange and marvelous things have happened before. If doom seems sometimes to hang down about us, marvels also wait upon us.

Consider one particular marvel: every plant that sustains us used to be a weed. Yet in time weed became food, and in the process we became other than what we had been. Consider, for example, the black-eyed pea. Cultivated in antiquity, from origins in Africa, the plant spread to the Mediterranean countries, and the Greeks and Romans knew it. Taken by the Spanish into the West Indies in the sixteenth century, it was established on this continent by the eighteenth century. The dried seeds of the black-eyed pea, *Vigna sinensis,* may be ground into meal for various uses, or taken as a coffee substitute. "The fresh seeds and immature pods," one source remarks, "may be eaten." To note that black-eyed peas "may be eaten" seems scant justice; black-eyed peas, especially in the company of onions and cornbread, are a staple of Southern diets, a necessity to the sustenance of a meager life, a delicacy to the palate of the knowing eater. Yet another writer, not given to Southern ways, says the *Vigna sinensis* is grown in warm regions for green manure and forage.

Ipomea batatas, the sweet potato, is sister to the morning glory. Common enough in most warm areas of the world, it is forsaken in some because of the great, long, trailing, space-usurping vines of its maturity. Apparently it came to these Western continents from the East by way of Polynesia. Not all of its history was lost in the strange voyage: a Peruvian dialect calls the potato *cumar,* a Polynesian dialect calls it *kumara,* and a Maori dialect calls it *umara.* However it came to these shores, it came early; a word for the potato occurs in many early dialects of Peru, the Yucatan, the Caribbean Islands. The word of San Domingo, *batata,* corrupted by Englishmen, gave us our word, *potato.* Columbus took plantings back to Europe from his first voyage. Now it is most commonly found in bins and piles at the grocery store, and some say it's attractive under brown sugar, molasses, and marshmallows, but it's still the sister to the natural morning glory.

The turnip, *Brassica napus,* is the civilized kin of *Brassica campestris,* which grows wild in sandy soils, originally and prolifically near the seaside in northern Europe, whence it came to be a chief source of food, filling though of no great nutritional value, to early Gallic, Germanic, and Celtic peoples. It remained a staple until it lost out to the potato, then dwindled into the present, when it is oftener remembered not for its taste but for its lack of blood. Even now, it has not lost its close similarity to the natural growth, the weed *Brassica campestris,* that grows near northern seashores.

The wild version of *Raphanus sativus,* our radish, is *Raphanus raphanistrum,* and they are scarcely distinguishable. The radish has a long history, but it has not lost its connection with weeds. There is a mention of radish in China in 1100 BCE. Herodotus tells of an inscription he saw in Egypt which proclaimed that the builders of the Great Pyramid ate prodigious amounts of radish. Perhaps it had already won its reputation for curative and generative powers: Anglo-Saxons in later centuries used the radish in recipes against madness, demonic temptation, and possession, and it occurred in poultices and drinks for headaches, pains in the joints, eye-ache, and warts. Withal it manages to be fetching when eaten raw, especially when it is coldly crisp. But the round red radish, cool in a bed of lettuce on the relish tray served smartly at your local restaurant, is not significantly different from *Raphanus raphanistrum,* the weed radish.

All of these—turnips, black-eyed peas, sweet potatoes, radishes—are growing now in our garden. So, too, is okra, which takes its name from *nkruman,* its name in the Tshi language of Ghana; Brussels sprouts, whose origins are unknown, though it has been of latterly centuries common in Belgium, whence its name; and onions, kin to the wild lily, common in Egyptian tomb paintings, unfit for Brahmins and yoga practitioners, object of fond recollection for wilderness Jews (see Numbers 11:5—when they remembered Egypt, it was for "the cucumbers and the melons, and the leeks and the onions and the garlic").

All of them once were weeds, natural growths, thought unusable.

Somewhere, sometime, perhaps along a lonesome stretch of the Nile in a time none can chronicle, a weed stretched and cast its spores into the wind, one to become a lily, another to become an onion, only to wait another eon before someone discovered it was edible. And elsewhere, in a cool, unknown place, a cabbage weed exercised itself and became Brussels sprouts. Elsewhere still, southerly, deep in Africa, someone saw the beasts eat okra weed and found that it was good. Someone cold and afraid of his hunger knelt near the sea along what would one day be a Danish shore, dug a strange root, ate, survived, and a weed became a turnip.

All of them once were weeds, natural growths, thought useless. Some are weeds still and useless still to parts of humankind. In some provinces black-eyed peas are not tolerable as food. To those who don't fancy pot-likker, turnip greens are less tasteful than poor grass, and the turnip itself seems merely a poor root. The radish is even to discriminating eyes much like the wild members of its family. All that became, became from weeds. Some things, like the turnip, may yet become weeds again.

And if all of them once were weeds, if everything used to be a weed, may we not, with some reason, wait and watch with glad surmise, dig strange roots, prune alien plants to fuller growth, discover that what is now a weed may yet be fruit, and all be fed?

Surely so. Such marvels do occur. But they need our making.

That brings me back to the lawn I was talking about a little while ago. Unattended, my lawn would be a weedy lot eight weeks from now. Everything that was a weed will go back to weed if it is not clipped and mowed and cultivated, and no casual cutting will do. What was alien weed must be trimmed to fuller growth, manured by work, and pruned by art. Just so are marvels made; just so are new worlds found and learned. The imagination, Whitehead has reminded us, has contagious power to construct new visions, to rekindle zest.

The ritual of today can free the mind to consider the possibilities of tomorrow. Thoughtless, hurried cutting won't do. Priesting to the lawn is no casual art. You don't just whir up the mower and go tearing across the grass catty-cornered or zig-zag. That's not the way at all. Oh, you can do it helter-skelter if you please, mow plaids, play X's and O's in the grass, if you're of a mind to. But that's not the way. Priesting to the lawn has its mysteries and rituals, has its proper liturgy.

I have two lawns to do, contiguous, mine and the widow lady's next door. First, I mow the small side of her lawn, and it must be done in decreasing rectangles. Then come the front slopes of both lawns, back and forth, neatly overlapping. The slopes done, I strain and heave the mower back up to the big flat area of our adjoining yards. That has to be done in diminishing L's, with one stop to trim around the red bud tree. There's little more: a quick strip down the south side, then diminishing squares do the last flat of the south yard, with genuflections at the elm, the mulberry, and six or ten stops for the drinking of holy water and general sagging.

Now there is some consequence to this ministry. It gets the lawn mowed, pretty clean, mostly even. Sometimes it mainly makes me sweat. Sometimes, my mind vacated, the ritual removing all need to think on mowing, I compose sharp rebuttals for use in day-old conversations. Sometimes, images of grief fill up the unused space in my mind, and I run behind the mower to shake them loose. Sometimes, I'm pretty sure the liturgy signifies nothing—other times, near the end, when I'm hot and the lawn mower is pushing back at me, I conclude that I'm caught in obsession, unable to mow another pattern.

But sometimes, maybe for a moment or two out of one mowing per summer, I think I get a sign and learn what liturgy is for, working back in my mind to the word's original signification of both public worship and public work, this last in the sense of a public duty a citizen is obliged to meet. Seven years ago I mowed a different pattern. Three years ago I mowed another. Now I've learned this way, the way. Each pattern got the lawn mowed. Each kept leg and eye and arm fixed to need. Now my sense of the slope and tilt of the yard and the bend of the grass and my sense of my own duration have taught me this way. And that's what liturgy is for: it gets the service done while we learn another way to name and know and locate God.

Over in our secular world, that's how marvels are made, how alien weeds become filling fruits, how new worlds are found. To the bitter weeds, the grinding losses, the searing terrors of the world, we bring the manuring of our work, the pruning of our art. We cannot go on being what we have always been. If we settle for that, we settle for weeds and woe. We can, instead, make a liturgy that will get done what needs doing. Sustained by that liturgy, while the work gets done, we can learn to reach out and enfold creation, making thereby new liturgies of life and re-generation. And then we shall not be afraid of the terror that comes by night or of the arrow that flies by day.

2

I have started here, in what must seem strange territory, because I want to propose an evolutionary conception of school teaching, which takes rhetoric, or at least some features of rhetoric, as its model. Weeds seemed a good enough place to start—an account of weeds is a way of sort of getting back to the basics. If the conception of teaching I hope to describe is evolutionary, that probably means that schoolteachers *never arrive,* but can at best be on the way. That, however, is another and later story, we all knew it anyway, and there's no cause for sadness in the matter.

At any rate, I want to work my way slowly toward an account of an evolutionary conception of school teaching. I think I would not be so concerned either with this conception or with the need for working slowly and cautiously toward it were I not so convinced that stasis, stagnation, and despair are so ready to hand and so little recognized in the profession of teaching.

In this section, I want to mention some evidences of stasis and stagnation, offering from time to time some modest alternatives. In the following section, I'll look a little more closely at the kind of despair teachers may always have before them, whether or not they succumb. In the final section, I'll try to suggest some ways out of stasis, stagnation, and despair by proposing an approach to an evolutionary conception of teaching.

I want to talk about certain mythologies and an intellectual attitude that are, I'm afraid, far too common among us. The mythologies are perhaps better identified as assumptions that we follow without question in our teaching and in our practice. I've called them mythologies because they have taken on the character of truth and because we enact them dramatically every term. They seem to represent or to display the truth about certain features of composition, though, in fact, we usually do not know where or why they arose and we do not question them. We have long since ceased inquiring whether or not they do display the truth; we have simply accepted them. The intellectual attitude I refer to is a certain pedagogical monism. I do not believe that we are mostly monists by overt belief, but our behavior often suggests that we have assumed there is one way of doing things right, one way of writing correctly, one way of judging writing, one way of teaching writing.

I'll turn first to the mythologies or assumptions that I mentioned a moment ago. I cannot and don't wish to be thorough— I'll only cite some examples of assumptions some of us have made without actually inquiring about the truth, and I should acknowledge that there is no particular order in the examples that follow.

For example, we have frequently assumed that there is a right way to construct paragraphs, and we have assumed that it is appropriate to insist upon clear topic sentences in every paragraph. We have done this despite the evidence shown in the work of good writers that probably fewer than 40 percent of paragraphs published have a readily recognizable topic sentence, and that paragraphs, oftener than not, far from being constructed by a *right* method, are forms of personal punctuation. I'll cite a single textbook (here and later I'll withhold names to protect the guilty) in which the entire section given over to "rhetoric" consists of five chapters on paragraphing, with such subtitles as "*the* basic principle of organization" (italics mine).

In our teaching and in our textbooks, we have often assumed that there is a right way to punctuate. The evidence we find if we actually read good writers—and do a little writing ourselves—is that, outside of three or four key spots, punctuation is highly variable.

My examples, as you'll see, range from the ridiculous to the ridiculous. We have somehow perpetuated such received truths as the notion that no sentence may end with a preposition, when once again the evidence we find if we actually read good writers shows us that is a notion we need not subscribe to.

Somewhere out there are some composition teachers who have taught whole generations of students that no personal pronoun may appear in a business letter, a research paper, or even an essay.

We have accepted convenient classifications as if they represented the whole truth. I'll cite the textbook that has a chapter claiming that there are six types of essays—not five, or twenty-seven, but six.

That kind of reductionist thinking is not at all uncommon. Another textbook, for example, treats all student essays as if they are and ought to be expressive forms, this despite the evidence that some are referential, some are persuasive, some are seventeen other things. The text in question displays nothing but expressive writing in the face of warnings by Kinneavy and others that preoccupation with any single mode of writing is perilous.

Textbooks, of course, are often presented as if the author had discovered the one, the true way to good writing. Consider the recent textbook, for example, that is entirely given over to sentence combining as if that alone were the sole guide to good writing.

Both in our texts and in our teaching, we often act as if it were easily possible to separate kinds of writing from each other. I'll cite a single recent text that assumes there are these separable forms: personal writing, descriptive writing, expository writing, persuasive writing, and critical writing.

In our monistic absorption with *right* ways of writing, we ignore, both in our teaching and in our texts, the effect of the very words we use. Any author or teacher, for example, who thinks of writing as giving *power* is probably singling out a single, legitimate feature of writing, but is otherwise violating the spirit of human communication.

Another text tells us that there are five reasons for writing, no more, no less—self-expression, informing, demonstrating, exploring, and persuading.

We tolerate texts that seem to know the truth, that announce, for example, that an exploratory essay must have a clear thesis statement early in the paper, never noticing, apparently, that if an essay is truly meditative and exploratory, it probably can't have a thesis sentence early in the paper.

In our teaching and in our textbooks, we sometimes assume that proper language is fixed and immutable, its laws to be followed rigidly.

In our teaching and in our textbooks, we often assume that the best language is the simplest, forgetting that one cannot always say a complex thing except in complex language. We sometimes assume that there is a universal audience, or that all audiences will require the same treatment. Sometimes we think there is a single *right* text, and having chosen it, we perpetuate it out of habit. (I'm almost moved to digress and lament for a moment our ways of adopting textbooks.) Time and again we choose or demand a *single* method. "Choose a single heuristic method and stay with it," one reviewer remarks of a text. "The text gives students too many choices," another says.

Enough. Any reader could provide a set of examples. These are reductionist, monistic strategies and methods. They sometimes work well for the short time, but to the extent that they are reductionist and monistic, they are a violation of the craft and art of writing, a violation of our students, a violation of our own professionalism. About the best we can expect of a reductionist, monistic form of instruction is momentary adequacy, and we may not get that much.

Which leads me, by a route the stages of which will not be immediately apparent, though I hope the connection will become plain in a moment, to the Sears catalog.

Our garden is under way this year, and the weeds are coming along as well as can be expected, thank you. For that reason, I decided I needed a new garden hoe. Before I went to hunt one, I browsed through the Sears catalog for this year. Many as old as I am or older and most younger than I am will not have been conditioned to the Sears catalog as I have been, and so may not understand how surprised I was to discover that there are no garden hoes in the new catalog. Some are available in the Sears store, to be sure, but none is exhibited in the catalog. It was for me an astonishing discovery.

I did what a scholar should do. I forgot the weeds. I neglected the garden. I got curious about the disappearance of garden hoes from the catalog, thinking that I had, perhaps, stumbled upon something of sociological and cultural significance. I thought first I had better check my memory of earlier catalogs. I went to our library, where, deep in the farthest recesses, we have a collection of Sears catalogs—not all of them, by any means, but about one for each decade as a sample—and as good fortune would have it, I fell upon a 1936 Sears catalog.

This was perfect. I would have been almost seven when it first appeared, and I could use it to check my memory about what used to be in the catalog.

You must understand that the Sears catalog was, when I was young, a thing of great moment. Its arrival signaled the start of a new year—school would be opening soon. It was particularly captivating because I knew my mother would study it closely and then make a careful order of our clothes for the year and somehow sneak in an order for our Christmas presents without our knowing it. The catalog was also a treasury for reading and drawing lessons, and in a rural community with idiosyncratic plumbing systems, it eventually found other uses. The catalog is still important, for that matter. Our vacuum cleaner came from the catalog. My wife picked our refrigerator and washing machine after first looking through the catalog, and sometimes my mother told people she got me from the Sears catalog.

At any rate, I still didn't get around to the garden hoe, thence to the weeds. Instead, I got caught up on the book and leafed slowly through it. The highest-priced dress was $7.98. An afternoon frock could be had for $1.98, a percale housedress for $.49.

Corsets ranged from $.94 to $4.98, depending, I suppose, upon how firm a foundation one sought. There were eleven pages of different styles of long johns for men, ranging from $.54 to $2.59. Men's shirts were available for $1.29, and separate collars were still available, at three for $.60. Ten different kinds of wood-burning kitchen stoves were displayed, and nine types of gas ranges. A complete living room outfit—sofa, two chairs, otto-man, table, and lamp—was priced at $58.95. School tablets could be had at two for $.84. There were nine pages of patent medi-cines. The universal joint assembly for a Model T Ford cost $1.45. There were eight pages of harness and gear. A good walking plow was available for $12.95. Three pages showed different styles of farm wagons. And surely enough, on page 908, there was a dis-play of garden hoes.

It seems a strange world, and yet it was less than my lifetime ago. Stunning changes have come since. That catalog showed an-other world, its features, design, style, and pace all foreign to us.

Well, at last I remembered where I had started, to get a new hoe to weed the garden. I took the 1936 catalog out to the big Sears stores, and you'd be amazed at what I discovered: They wouldn't let me order a hoe out of the 1936 catalog.

The problem is that a catalog describes a fixed world. It was present and real once, but now it's gone. It gives us a glimpse of a particular world, real and right enough when it was present in time. That seems to be what happens to single, reductionist, monistic visions. They are linked to particular times, particular places. They may be right enough, even moving and evocative, in the then and there they belong to, but if we perpetuate single visions, always see by a single vision, always judge by a single vision, then sooner or later we fall victim to arrogance, igno-rance, dogma, rigidity.

I can't order a hoe in 1982 from a 1936 catalog. We mustn't try to live forever with only the knowledge we now have. If we accept only the knowledge we now have—our current catalog— then sooner or later it becomes our dogma, and we will be either arrogant or ignorant to the extent that we follow it rigidly. We must learn to see with many eyes, learn to use many catalogs. Diversity is to be enjoyed. All creation opens itself to the free search of free students. If we don't bind ourselves to what we already know, to a single vision, to a single catalog, then we each have a startling gift: we can think our own thoughts, unenslaved by the thoughts of others, and we can be our own spokesmen. Everything is full of wonder if we watch and see in many ways. Creation is too full and rich, too varied and copious to be comprehended through single visions, or detailed in single catalogs.

I'll illustrate by veering aside again to Fort Phantom Hill, which is all right—weeds grow there, too. The ruins of Fort Phantom Hill lie some twelve miles to the north of Abilene, Texas. I had never been there before a year or so ago, though I had erected the fort many times in my mind.

Construction of the fort was authorized in November 1851, by General Order 91. Major-General Smith, commanding the Eighth Military Department, which included Texas, thought he was establishing a fort on the Clear Fork of the Brazos to protect settlers on the upper Brazos and Trinity Rivers. The site, he was told, was "alive with deer, turkey, and bear." Truth was, the area lacked timber for construction, and water for the fort's troops had to be hauled from four miles or so away. The fort took its name from a nervous sentry. On night duty during the first encampment, he fired at what he later testified was an "Indian on the hill." When no trace of the marauder could be found, the others concluded that it was a phantom—a phantom on the hill, hence Fort Phantom Hill. It's a grand name, full of wonder and romance, a name that might have resonated with sounds of heroism under desperate circumstances, a name scarcely matched by John Ford, or John Wayne, or the makers of a hundred cavalry fictions.

The fort, as it turned out, was not equal to the romance of its name. Not quite three years after it was established, it was abandoned, in April 1854.

I had built Fort Phantom Hill long since from the lumber of a hundred movies, five hundred Western fictions, and God knows how many cavalry stories, and I had peopled it long since with such folk as filled the pages of *Beau Geste*. When you're a boy and you live in another world and you haven't yet learned that war is wicked and ugly, and that most of the games men play, in uniform and out, are at best foolish posturings, at worst forms of oppression—when you're a boy in such a world, I was about to say, a fort is a wondrous place where it's possible to be heroic.

Later, I learned about Fort Phantom Hill in different ways, in the words, written years later, of a lady who had lived at the fort as a girl. "The soldiers were soon in battle array," she wrote. "The whole tribe of Northern Comanches was coming in sight, the head chief Buffalo Hump in the lead, followed by his subordinates; then came the warriors, squaws, and papooses, 2500 in all. Seeing the preparation for their reception, it was too much for the noble red men and they passed on with scowls and angry looks, going in a westerly direction."

Later still, I learned more—or rather, I learned to accept less of what I thought I had learned. A historian, quoting the lady's account of Buffalo Hump's visit, suggested that for the sake of accuracy it would be a good idea "to divide the good old lady's 2500 by ten and subtract a hundred." He reckoned, in other words, that there could not have been more than about 100 or 150 in the Indian band, though to an old lady remembering what she thought she saw, it might well have seemed 2500.

And still later, I discovered that if there was heroism in that province, it didn't all belong to white people. On August 25, 1869, Major George Thomas and his cavalry troops came across a fresh Indian trail near Abilene. They followed it and finally sighted the Indians in the vicinity of the Double Mountains. The troops were clearly gaining on the Indians. One old Comanche warrior apparently decided that he was expendable. He dropped out of the Indian party, dismounted, and attacked the cavalry as they approached. Twice he wounded Major Thomas with his arrows. He wounded three troopers, all the while loudly berating the soldiers. And then he died in the cavalry fire. But in the confusion of his delaying fire, his fellow warriors escaped.

Finally, I learned one more thing, which I've already mentioned. I had pictured Fort Phantom Hill in my mind along with the others—Fort Richardson, Fort Griffin, Fort Concho, and the rest—and had conceived them as, if not permanent, at least durable, continuously present in the landscapes of fantasy where warfare might be noble and men might be brave. But then I learned it was all a mistake: the army blundered and built the fort in the wrong place: there was no timber; there was no water; and the fort itself was occupied for only three years.

Perhaps you will understand, then, that when I drove twelve miles to the north of Abilene and stood for a moment in the ruins of Fort Phantom Hill, I didn't know which Fort Phantom Hill to look at. I didn't know which Fort Phantom Hill was real. Was I to look at the fort of my old imagining and picture myself bravely at the ramparts? Was I to see the small, beleaguered, but noble band of troops in that old lady's fort? Was I only to see the small ruins of an old mistake? Was I to see Buffalo Hump's fort? Was I to see the sane and sober historian's fort? I stood there a while that morning, and after a bit I came away.

It's hard to find Fort Phantom Hill.

Must I learn to see Fort Phantom Hill in only one way? Must I see forever only the small and scattered ruins that I saw that morning? Must I give up seeing it as the old lady saw it, remembering her girlhood, when a company of troopers stood against the odds? Yet if I see it only in her way, I surrender the power to see it as the historian sees it. Must I forget the dream fort I erected before I ever saw Fort Phantom Hill? Must I cease trying to see it as Buffalo Hump saw it? I choose not to.

That fantasy fort I imagined as a boy is dear to me, but it is not Fort Phantom Hill. That old lady's remembrance of the place is sweet to me, but it does not tell me the whole truth. I have to read the historian's account. I have to try to see it as Buffalo Hump saw it. I have to go and see the ruins. I have to keep looking. Fort Phantom Hill exists and has its identity in all of the versions of it that exist.

I began this section with some account of reductionist, monistic practices, evidence, I think, of some stasis and stagnation and a consequent manifestation of arrogance or ignorance or dogma. Over against that, I mentioned some of the perils of relying on a single catalog and the risk of seeing Fort Phantom Hill in only one way. Here at the end of this section I want to return for just a moment to some of our rigidities.

We like to think that we expect good speaking and good writing of our students, and some of us are grand in our proclamation of high standards in these arts. Yet university faculties don't have a very good or convincing record of their own belief in or practice of these arts. I'll cite five last examples briefly. One set of examples could be provided by almost any editor of almost any journal with his or her account of the state of writing manifested in the manuscripts submitted by professionals. Another kind of example is available in almost any university catalog. Do I need to say more? They needn't be models of elegance, but they might be models of the plain style. They mostly aren't. Yet these are the instruments by which most students first come to know us, and they are the chief display of our educational belief. Almost any university committee meeting might provide a third kind of example. Do I need to say more? For a fourth kind of example, consider our textbooks. Do I need to say more? They needn't be poetic, but they might be lucid, strong, and economical. They mostly aren't. Yet these are the only documents many students will ever see as displays of our subjects. For a fifth and last example of our own failures—and rigidity and reductionism—I'll cite from our schools another standard feature which requires neither speaking nor writing. I mean here to refer to such abominations as evaluation forms and short-answer examinations.

Well, enough of that. If we get started upon the enterprise of counting each other's failures, we'll all still be here next month, counting. I want, instead, to consider, as I promised earlier, why teachers always might, but need not despair.

3

In 1982, a citizen would have to be wonderfully innocent, unaware of television, unfamiliar with newspapers, uncommonly insensitive, and in general about three bricks shy of a load not to suspect that the future may be perilous for all of us, for education and educators in particular. I'm inclined to think, as I've heard it said, that if on some days at least we're not fretful, worried, and a little psychotic as we contemplate the future, that probably means that we don't have a very good grasp on reality.

When I was young, alone, say, in the house with my family gone, and trees or something mysterious scratched against the roof and a settling in the house made steps creak, or alone, say, walking home in the dark after seeing *The Mummy Walks,* I thought that if I would go ahead and name the ghosts that were out there, it would somehow be better and I could breathe again. I expect I still feel that way. If we acknowledge and name the anxieties, fears, difficulties, and problems that are out there waiting for us, they don't go away, to be sure, but they're not quite so scary. It's easier to deal with the ghost behind the next tree if you have a name for it.

We look ahead and wonder if there is a future for education. That future is probably always at stake, but we don't always know it. We know it now. Our conception of ourselves as teachers is at stake, too, and our vision of education is in doubt. Out there (in the future we are sometimes unwilling to look at) the possibility of liberal education seems in doubt. If we don't look and see what's there, we can't go except with stumbling, halting steps, and partly blind.

But of course we can't see all that is out there. The future isn't here yet. We see signs and portents, but not all are revealed to us, and we don't understand some that are. We can't be perfect in wisdom, but we can learn to face the frights, perils, and signs of despair that we see.

Sometimes, everything seems to be coming loose. Part of what startles us and sometimes very nearly renders us inactive is that the myths, assumptions, professional dicta, and good advice we started with all appear, on some days, to be little more than an accumulation of debris, a pile of things that were obsolete long before they were discarded. Somehow or another, we were all taught that thrift is important, but through most of our lives no one has acted as if it really were. We were taught the need for human community, but we move, disband, and dissociate. We were taught, or we thought we were, the rewards of love, marriage, and fidelity, but everyone knows what has happened to those things. We were taught that the world is spacious and full of promise, but it shrank along with our expectations. We were taught the proper content for our disciplines, but they have changed six or twenty times, shifting out from under us. Disciplines come and disciplines go, and subjects we held dear are prized no longer.

I don't want to linger indefinitely over the possibilities of disaster, but I do want to display for a moment a bit more of a quick catalog of fears. My list of impending woes is not complete, nor is it the same another would compile, but it will do for now.

The newspaper one morning this week detailed again on the first page, and for column after column inside, the effects of proposed federal budget cuts. Naturally enough, education is one of the first places likely to experience further budget reductions. This news won't be the last such news—there won't be enough money. Elsewhere in the same paper, a visiting expert taught us that "less is more," that it really feels better to have less. If that is so, then we'll all probably get a chance to feel just fine.

But we don't have to look outside educational establishments for problems. Inside, we have often acted as if our work were sacred. We have often acted as if things must continue to be what they have been, as if our disciplines must remain inviolate as we first conceived them, when in fact we have in many instances long since lost any sense of rigorous definition or clarification of our hopes and expectations for the humanities, the social sciences, and the natural sciences. It's already apparent that traditional programs will probably not survive in the next generation or so, at least not in their present form. But we seldom look at the signs, therefore don't know what's happening, therefore can't anticipate what to do next.

But other problems wait inside the academy. We forget that education should be first of all concerned with the free spirit of free citizens. We forget that all of us are first men and women, and in our schools move instead to train students as if they were first lawyers, management entrepreneurs, doctors, English scholars, chemists, accountants.

If the prospect for education seems gloomy and chancy, in other words, we are ourselves partly responsible. We are not prepared to provide or willing to provide what the world may ask for or need. We create false divisions among ourselves, and we don't talk across the boundaries of our disciplines and departments. We divide ourselves into parts, and then each part or discipline or department cherishes itself as the only or at least the best source of truth. Our own language betrays us, and we splinter into a new Babel of conflicting groups, each with its own strange tongue. On the rare occasions when we gather to talk about planning for the future, we talk about tight money, retrenchment, FTEs and faculty/student ratios, and credit-hour production. We get lost in instrumentalities and seldom talk about an imagined future that is both proper and exciting for our work.

If we look, the problems increase and multiply, both without and within. We haven't yet taught our students to be men and women of understanding and learning; they and we are still creatures of ambition, greed, and war. We haven't yet learned ourselves or taught others how to face crucial shortages in energy and food, pollution of water and land, tense overcrowding in some pockets, barrenness and empty poverty in others. Political uncertainty and economic confusion have shaken the people's faith in education as a key to the future. Education has been the presumed path to upward mobility. Now both the path and the goal are under question. Educational institutions have come under serious doubt; some people tell us, "You are not doing your job very well," and others say, "We really don't need what you have to offer." Some already think upward mobility is impossible. If education is not worthy and upward mobility is not possible, we may face the spectacle of a stratified, class-bound society ruled by a self-perpetuating power elite. Signals have already flared: the back-to-the-basics movement that has swirled around us—and it will not soon go away—promises, if we are not vigilant, to turn into a profound reactionary movement that is social and political before it is educational.

If we look, we can indeed see failures, perils, and fears. Robert Lekachman ended an essay on the future of education in a recent issue of *Change* in this way: "As a good American should, I should like to end on a note of cheer. My misfortune is that I can't identify a single valid reason to be cheerful about the outlook for education."

To be sure, another would explain our problems in a different way. One thing seems certain, however: We can't be what we are *and* become what we should be.

If what I have said seems too dismal, too full of woe, too narrowly pessimistic, perhaps there is a small remedy. Looking a different way does often let us discover something different to see.

I want to tell about a house—more accurately, a small ruin. The walls still stand, and part of a rotting roof, from which protrudes part of a rusty stove pipe. Even if I offered explicit directions, many would not find it. You'd have to go west from Fort Worth, Texas, about 225 miles, through Weatherford, Mineral Wells, Breckenridge, Albany, Stamford, Aspermont, Swenson, to Jayton. By now, you'd be in territory from which it costs about fourteen dollars to send a letter to the world, but you'd still not be there yet. Jayton, with a population of about seven hundred, is the last big city before you get there. You drive four or five miles out of Jayton, turn onto a dirt road, and drive deep into the Croton Breaks for seven or eight miles, and after a while you'd come to the little community known as Golden Pond (which bears no resemblance to the setting of a recent movie). It's not close to anything. Nobody ever goes there. It's no longer recognizable as a community. The only inhabitants are ghosts, and the northwest wind keens and moans through rotting planks of an occasional ruined shack.

Not far from Golden Pond—some two miles or so—is the house I mentioned. It's a little house made of native stone. It measures about twelve feet by fifteen feet, and there is a small wooden lean-to on the back. You can see through the walls. It's empty, obviously has been for years.

My family and I happened onto this house a few years ago. We stopped to photograph it—to city folks, it looked picturesque. Not long afterward, I chanced to show the photograph to one of my aunts. She shuddered, quite noticeably, and said she didn't want to see it, or to think about it.

As it turned out, she lived in that house with a family during the school year of 1933–34 while she taught at Golden Pond. It was her first teaching job, and she made twelve dollars a month with room and board thrown in. She remarked, incidentally, that you could see through the walls in 1933, too, and feel the wind coming through.

For a moment, it's worth remembering that house, that school, my aunt, and that school year, 1933–34. It's worth trying to think what it was like, that first teaching job at twelve dollars a month, living in that house in that place.

She was far miles from home. There were no telephones in Golden Pond, and she had no transportation save what her feet offered. Even in 1933 there were no cars in Golden Pond. She was there among strangers in a barren, twisty land. That area, the Croton Breaks, is broken, eroded desert land; dry creeks, ravines, gullies, and canyons break the terrain for thirty miles and more. Even in 1933 it was rough country, nearly forgotten country.

There were no telephones, no electricity, no running water, no way to wash except in a pan or a round metal washtub. And the wind whistled and moaned through the rock walls.

If you stand on the little rise between ravines where the rock house is, if you stand there even in bright daylight, in every direction you look the distance is blue and far and melancholy. It is the lonesomest country I know. If you stand there at night, imagine what the dark is like when you're far from home and there's only one dingy, smoky kerosene lamp, which, for the sake of economy, can't be burned long.

Imagine lying in a narrow bed with the wind coming in between the rocks and across you, or moaning over and through the inadequate roof.

Imagine that, if you will, and then inquire: Lying there in the lonesome dark, with the northwest wind keening and moaning over you, how could you possibly imagine a bright future?

I've told about this house in that place so that I could come to this: At any given moment, the future can always look grim, as it must have then. Indeed, since going into the future means becoming something other than what we are now—that is, it's always risky—then the future can always look grim unless someone makes it otherwise. A future always happens; a good future has to be made.

Future-making is teachers' work. The myth of Sisyphus, Camus taught us, tells much about human work and human futures. Everything depends upon how we feel about the rock and the work of pushing it. If sadness and defeat clench us and melancholy rises in our hearts, then the rock wins. But if we know that we always have the chance to keep making a future, that next time we'll get the rock to the top of the hill, then we and the future win. If we know this, it's because we learned it from a good teacher, wherever he or she happens to be located, whatever he or she happens to be called at the moment. It's always a good teacher who makes the future for us. Some teachers, of course, just reiterate the past. Some grab the prevailing fashions of the present. But good teachers make the future.

Because we are mostly pretty complex, we are easily lost to each other. Sometimes our vanity teaches us that other people are only what we perceive them to be, and we lose each other by our ignorance, our unwillingness to search each other out and know each other. Sometimes we are apart, sometimes forlorn, sometimes afraid. We are segmented, divided into parts; we focus narrowly sometimes so that we can see more intently. But a good teacher can unite us in the imaginative consideration of learning. We are isolated from each other and often compartmentalized, but a good teacher can teach us to touch hands with others, to learn from others, to take the encouragement we need from others, to remember that there is no sure sign of wisdom that marks a single department, discipline, or college. A good teacher can teach us that it is splendid to be human together.

A good teacher can teach us to know that each of us is blessed with a startling gift: Each can be his or her own advocate, judge, critic, spokesman. A good teacher can teach us that change did not cease when it reached us, that we can go into a new world clasping to our memories what was dear in the old, but expecting to make magic hereafter. A good teacher can teach us that it is all right to question orthodoxy, that everything is full of wonder if we watch, that creation is too rich and varied and copious to be comprehended by single visions. There are many ways of looking, and a good teacher can show us many visions, each holding something precious and dear. Dear and deep as the past may be to us, a good teacher will teach us that we are free to remain unimpressed with what we have been and to be intent instead upon what we are becoming. Good teachers have the surest, boldest, loveliest validation for their work. Teaching by its nature takes hold of the past in order to proclaim and to create the future. However dark the time may be, good teachers are always making the future.

When they refuse to lock themselves into some pattern of the past, when they refuse to acquiesce in prevailing fashions, when they teach the nation's citizens the ultimate practical and spiritual uses of education, the liberating uses of knowledge, when their own behavior is self-luminous, then good teachers will teach us to make a future brighter than any we can now imagine. And then the rest of us will not be alone and frightened by a mournful, moaning wind in some small rock house in a dark and lonesome country.

4

I am trying to say that because there are in rhetoric certain lessons and hopes that can change our ways of seeing, being, and acting, we need not despair, though we sometimes do, we need not fail, though we often may.

What are these lessons and hopes? I won't presume to tell teachers that I know all *they* need to know. I haven't come this far in order to tell teachers what to be or how to proceed as teachers. I do want to suggest some things we can learn about being teachers—all, I think, evolutionary by their nature—first, by borrowing a lesson from some rhetorical categories; second, by taking a lesson from a profound rhetorical problem we and students always face; and third, by learning a lesson from some of the twists and turns of the rhetorical mode known as *ethical argument.*

A. *Speaking through time.* The first lesson and hope are implicit in what I was saying just at the end of the previous section.

Observing that discourse sometimes has different needs and different characteristics on different occasions, classical rhetoricians eventually came to describe three kinds of rhetoric. The descriptions, naturally enough, vary from text to text, but generally acceptable terms for the three kinds are *judicial rhetoric, epideictic rhetoric,* and *legislative rhetoric.* Their primary time orientation provides a useful way of distinguishing among them. Judicial rhetoric looks toward the past, as in courtroom discourse, in historical writing, or, for example, in a poem like Dryden's "Religio Laici." Epideictic rhetoric looks toward the present, as in July Fourth oratory, for example, or in introductions, or in other kinds of ceremonial discourse. Legislative rhetoric looks toward the future, as in much polemical writing and some political oratory. The first explains or examines the past, the second celebrates, or observes, or serves the present, the third wants to influence the future. Sometimes a whole discourse has a single orientation; sometimes a single discourse must move in different ways and do different things, as Lincoln in the Gettysburg Address catches the past in his opening, then moves to commemorate the present and to call for a new kind of resolve in the future.

When teachers are at their best, they are always moving in time, speaking through time, enacting what they know now, showing where it came from in the past and why and how, and exploring its consequences for the future. A teacher cannot stay fixed in time and remain a teacher; a teacher must constantly practice judicial, epideictic, and legislative forms of rhetoric. When a teacher stays in one time, without demonstrating the full context of what gets said, he or she is asking students to accept assertions rather than to learn. When a teacher stays in the past, he or she is only remembering and asking students to accept memory as education. When a teacher stays in the present, he or she is only making an inert and historyless display and asking students to accept the display as education. When a teacher stays in the future, he or she is in the business of indoctrination. Speaking through time is a means of evolution in teaching, as suggested earlier: A good teacher can teach us that change did not cease when it reached us, that we can go into a new world clasping to our memories what was dear in the old, but expecting to make magic hereafter. Dear and deep as the past may be to us, a good teacher will teach us that we are free to remain unimpressed with what we have been and to be intent instead upon what we are becoming. Teaching by its nature takes hold of the past in order to proclaim and to create the future.

B. *Ministering to mavericks.* A little earlier I spoke of a profound rhetorical problem we and students always face. To explain what I mean, I must talk a little about mavericks. The word *maverick* comes from the name of Mr. Samuel A. Maverick, a Texas lawyer and cattleman who did not brand his cattle. It originally meant an unbranded, orphaned, or strayed animal, typically a calf. But then in informal American usage it came to be applied to human-kind, and signifies one who is unorthodox in ideas or attitudes, one who *will* stray from the herd, one who *will* wander off, one who does not get branded.

I'm much interested in mavericks, but must come upon them the long way round. Not long ago, a student I know began an essay, echoing Michael Halloran, with this sentence: "For the modern speaker to communicate modern ideas in the modern world, he must be a speaker 'without letters'—an illiterate." I'd not want the sentence to be taken too simply. The author is talking about illiteracy as we commonly think of it, to be sure, but she is also talking about being "without letters" in a much larger sense. I'll try to illustrate.

The Latin rhetoric and composition manual that John Milton used as a schoolboy in the early seventeenth century had been in continuous use across Western Europe and England for the better part of a thousand years. That is a set of letters that thousands in many generations shared. For centuries, Latin and Greek languages and literature were central to all schools in the western world; they were vital to most curricula until at least the 1890s. Few American universities introduced any study of English or American literature until after 1850, holding instead to a classical curriculum, and the practice of teaching composition in English did not become well established until after 1875.

Indeed, it does appear, at least to our nostalgic eyes, that there was once a core of knowledge, a canon, a set of letters, if you will, that was steady, dependable, and shared by all, generation after generation.

But we are without the *Iliad,* the *Odyssey,* the Bible, the *Song of Roland,* without Greek or Latin. We are without the mythologies many once knew, without the scriptures that once formed a part of education. We are "without letters" in this sense. Milton's composition text in Latin was known by his kind for a thousand years. Now it's uncommon for such a text to survive upwards of three years in a single school. That means that it's likely no two generations will parse the same sentences or read the same texts. We are "without letters" in the sense—so it seems—that there are no letters, by which I mean texts, discourses, documents, that are shared either chronologically or geographically.

We are inclined to believe that in antiquity—which to a fresh-man and to some of us may be any time before 1950—there was a canon of art, literature, and historical, scientific, and philo-sophic discourse that could be known and shared with an audi-ence. Thus, so we are inclined to believe, a speaker shared with an audience certain knowledge and values which provided a ba-sis for discussion, argument, and understanding.

But we are "without letters" and seem therefore speechless before each other to the extent that we do not seem to share a world. That means that the gap between speakers and hearers now may seem or be far wider than ever before. When a speaker and a hearer inhabit the same world, it is enough, commonly, that both attend to the discussion at hand. But when a speaker and an audience inhabit different worlds, when they are "with-out letters" that can be shared, then the audience may never be able to hear what the speaker is saying. Thus the modern speaker, apparently deprived of a given world, is also apparently deprived of a shared way of communicating.

To the extent that this is true, then, the speaker must consti-tute his own world, must constitute himself by his own discov-ered language, enacting that creation so as to make himself and his words knowable and known to others. The modern speaker must create a world that has sufficient magnitude for others to enter and share. If he's to do that, a teacher must be there to help.

The trouble is, we mostly don't know how either to speak or to help, and so we find ourselves sometimes fretful, sometimes alone, sometimes afraid, sometimes hostile. We are uncertain how to achieve authentic discourse with each other, uncertain how to manifest our own humanness, uncertain how to show others a way.

And worse: Some of our habits of behavior stand in our way. I'll cite only three—fear, idolatry, and our fondness for time traps.

I'll take the last first, and only briefly, since I've mentioned it at some length before. We trap ourselves in moments of time and act as if there were no other. Some choose the past, and muse nostalgically over our vanished greatness, over the time when school was serious business, over the time when folks had a real sense of values. Most fall into the trap of the present, finding no solace in the past, and, caught in the whirl of present expedients, in the clutter and clamor of the moment, thus have no way to expect joy in the future. We only know we are busy, doing work that has to be done, though we'd rather be doing something else. So trapped, we cannot speak, having neither past nor present in common. We are "without letters."

Idolatry, too, stands in the way. I can't begin to list the things we worship. Recently, some have come to idolize "the basics," imagining that there was a time in the past (the time usually coincides with the early schooling of the person speaking at the moment) when we knew how to educate folks right. Some idolize vocational training, neglecting to notice that upwards of 70 percent of bachelor's degree holders soon shift to jobs unrelated to their undergraduate degrees. Some bow down before an economic secularism that will use even presumed religious beliefs as a means of perpetuating poverty, segregating wealth to the few, and exalting "right" values. We practice idolatry in schools, which should be nearly its last home, worshiping established curricula and the "standard" way of doing things, presuming that curricula and methods once learned are always right, idolizing our own territories, ignoring and debasing others, presuming that we, wherever we are, are the last guardians of liberal education, upholding a pretentious rigor uninformed by vision.

And plain fear stands in the way of our teaching. Tight budgets and chancy enrollments scare us. We're a little afraid that the community, or at least a growing part of it, has repudiated the academy and will burn our books. We're pretty much afraid that the world has clearly repudiated liberal learning, and so we retreat behind the walls, waiting fearfully for the barbarians to beat down the gates. We're more than a little afraid that we will have to teach without hope. We fear, perhaps as much as we fear death, that we will perish of insignificance.

When to these perils one adds our sometimes lust for efficiency, the scene seems to be set, not for our humanity to enact itself, but for us always to become less than human. We sometimes seem to be seeking a perfect efficiency: "Let's get precisely the right input in our scenario," we say, "so that at the bottom line we can assure the right output."

And that brings me back to mavericks.

I put uncommon hope in the maverick strain among us humans. We are the marvelous works of God. We are, or can be, beautifully bullheaded. We will wander from the herd. There remains in us a capacity for a wonderful inefficiency. There is in us the perverse beauty of a marvelous impudence. The maverick strain will save us, if we cherish it. We will save and make letters, and some teacher will show us how.

When the last wall of the last time trap is built around us, enclosing us with our idols and our fears, our mere efficiencies, someone will amble up to that wall, scrawl "Kilroy was here" across it, climb over, and see a new earth beyond. When the pretentious rigors of our imperfect standards seem to violate the sanctity of the human soul, some Huck Finn among us will say, "All right, then, I'll go to hell," and wander off from the herd, heading west.

I'm not proposing anarchy—I'm much too mild for that. I'm not opposing a prudent and beautiful sense of community—I'd be much too lonesome without that. But I do want to talk for a moment about how we cherish that wonderful impudence, that magical inefficiency, that maverick strain.

Obviously, I can't say once and for all how it's to be done, and if I did, some maverick would kick both the milk bucket and my proposal over. But I can propose a few hopes.

First, in the university, we can forget for a moment our customary territorial expansionism on the one hand and our customary territorial parochialism on the other, and go in aid of nonterritorial studies.

Second, we can forget our pretensions that all of the liberating arts have already been devised, and recognize new liberal studies that have emerged or are emerging, acknowledging the liberating moment wherever it occurs. There is no single set of educational truths that will take us to Eden. There is no single course of study that is inevitably perfect and available in one university. All forms of speaking are imperfect. All forms of study and organization are imperfect. Few anywhere are already wise. At our best, we yearn to be wise. We are not already learned; at our best, we are learning. Our imperfections are plain enough if we choose to look, but at our best, we are learning, yearning to be wise.

Third, we can summon ourselves to afford good teaching, to keep becoming teachers wherever we are. Teaching does not occur only in the classroom or in the library or in the laboratory. Anyone anywhere has the chance to keep becoming a good teacher, and good teaching is a grace we always owe each other. In a world "without letters," good teachers have to save texts and re-create texts, to be sure, but that isn't enough; they must also *make* texts themselves, perpetually imaging the process whereby students may learn to make texts, to know, show, and share their world, to create larger worlds in generative texts. All together must find and make the liberating texts.

Will all of that free us to be ourselves? To be human? I'd not guarantee it for a moment.

But we do still have in our own safekeeping yet for a while our own impudence and bullheadedness, our own inefficiency, our own maverick strain.

I started out a while ago with the difficulties of the modern speaker "without letters." Let me end this section with the modern speaker as maverick.

We have the gift to go out into the future, that extraordinary gift to be our own spokesmen, mavericks all. But with that gift of freedom there comes a responsibility: To use creation wisely, to treat others kindly, to ransack our own talents and to give them away as we make and save letters.

We keep trying to tell our identity to others and say how we want the world to operate. We want definition, and don't know what life means until we say it. We are always needing to speak in a variety of ways, *from* the heart, *to* the point, *up* in discussion, *out* in controversy. Yet we don't know how; we are "without letters."

And so we are left in a dilemma. If we are mavericks only and use our private languages only, then, as Georges Gusdorf points out in *Speaking,* we will not communicate but sink into incomprehensibility, excommunicated from our fellows. Yet if we use the language that everyone uses, then, while we may communicate, we risk inauthenticity and self-denial.

And so we go on, "without letters," doing our work, trying to be free citizens, trying to know the world, trying to name its parts, trying to proclaim its riches, trying to identify ourselves to others, trying to speak the future into existence. Good teachers will let us go on, will show us letters, will make letters, will lead us to make letters, liberating us to go on. We hope then someone will hear us, now or later, understand our words, and join us in completing the text we are making toward them.

C. *Emerging toward others.* But I must hurry on. I promised at the beginning of this last section to mention three kinds of lessons and hopes discernible in rhetoric. I want to turn to the last of these and propose again that some features of rhetoric show us the way to an evolutionary conception of teaching. [. . .]

First, you must remember the goddam weeds I started with. Every eon or so, a weed does turn into a potato or a black-eyed pea. The world is not yet ended, not for a little while yet, and change didn't cease when we reached maturity, chronologically if in no other way.

Second, I urge you to remember the cyclical, naturally replenishing nature of rhetoric. Invention feeds and informs structure and style and is fed and informed by them, the potential process of growth never ending, never tiring, unless we settle for less, unless we stop along the way and content ourselves with fatigue, fragmentation, and some monistic view of creation.

The third reason for hope requires a somewhat longer explanation. I'll ask you to return with me to consider some of the earliest stages of instruction in classical rhetoric. Among the subjects studied and the procedures practiced were the contemplation and display of how arguments get made, how arguments reach an audience. You'll remember some of the distinctions among logical argument, emotional argument, and ethical argument. I want to focus a little while on this last, argument that arises from *ethos* or character. [. . .]

Good discourse is always moving toward completeness. What complicates and intensifies the process is that discourse is a closure, a stoppage, hence in itself an incompleteness. We do not speak these words unless we have already chosen or unless we have already been directed not to speak those. The act of speaking eliminates possibilities for speaking; when something is named, it is not named otherwise. There is always more to be said than can be said. The language of generative *ethos* moves toward completeness, beyond closure, reaching somehow beyond its synecdochic nature.

One way this begins to become apparent in discourses is in their demonstrable extension in space and time. A generative *ethos* in one way or another opens the borders of the discourse to hold extraordinary time and space. The speaker in the Gettysburg Address makes space enough for all to come into the future he is summoning them to create. The speaker in "The Deserted Village" distances himself from the village, largely ridding himself of self-interest, and as he does so begins to see the village so well that he can also see into its future. [. . .] The speaker in *Amos* makes a world full of time and space, getting far beyond tribal boundaries and seeing what consequence looks like as it works itself out into the future. Each of these speakers—and I've mentioned only a few and those briefly—is a steward, not an owner of space and time. [. . .]

What frequently stands in the way of communication is some violation of space or time or both. We believe that the flood of language around us often blocks human correspondence; if that is so, it is not just because language at floodtide is all too often careless and sometimes corrupt, but also because the volume crowds our living space and our time, sometimes generating frenetic speed, sometimes a paralysis. We understand, too, that communication is often blocked because, as Geoffrey Wagner has mentioned, "[W]e are, in short, our own enchanted listeners." We may hear ourselves, not another; the other's words may act only as a trigger to release our own, unlocking not the other's meaning, but the one we already possessed. When this happens, we are bound in space, caught tightly in our own province. Specialized languages—slang, cult tongues, professional jargons, and the like—stand in the way of communication because they bind space, the specialized language of the speaker prohibiting entry by a hearer into the speaker's discursive universe. [. . .] The languages of television and other mass media crowd our time and hurry our responses, or stop our responses entirely. The languages of confrontation set space against space, universe against universe, and cannot wait for meditation time. Many instances of failed communication and many instances of communication never attempted are consequences of some violation of space or time or both.

Ethos is generative and fruitful when the time and space stewarded by a speaker give free room for another to live in.

[. . .] The self-authenticating language of such an *ethos* issues an invitation into a commodious universe. What makes that possible is its extension in space and time. Argument is partial; when a speaker argues a proposition or develops a theme or makes an assertion, he or she has knowingly or not chosen one proposition, one theme, one assertion from all available. When we speak, we stand somewhere, and our standing place makes both known and silent claims upon us. We make truth, if at all, out of what is incomplete, or partial. "An individual utterance," Bonhoeffer said, "is always part of a total reality which seeks expression in this utterance." Yet language is a closure, for we cannot speak two words simultaneously. Generative language seeks to shove back the restraints of closure, to make in language a commodious universe, to stretch words out beyond our private universes. Extension in time and space seems to be one effort that makes this possible. A last example may further clarify what I am trying to say.

The fourteenth chapter of *Corinthians 1* discusses two forms of behavior, *speaking in tongues,* quite outside the range of normal behavior, and *prophesying,* two spiritual gifts here set in contrast with each other. Speaking in tongues, we are told, was common in at least some early churches, as no doubt it is common in some churches today; the gift manifests itself in an ecstasy that realizes itself in a torrent of sound typically untranslatable by a hearer. The gift appears to have been highly coveted as evidence of immediate communion with God, though it was recognized as dangerous since the possessor might prove susceptible to spiritual pride. Prophesying, on the other hand, far from being the act of foretelling the future, may be better understood as a kind of preaching, or teaching, or a speaking out of the message of God. While Paul concedes that the speaker of tongues indeed speaks to God and acknowledges the vitality of the gift in the fifth verse ("I would that ye all spake with tongues [. . .]."), he nevertheless focuses on the error of speaking in tongues:

2 For he that speaketh in an unknown tongue speaketh not unto men, but unto God: for no man understandeth him; howbeit in the spirit he speaketh mysteries.

The speaker in tongues, Paul says, profits no audience, for no audience can distinguish meaning in the sounds (14:6–7). If men come together speaking tongues, they must remain aliens:

10 There are, it may be, so many kinds of voices in the world, and none of them is without signification.
11 Therefore if I know not the meaning of the voice, I shall be unto him that speaketh a barbarian, and he that speaketh shall be a barbarian unto me.

The gift is powerful, Paul continues, but edifies no one unless interpretation follows:

14 For if I pray in an unknown tongue, my spirit prayeth, but my understanding is unfruitful.
15 What is it then? I will pray with the spirit, and I will pray with the understanding also: I will sing with the spirit, and I will sing with the understanding also.
16 Else when thou shalt bless with the spirit, how shall he that occupieth the room of the unlearned say Amen at thy giving of thanks, seeing he understandeth not what thou sayest?

And finally, Paul concludes, should a congregation come together speaking in tongues, the unlearned, the ungifted, and the unbelieving must conclude that all are mad.

Better for the church, Paul argues, is prophesying, the speech that "speaketh unto men to edification, and exhortation, and comfort" (14:3):

4 He that speaketh in an unknown tongue edifieth himself; but he that prophesieth edifieth the church.

And so, while he is himself gratified by the gift, he exhorts men to edification:

18 I thank my God, I speak with tongues more than ye all:
19 Yet in the church I had rather speak five words with my un-

derstanding, that by my voice I might teach others also, than ten thousand words in an unknown tongue.

In the distinction between speaking in tongues and prophesying is a last guide to talking about "generative *ethos*" and school teaching. The speaker in tongues inhabits a bound universe; his time and space are small, and can accommodate no other. The other must stay outside; he cannot enter. The speaker in tongues does not predicate; he does not speak forth to embrace and be embraced; his world has his own dimensions. He lives in a bound universe. And this is no alien experience; we are all speakers in tongues. He who prophesies, however, speaks to edify. He predicates; he speaks forth to another. Space and time come thereby into his speaking, and his universe begins to slip its bonds. "Generative *ethos*" exists in a universe in the process of unbinding itself; it is always speaking itself into existence in commodious time and space.

In *Speaking*, Georges Gusdorf remarks that "each sentence orients us in a world which, moreover, is not given as such, once and for all, but appears to be constructed word by word." A little later, he continues, "Living speech acknowledges the requirement of the spiritual life in travail—not at all a closed system achieved once and for all—but an effort of constant regeneration." If we remember that, and if we can learn from the study of *ethos* that the creation of a "generative *ethos*" can never be wholly done, then we may remember not simply to *be* teachers, reiterating the past and displaying the present, but always to *become* teachers, reiterating and recreating the past, displaying the present, in order to make a future.

Editors' Note

As a rejoinder to this essay's etymological, horticultural, and cultural play with weeds and their culinary "evolution," W. Ross Winterowd offers the following sly lyric:

> **Okra** (at the request of Jim Corder)
>
> Family mallow's diverse stock
> Includes both okra and hollyhock,

Althea shrub, and, indeed,
Rose of Sharon, and velvetweed.
When you served your okra gumbo,
You undoubtedly didn't know
That your soup was pleonastic—
Rich and spicy and bombastic.
As the dictionary tells you,
Gumbo's "okra" in Bantu.
Consider, then, this irony:
Okra came across the sea
To pick that field, to cut that cane,
To labor on in woe and pain,
While its cousin sat in state,
King Cotton, mallow's line enate.

A prominent rhetorical theorist of Corder's generation, Winterowd remained Corder's appreciative reader and regular correspondent.

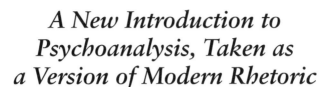

CHAPTER SIX

A New Introduction to Psychoanalysis, Taken as a Version of Modern Rhetoric

Human frailty sets immediate and overpowering limits. What follows is what I can presently do, and I have scant time or patience for all I ought to know. The choice, then, as James Hillman has remarked, is in due wisdom to stop speaking or to speak in consciousness of folly. Since that's hardly a real choice, I'll go on, believing that there is no justice anyway except, as in the words of an old papal directive against disobedient priests, "to be deposed and made to do penance in perpetual pilgrimage, deprived of all honor."

I started to use in my title a term coined by Thomas Szasz in *The Myth of Psychotherapy.* The term he offers is *iatrology,* which he renders as "healing words." However, I chose not to use Szasz's term. In the first place, I did not in any way want to suggest that the medical connection psychoanalysis now has should be minimized or lost. Further, I wanted even any distant association with Freud's work that I could attain.

The term *iatrology* was and is appealing. We humans are frail and unreliable, but words abide. In a little while, I will not be a memory, but with a little luck, words will last and signal welcome to someone long after. Words celebrate life; they cast magic spells. I want to linger a moment over these qualities of words. Doing so, I believe, may help to make sense of other things I want to say later.

Words name, identify, preserve; they let us hold and celebrate life. The first thing we did when we came into creation was

First published in *Pre/Text* 5 (1984): 137–69.

to try naming its parts. Even if we lost all else in Eden, even if there was no Eden, we have the words to name things, and when we call the words to mind, we can cherish all the parts of that Eden of the mind. We can keep life, treasure it, and never lose it, for we have the words. Gloria Emerson reminded us in *Winners and Losers* that we can save the names of things and say them well, and then we'll remember the provinces we've lived in and remember what happened there. In *Ceremony*, the novel by Leslie Silko, an old medicine man says, "That was the responsibility that went with being human. . . . [T]he story behind each word must be told so that there could be no mistake in the meaning of what had been said." Loren Eiseley has helped to teach us that we can name life and hold it. In "The Cabin," one of the poems in *Notes of an Alchemist,* he imagines the former inhabitants of an old, ruined cabin:

> Think of us, please. We shall be
> nameless,
> lonely.
> There will be no one to explain why we forgot
> the washbasin or one shoe on the floor.
>
> We will appear odd, yet there was
> possibly a reason.
> We were
> like you.
> Remember us. This is all that is left.

When a child acquires words, he or she can say a sentence that's never been said before, can understand a sentence that's never been heard before. All human capacities to do are introduced, made known, acquired through words. The process of language-making, diligently pursued, honestly undertaken, is a liberating process, affording freedom in many ways. We are not bound to a single way of speaking unless we deceive ourselves or succumb to prisons of the mind. Words will let us say contrary things, will let us speak in opposition, will let us speak in various tongues, will let us speak ambiguities, even mysteries. We have the liberty to be ourselves, to speak ourselves into existence, come what may.

Words, too, have let us learn what we might of happiness. We have found our identity and learned what we might pursue by magic, spell-casting words. Think of the spells that have taught us what to seek, that have taught us what happiness is and where it might be found. Remember the spells.

I don't know what list another would make, and I can't give all of mine, but remember the spells. Think what we learned about the indomitability of the human spirit from that simple spell, "Kilroy was here." Think of the lesson of calm courage set out by that spell, "Tranquility Base here. The Eagle has landed." Think how we learned from Lincoln at Gettysburg the possibility of one day binding people together. Think how we learned that a life of service and sacrifice was possible from Gunga Din. Think how we learned ways of friendship and identity from the Virginian's "When you call me that, smile." Think how we might learn at last to study war no more if we would attend to such spells as Housman's epitaph for British soldiers:

> Here dead lie we because we did not choose
> To live and shame the land from which we sprung.
> Life, to be sure, isn't much to lose;
> But young men think it is, and we were young.

Think what we learned from Huck Finn about the sanctity of the human soul when he decided, "All right, then, I'll *go* to Hell." Think what we learned about love and valor from the brave model of Beau Geste. Think what we learned about the possibility that gentleness and strength could go hand in hand when we read about that season when Boo Radley came out. Think what we learned about the hunger of the imagination, about the inexorable drive for worth yet to be achieved from Samuel Johnson, writing in 1764, "I have done nothing; the need of doing therefore is pressing," or in 1777, after most of his mighty work was done, "When I survey my past life, I discover nothing but a barren waste of time [. . .]." Think what we have learned from words. And more: they deliver us from time. We can say to creation, to all time, "I exist; I am still here, brother, sister, take my hand." We can say grace, companionship, love.

For such reasons as these, I tilted for a while in favor of the term iatrology, hoping to catch the magic, the healing, incantatory sense of words. But I came back finally to *psychoanalysis*. It's a good word: it keeps its medical connection; the term has signified to some "the cure of souls"; an early patient called it the "talking cure." The term is good enough.

I have not yet begun, but I want to stop and come at things in another way so that I can sneak up on what may be my subject from another direction. What I want to talk about later will make a little more sense, I think, if I sketch out its origins and reveal something about the habits of mind that led me to this essay. One set of interests I have entertained for some time is the possible uses of rhetorical language to describe some mental disorders, including schizophrenia.

Rhetorical study suggests useful approaches to subjects not ordinarily associated with rhetoric. I don't suggest that rhetoric can always do in other fields what their own methodologies have not yet made possible. Rhetoric will not invariably solve problems outside its own territory, but it is useful, and looks on toward becoming more useful.

We can begin to understand why, I believe, if we approach things in this way. Every utterance belongs to, exists in, issues from, and reveals a rhetorical universe. Every utterance comes from somewhere (its inventive origin), emerges as a structure, and manifests itself as a style. All of the features of utterance—invention, structure, and style—cycle, reciprocate, and occur simultaneously. Each of us is a gathering place for a host of rhetorical universes. Some of them we share with others, indeed with whole cultures; some of them we inhabit alone, and some of them we occupy without knowing that we do so. Each of us is a busy corner where multiple rhetorical universes intersect. Ordinarily, we keep some consonance among these multiple universes, and hold order and relation among them. But not always. Sometimes the traffic within a single rhetorical universe stalls; sometimes the traffic from one universe collides with that from another. I'll consider the former for a moment or two.

A particular mute compulsive goes through the same series of motions—vaguely like the motions of chopping wood with an axe, though somewhat more complex—some thirty or forty times an hour. He is trapped in a structure, unable to explore or to use his own inventive world, unable to realize himself through a style.

In rhetorical terms, his circumstances might be described by saying that structure has obliterated invention and style. He cannot reach back to know the origins of the structure he is trapped in, and he cannot reach forward to speak. The extraordinary popularity of how-to-do-it-with-joy-and-more-joy books on sexual practices, to cite another example of blocking or stalling, seems to reveal a social preoccupation with style. In the lives of sensuous men, women, groups, widows, and kangaroos the complexities of inventive history and the possibilities for creating structures of human relationships scarcely seem to matter. *Playboy* converts love into an inventionless style, and lovers are to be admired not so much for the depth of their feeling as for their schemes and tropes.

Other instances of disorder occurring when traffic stalls within a single rhetorical universe can be cited briefly.

1. Anxiety reaction, sometimes defined as a chronic and mostly vague and unfocused feeling of unease or fear, may be described in rhetorical terms as the oppressive sense that something in invention is not getting into structure and style. Something waits, impends, looms. Something is there in invention, but is not known or grasped. Something is caught, stalled there, waiting to come out.

2. Obsessions and compulsions are forms of stalling or blocking within a rhetorical universe. The obsessive or compulsive stalls, for example, in invention, perpetually returning to it. Sometimes the obsessive and the compulsive get blocked in a structure or a style.

3. The form of hysteria known as dissociative reaction is an instance of blockage in invention, where the victim refuses conflicts by refusing to come out into structure and style.

4. Amnesia, an extreme form of dissociative reaction, is a reversal of the circumstances I just mentioned. The amnesiac can still perform (usually) in structure and style, but is caught there, unable to penetrate his or her invention.

5. In multiple personality, another extreme form of dissociative reaction, segments of invention are blocked from structural and stylistic realization, so that a single segment of invention becomes the breeding ground for different sets of structure and style.

6. The depressive phase of manic-depressive psychosis seems to occur in two distinct rhetorical ways. In one, sufferers conclude that their invention is empty and therefore offers no source for appropriate structure and style. In the other, sufferers know that their invention is full, but they conclude that, for whatever reasons, it is hopelessly contained so that nothing in it can reach elsewhere through structure and style.

7. The manic phase of manic-depressive psychosis seems to be a manifestation of a swollen and delusively prodigious invention. Sufferers are led to conclude both that their invention holds everything and that everything in it can emerge simultaneously in multiple forms of structure and style.

8. Catatonic schizophrenia may be described as a condition in which the sufferer blocks into a portion of his or her invention so private, so secret, so primitive, that it not only will not sustain communication with others, it also will not give rise to even rudimentary forms of structure and style.

9. In hebephrenic schizophrenia the sufferer is blocked from those portions of his or her invention that would support public forms of communication and can only make private forms of structure and style.

Instances of traffic colliding as it tries to cross from one rhetorical universe into another are sometimes dramatic, as in acute undifferentiated schizophrenia. This state is known in an often severe disordering of the thought processes, in frequent interruption of the flow of ideas, in apparent illogicality, in the occurrence of strange words and coinages, and in hallucinations. These forms of apparent disorder can be described with rhetorical terms. The disorders associated with acute undifferentiated schizophrenia appear to occur when crossovers and collisions take place between universes, or when slippages or leakages occur from one universe to another, when the "normal" sequences of one universe mix in those of another.[1]

Some illustrations and extensions of this notion can be noted quickly.

1. Invention in any individual is vast and diffuse. All of a person's time is held there, much of it unused and unrecognized. Sometimes a portion of the unused invention slips through into "normal" forms of structure and style, disrupting them and accounting for the apparent illogicality of the schizophrenic, perhaps also accounting for the strange words and bizarre thought processes, as the diagram below may suggest:

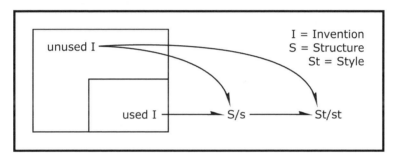

When this happens, the words are not really strange, the thought processes are not really bizarre, and the illogicality is only apparent. Could they be tracked back to their secret source in the unused invention, they would have their own normality.

2. Ordinary affectations may show how the crossover effect works. An affectation occurs when a person with a given invention practices forms of structure and style that do not normally evolve from that invention, as the diagram below may suggest:

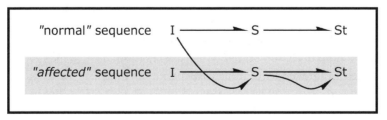

An affectation may be mild enough, but it is easy to anticipate the gross symptoms of disorder if we imagine the two worlds as being markedly disparate and see a person thrown out of one world into the other. Both sequences will make themselves known, if garbled, even through the structure and style they don't belong to.

3. Sometimes different portions of invention try to move simultaneously into structure and style. In a usual sequencing, structure and style seem to arise out of a given, limited, inventive set, but in this simultaneous move two different inventive sets clamor to be known through one sequence of structure and style. When that happens, if we are fortunate we can still act in the presence of contradiction and diversity. Sometimes, however, any action or utterance that occurs will be undercut or even betrayed by the persisting whispers of that other inventive set that was trying simultaneously to be known, as this may indicate:

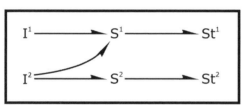

The presence of those persisting whispers can generate paralysis, of course, if the person is so compelled by the offered choices that he or she cannot choose. The persisting whispers can also produce a vague but powerful hostility and cynicism as the person acts or speaks but in the very act of doing so is unrelentingly reminded that other acts or utterances, perhaps equally appropriate, were possible. Finally, these whispers, crossovers from one world to another, can account for some of the signals of schizophrenia—bizarre associations, peculiar logic, strange language, all trying to occur in a world where they don't belong.

4. The distance between a word and the thing it stands for narrows sometimes, sometimes widens. Sometimes the distance grows so great that word and thing lose their association. At other times the distance disappears and word replaces thing. In schizophrenia, what appears to happen is that an object is perceived in one

rhetorical universe, but named afar with a word from another universe.

5. Ordinarily, invention, structure, and style form a reciprocating sequence, where invention feeds structure and style, which in turn feed new possibilities to invention. Ordinarily, too, a change any where in the sequence will generate a change somewhere else in the sequence. When invention grows, for example, that makes it possible for structure and style to change; when new structures and styles are devised, they turn back to become new inventive resources. The customary sequence, then,

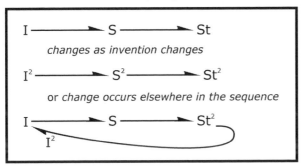

But if change occurs in one part of the sequence without an accompanying change in the other parts, then sooner or later the change will manifest itself anyway as a whisper trying to be heard from one universe into another.

I am suggesting, remember, that each of us is a cosmos in which multiple worlds circle and sometimes collide. Interruptions in the train of thought, apparent illogicality, occurrence of strange words and ideas, hallucinations occur when worlds normally kept in their own orbits mix, so that crossovers take place. The "Freudian slip" is an intrusion from one world to another.

6. This cosmos of rhetorical orbitings is the hunting ground for analysts. Invention, structure, and style are never lost. They remain, though they may at times, when the past seems to close or the future seems to close or when worlds mix, slide off into depths we cannot easily reach. All rhetorical universes are still present. The debris of all our generations is around us and in us. Full worlds, barren worlds, lonesome worlds circle about us and in

us, and they are ours to explain. For this reason, it is necessary that the analyst become a historian of rhetorical universes. The crossovers I have been talking about may occur over a long and complex history.

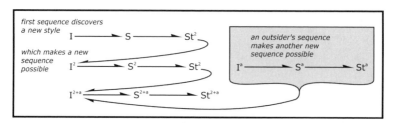

Such a pattern of growth and change in rhetorical sequences might be drawn out for pages and still not even hint at the complexity of a human life. Then, if we imagine the possibility of crossovers occurring between *any* elements *anywhere* in this series, we can understand why an analyst must become a historian of rhetorics.

7. Other kinds of disparate worlds exist between which crossovers may occur. For example, people who act upon the basis of messages they believe they have received from others may find their actions, thought, and language disrupted and undercut by the entrance into their world of messages from others that they have heard but not heeded. Messages often, if not always, persist. A message not heeded may persist to cross over into the midst of an action, thought, or utterance based upon a message that was only heard. This may suggest that change itself is a source of disorder. A person may customarily act or speak upon the basis of understandings he or she already has. Any change, particularly any radical change, may then be ignored or resisted, only to intrude later into the person's world as a crossover from another world.

That set of thinking is a source for this essay. Another occurred when I thought I saw similarities between certain medical practices and certain rhetorical practices. Then I realized that they weren't similarities or analogs, but identities.

When you look outside the discipline of rhetoric along the lines of vision provided by rhetoric, you sometimes see only old things in new ways. That, of course, can have great worth. The penicillin-producing mold had been grown, kept, and observed in more than one laboratory before someone decided to look at it in a new way. Often, when you look along rhetorical lines toward other things, you only satisfy your curiosity. Once in a while, perhaps, you see something new. Often, too, you discover that rhetoric—our chief occupation—quite unsurprisingly allows you to talk usefully about human concerns not otherwise thought to be connected to rhetoric.

I want now for a little while to use rhetorical terms to describe some practices of some physicians, from time to time noting especially some practices of psychiatrists and psychoanalysts, so that I may suggest why physicians are, or should be, not just historians, but conscious rhetoricians. The idea is not new; Gorgias suggested it in the "Encomium to Helen":

> The effect of speech upon the condition of the soul is comparable to the power of drugs over the nature of bodies. For just as different drugs dispel different secretions from the body, and some bring an end to disease and others to life so also in the case of speeches, some distress, others delight, some cause fear, others make the hearers bold, and some drug and bewitch the soul with a kind of evil persuasion.

I have no credentials in the practice of medicine or of any form of analysis and therapy. However, what I learn about the work of those who do sometimes—certainly not always—translates for me into certain rhetorical practices. I cannot pretend that I have made a thorough catalog of the most striking or pertinent practices of physicians. Neither can I claim that I have made a thorough catalog of rhetorical equivalences. I don't know enough to catalog all medical practices, and I doubt there are rhetorical equivalences for all. Some equivalences do occur, I think, and I want to cite some that seem particularly interesting, perhaps even provocative. Equivalences should not surprise us. We already know that physicians have to be good historians; I am suggesting now that they must also be good rhetoricians, whether or not they use the title. The various arts I mean to mention—medicine, psychiatry, psychoanalysis, rhetoric—have some common roots in the sometimes rocky, sometimes blessed ground of human communication.

Physicians, psychiatrists, and psychoanalysts, like rhetoricians, use *oxymoron* to establish new ways of thinking, new ways of finding meaning. Oxymoron brings contradictory, or at least unlikely, terms together for emphasis or to give point or inclusiveness to a statement. If I say that on my vacation I am going to enjoy a "strenuous idleness," or if I say to an acquaintance, "I admire your conviction, but I question your judgment," those are oxymoronic uses. At its best (which I'd not claim for my examples so far), oxymoron brings two worlds into collision so as to produce a meaning not possible in either alone. Each term in an oxymoron conditions and shapes the other. Oxymoron is common in epigrams, which by their nature are trying to bring a great deal of experience together in a single statement and for that reason frequently use the antithetical oxymoron. The practice is common, though not frequent, when writers are trying to get much meaning in little space. In a poem titled "Near Idaville" (*Signs and Wonders,* Princeton UP, 1979), Carl Dennis speaks of someone who, though living alone, wants visitors,

> A congenial race of enlightened souls
> Walking arm in arm in graceful pairs
> Slowly along the hills and down,
> Greeting each other with warm ceremonious smiles.

The words *warm* and *ceremonious* might not always, or even commonly, be used together, but here they give each other meaning that would not be held in either separately, preserving the comfort of ritual and the intimacy of warmth, converting the two terms into a meaning that neither achieves alone. Something of the same effect occurs in Samuel Johnson's *The Vanity of Human Wishes,* when near the end he urges the reader [italics mine] to

> Pour forth thy fervours for a healthy mind,
> *Obedient passions* and a *will resign'd* . . . .

Since I've come this far, I might as well go on and reach for the foolhardiest equivalence I'll try to establish between the work of rhetoricians and the work of physicians. As I am given to understand the matter, electric shock treatments are a version of oxymoron. Oxymoron works by bringing two worlds into collision, where they fuse for a moment to create a new meaning. In the example by Johnson above, we do not customarily expect *passions* to be *obedient*. The juxtaposition of the two words wants obedience to be given some zeal by passions, but also wants passions to be given some control and direction by obedience. In some forms of therapy, the briefest possible electric shock is administered to the patient through electrodes applied to the skull. This may be done bilaterally, where an electrode is placed on each side of the skull, or unilaterally, where both electrodes are placed on the same side so that the shock is felt in the nondominant side of the brain. The bilateral mode works faster, but is also more likely to produce momentary confusion and some memory lapses. The unilateral mode is slower, but produces less confusion and fewer memory lapses. When the shock is administered, a convulsive reaction *has* to occur, however mild, or there is no discernible effect upon the patient. A chief use of the electric shock treatment is in lifting depression. The convulsion is expected to awaken or to uncover or to animate or to energize dormant or dulled or ineffectual thought paths, lifting depression by jamming other thought paths against the depressed path the brain has been taking. This sudden encounter of diversities creates a set of new possibilities for the mind, as oxymoron does. And all of this can begin to happen in far less time than we might think—from the time the patient stretches out on the appointed bed, through the shot that reduces the violence of the convulsion, through the shot that puts the patient to sleep, through shock, and on to awakening, all in something like three to five minutes.

Physicians also use the writer's technique of *incremental repetition,* a method most commonly associated, I suppose, with medieval ballads. Probably the best known version of incremental repetition, as in "Edward" for example, uses the same pattern for each stanza, and each stanza typically repeats some lines or phrases, only to add a new piece of information in, say, the last line of the stanza. The writer, as the term says, repeats incrementally, using a frame of repetition that grows with each utterance. In some forms of therapy, everyone involved may have to figure out who the poet of incremental repetition is. Sometimes, apparently, the patient thinks he or she is the writer, telling the doctor just as much as the patient thinks the doctor can take in each time they meet, withholding other news until later. The patient fancies that he or she is doling a life out in parcels each day, trying to add a new touch from time to time. Sometimes the doctor thinks that he or she is the poet, pulling a little more information or insight out of the patient each time they talk. But then doctor and patient sometimes realize that both are conspiring as one poet to form a pattern of incremental repetition.

I'll cite a sample case, that of a male patient in a psychiatric ward in a hospital that is part of a large medical complex that also includes a medical school. The patient's primary doctor is a psychiatrist, the one chiefly responsible for the patient's admission, treatment, and release. The patient sees the psychiatrist at least five times a week in his own hospital room. The psychiatrist calls in a psychoanalyst, who sees the patient separately five times a week in his office across the street. The psychiatrist has a "physician's assistant," who sometimes accompanies him, but more often sees the patient alone. In addition, senior medical students sometimes accompany the psychiatrist, but more often come alone. This means that whatever was on the patient's mind on a given day, he could count on talking about it twice, and might sometimes talk about it four times. In the course of, say, five consecutive days, the patient would inevitably repeat himself, but through a combination of the visitors' questions and promptings and the patient's sometimes faulty memory, no doubt it is an incremental repetition. That is to say, when the medical staff periodically conferred about the patient and what he had said, there was, I expect, a common core that they all heard, but the likelihood is that each also heard something that the others didn't hear. Thus, whatever story finally emerged, it emerged partly through incremental repetition.

If they are good, writers create for us new analogies, new maps, new metaphors for seeing the world, or some portion of it. Among other things that physicians do is to probe about in our histories to learn what we are like so that they, too, may show us other analogies, maps, metaphors, other ways than ours of seeing what troubles us, or other ways of taking the world so that what troubles us is put in different and/or better perspectives.

They assist us, that is to say, in creating and distinguishing among different realities.

What I've been trying to lead to in the preceding paragraphs is the observation that physicians must practice rhetoric as well as medicine, analysis, and history. They must explore our *inventive* worlds, our ways of making *structures* of meaning, and our ways of identifying ourselves in the *styles* we manifest.

A patient's inventive world is the richest, though clearly not the sole, territory to be mined by the physician. If the doctor is to be able to talk fruitfully—the chief art of both physician and rhetorician—he or she must first plumb the patient's inventive world, must probe about and learn the patient's past, or what the patient *thinks* the past is, or what others think it is like. The doctor has to learn what is already present in the patient's mind, what is there but forgotten, what is there but covered over or masked. If the doctor is going to assist in the modification of physical or behavioral aberrations that range from the mild to the monstrous, he or she is going to have to learn how we think and inquire. In other words, the physician is going to have to understand rhetorical *invention,* which is a word signifying all of the patient's past, all of the resources available from that past, the complex, often muddled capacities, creative, repetitive, or otherwise, that let a patient be and speak in the present. The physician is also going to have to understand what rhetoricians describe as a part of the inventive process, that is, the *topoi,* or customary ways of thinking that people use with varying degrees of success. Sometimes, customary ways of thinking work; sometimes, physicians have to show us new ways.

But the past doesn't stay past. A patient's inventive world keeps coming into the present and the future, and may alter itself in the process. The doctor, then, must watch the way a patient makes *structures* of meaning, if necessary then showing the patient how to see other structures, how to re-create structures, how to find structures lost in the mind, how to make new structures. To complicate this, the patient's inventive world may at the same time keep moving and changing.

The doctor also has to observe and understand the patient's *style*, recognizing, what is more, that the word *style* probably ought to be taken in at least two senses. In the first, *style* means something like identity; it is the patient's way of making himself or herself known. In the other sense, *style* means something like an enabling capacity, an art or skill or technique that the patient can perform without necessarily appropriating it as identity. Understanding style as enabling capacity may be a way of helping the patient learn new ways of doing and being, rearrange old styles, and generate more new styles. Understanding style as identity at least suggests the possibility that a patient may be assisted in making a new person with a new future.

Each patient is a rhetorical creation. Out of an inventive world (a past, a set of capacities, a way of thinking) a patient is always creating structures of meaning and generating a style, a way of being in the world. Each patient is, as I've said, host to multiple rhetorical creations. For that reason, the doctor has to watch for and if possible aid the patient in understanding disparities both within a single rhetorical world and among multiple rhetorical worlds. I can cite only a few examples of what I mean. One patient may keep trying to make structures and styles not grounded in his or her own inventive world, erecting a form of living that has no life. Another patient may fall silent because he or she does not have the inventive background he or she wants to manifest in structures and styles of living. Another patient may suffer because multiple inventive impulses are trying to emerge simultaneously in structure and style, which they cannot do—some forms of living cannot coexist. Still another may suffer because, at that intersection where rhetorical worlds pass, shift, or collide, inventive impulses from one rhetorical world are trying to cross lanes of traffic and make themselves known through the structures and styles of another world. I'll be so bold as to suggest even that a gene may become an oncogene when, because of some inner necessity, it tries to become something (that is, be a structure and a style) that its biogrammar (that is, its inventive set) won't support.

Classical rhetoricians observed that humans tend to practice three kinds of rhetoric: *judicial,* concerned with what has already happened; *epideictic,* concerned with what is going on at the present moment; and *deliberative,* concerned with what is yet to happen. In the normal course of events, in however large or small a circle, most of us practice all three kinds of rhetoric. Sometimes, however, we get trapped in time, able to speak only of the past, or only of the present, or only of the future. If a patient can practice only one kind of rhetoric, is thus trapped in time, the doctor-as-rhetorician needs to know why if he or she is ever to assist the patient toward freedom. When I say that a patient may be trapped in time, I mean to refer to things as apparently simple as a patient's clinging to ingrained but inappropriate dietary habits, or to things as apparently complex as a patient's clinging to sophisticated but confused thought patterns.

If I take some pleasure in finding certain identities in the arts of medicine and of rhetoric, I am also obliged, I think, to inquire whether or not the physician can find gain in what I am suggesting. Some gain is possible, I believe, if we look a moment longer at the process of language-making. We don't get things said all at once. In our frailty, we keep trying to say things right, but more often than not, we miss. To complicate matters, we are sometimes caught by our habits, our arrogance, ignorance, dogmas, and miss again. Against our frailty, against the traps we sometimes fall into, there is the hope of revision.

In writing, genuine revision demands more than tinkering and adding commas. Revision is RE-VISION, a new seeing, a seeing again. In the process of revision, the physician is the editor, but the patient must be the writer. Both must plunge into whatever illness or apparent disorder that presents itself, learn its character, shape, and consequence, live with it, and re-see it and the self of the patient. If the free self of the patient is to be realized, or if the self of the patient is to recover into freedom, then editor and writer must fully know the self that has so far been written or said if they are to conspire in the revision.

That may require continuing exploration through conscious usages such as deliberate experimentation with varieties of oxymoron, deliberate experimentation with incremental repetition, and deliberate experimentation with the cycling process of invention, structure-building, and style-making, all parts of which can feed, reenforce, or destroy each other. It may require even stranger usages, as the rhetorician's methods suggest therapeutic possibilities. If the patient-writer cannot see connections, causes, or consequences, then the physician-editor may have to teach *polysyndeton,* the practice of deliberately inserting connective words even where they are not always necessary. Or the physician-editor may have to teach *epistrophe,* the practice of deliberately ending a series of statements with the same word or phrase, so as to drum home a meaning. Or the physician-editor may have to teach *epanalepsis,* the practice of deliberately starting and ending statements with the same word or phrase, so that the impact of the word or phrase cannot be escaped. Or the physician-editor may have to teach *anadiplosis,* the practice of deliberately using the last word or phrase of one statement as the first word or phrase of the next, so that continuity and connection cannot be avoided. At the intersections where our genetic markings, our training, our education, our habits of thought may be overwhelmed by the traffic of change, all arts may be necessary for our salvation.

Revision can be guided by an editor, but ultimately it must be done by a writer, else it's only a way of seeing that belongs to someone else. Revision is sometimes simple, but sometimes it requires radical transformation. Medicine may be enough, but soul-curing may be necessary, too, and that requires listening and talking and listening again and talking some more.

That set of thinking was also a source for what I have still to say, and there are other sources, other initiating impulses. (See how far I've come: still talking about origins, sources, initiating impulses.) I think it important for any present to know what I've been thinking. If I can convey that, it will set a context for what follows and perhaps clarify what I want to say. Some other initiating impulses, then.

One is my own growing conviction—however wrong it may be—that in an indeterminate, shifting world, all knowledge is rhetorical and all behavior is rhetorical. Rhetorical study and practice are not subordinate to other studies and practices that define them, and there are no structures of being prior to rhetoric, as Walter Carleton suggests (see "On Rhetorical Knowing," review of Gregg, *Symbolic Inducement and Knowing: A Study in the Foundations of Rhetoric,* in *Quarterly Journal of Speech,* May,

1985). We can conceive of rhetoric itself, Carleton says, as generating both what is and what is known.

Another initiating impulse rose from recent reading of sharp attacks on psychoanalysis (such as Szasz, *The Myth of Psychotherapy*). While some attacks are in many ways convincing (*e.g.*, attacks on the tendency to accept societal—that is, political—standards for what is normal), and while I do not at all mind seeing psychoanalysts under attack, I found myself thinking, "Wait, now, there's more to be said than that for psychoanalysis." Then I thought I began to understand that the attacks rose from anger—anger that psychoanalysis should presume to be a science when it ought to be a religion, anger that psychoanalysis should not presume to be a religion when it ought to be a science—and from fear of the nonsystematic and indeterminate. Jung did remark in a letter to J. A. F. Swoboda (January 23, 1960) that there could be no such thing as a systematized theory of psychoanalysis. Then I began to think that psychoanalysis does not belong to either science or religion; it belongs to rhetoric. It *is* the "talking cure," and it must plunge right past foible and freshman composition into moral conflict and human tragedy.

Another initiating impulse is my own perhaps irrational resistance to any deterministic view of human conduct, to any conviction that we can finally be measured. The recent spate of books on the brain, on neurological behavior, and on neurochemical behavior report uncommonly exciting discoveries. I am referring to such works (all recent) as Nancy C. Andreasen, *The Broken Brain: The Biological Revolution in Psychiatry* (Harper and Row), Floyd E. Bloom, Arlyne Lazerson, and Laura Hofstadter, *Brain, Mind, and Behavior* (W. H. Freeman), Richard M. Restak, *The Brain* (Bantam), Morton F. Reiser, *Mind, Brain, Body* (Basic Books), and Jonathan Winson, *Brain and Psyche* (Anchor Press/ Doubleday). Almost always exciting, some of these works also flirt with, or sometimes embrace, neurochemical determinism. Many suggest that schizophrenia and other forms of mental illness result from chemical imbalances in the brain; Andreasen, for example, says that "a large amount of evidence has been amassed suggesting that mental illness is caused by biochemical abnormalities, structural brain abnormalities, and genetic abnormalities." The view is reflected by Martin L. Gross (*The Psychological Society*, Random House, 1978):

> What we call the Unconscious may instead be a complex, gene-determined neurological-biochemical circuitry. It responds to stimuli, creating ideas and feelings to suit the DNA-coded needs of the particular human animal. Reactions to love, adventure, threat, sex, friendship may be partially learned, but they are also biologically hidden—not in the romantic Unconscious—but in thousands of protein-coded genes each of us has been endowed with since the moment of conception. This, not the mystical Id, Ego, and Superego, may be the unknown psychology of man. (44)

Some of these works, as I have suggested, veer toward neuro-chemical or neurophysiological determinism. MIND does not seem to count; they appear unable to conceive that word, sentence, utterance, mind create the interior as well as the exterior world.

Some folks seem to need to get us fixed, settled, determined. The same folks are inclined to think they can measure us. I have been baffled for a long time by the physician's assumption that he or she can determine the sugar level in human blood by examining a specimen of blood taken from *one* place at *one* time.

If I open my left wrist and blood runs, and if I open my right wrist and blood runs, it will not be the same blood flowing from my right wrist that flows from my left. In the laboratory, they take blood from my left arm, scrutinize it, and imagine that they learn what my blood is like. If in surgery they take the tiniest piece of the tiniest piece from my brain, scrutinize it, and find chemical neurotransmitters flowing across synapses as one cell teaches the news to the next cell, then they imagine that they have learned how my brain works. But no: I am in here, between my two wrists and beyond that tiny piece of brain, and they haven't found me. I am in here. I think. I am often if not always at war. Habit wars with new vision. Ambition wars with laziness. The need to search out new country wars with the need to lean back and know the old. Pride wars with the realization that there is no occasion for pride. I send conflicting messages to myself and to others. I deceive myself. How can my blood be uniform?

The energy of word and thought is real in here between wrists, and it is always conserved.

Language borrowed from one field (say sports, as in "game plan") into another field (say politics) does not lose its association with the first field. That energy persists. A structure and a style always have their invention, even if it appears to be lost. That energy persists. The energy of the reciprocating system (invention-structure-style) is always conserved, always acts in some way, always exerts itself in some way.

This energy tells the blood what to be. This energy mobilizes chemical neurotransmitters (or whatever metaphor suits the science of the day). If this energy is multiple—as it always is— then blood and brain will be multiple: what flows in my left arm will not flow in my right; what leaps across a synapse will be accompanied by the mysterious other. I am in here between my wrists. Ideas have consequence. Words have consequence. They are energy and carry energy. Of this, more later.

Enough. I expect I've talked long enough about originating thoughts. I should get to what I came for.

Let's loosen the dimensions of psychoanalysis and let it become as wide-ranging, as pervasive as rhetoric, let it *become* rhetoric. Let the divisions of rhetoric and their relationships become stages of psychoanalytical investigation and understanding. Let rhetoric stretch psychoanalysis beyond its usual reaches. Let rhetoric provide new descriptions of symptoms. Let rhetoric generate a new taxonomy of mental illnesses. Let rhetoric suggest new therapies.

That gets me started, but now I have to stop again. Before I go on, I want to try to identify certain presiding ideas that influence and work through what follows. I am trying to remember James Hillman's remarks that "Each psychology is a confession, and the worth of a psychology for another person lies not in the places where he can identify with it because it satisfies his psychic needs, but where it provokes him to work out his own psychology in response" (*Re-Visioning Psychology,* Harper and Row, 1975, p. xii).

I am supposing, in the *first* place, that the world is indeterminate, that knowledge is not fixed and stabilized, that all of us, as the rhetoricians we always are, say the world into existence, often getting it all wrong, sometimes getting it beautifully right.[2]

Second, I want to contend, given what I have just said, that when we bring the search for an understanding of psychoanalysis and with it the search for an understanding of mental illness up and out to the dimensions of rhetoric, then we must recognize that there is no normality. In my own earlier efforts to think, which I have tried to record in previous pages, there was some presumption of normality. Now I believe that, while there are some commonalities among us, there is no normality, that each of us must continually be constructing a normality.

Third, I want to disagree with my betters (psychoanalysts, among others) and say that much is put away in our minds but not subterranean. There is more floating and darting about in the mind than either therapists or patients have acknowledged. I do not mean to deny the existence of the unconscious or of the strange, perhaps censored rhetorical enactments in our dreams. I do want to say that we hold much, not hidden always in the unconscious, but in such close confidence that we won't let it out—I mean lies, dramas we create of ourselves and for ourselves, yearnings that can't be spoken because they lie too close to sin or to mystery. We *know* these things; they do not have to be translated from our hidden texts, but we put them away from ourselves and from others. We can deceive ourselves, allaying anxiety by distorting awareness; what may be even more harmful is acting in full and excruciatingly painful consciousness of our own lies, dramas, and yearnings.

That much said, I'll hurry on to add that there is far more deeply buried than we can customarily get to, a grammar of the soul—or call it a biorhetoric, the genetic markings that come from the time before each of us was born, or a rhetorical imperative, an unspoken, perhaps unrecognized, but nevertheless real theory of communication that informs everything each of us says. A rhetoric assumes a view of the world and of human nature, and each of us assumes a rhetoric. Each of us is a rhetorician, and each of us is obliged to be constantly writing a modern rhetoric. Often as not, we don't. Most rhetorics have not explored the world they assume, the world they rise from. Most rhetorics have accepted a worldview, or some set of views, and rhetorics are still being written and lived in one world that belong over in another world. I want to suggest that each of us must search to know which worlds reciprocate with his or her rhetoric. We should come to each other as rhetoricians in the company of our view of things, knowing and declaring our origins, claims, and imperatives, revealing our inventive resources to ourselves and to others, recognizing what our structures and styles signify. We have to keep on examining and keep on proclaiming the circumstances of our own existence and way of speaking.

In the *fourth* place, I always want to defeat time. In this case, that means trying to defeat the metaphors of the day. There is probably no way to do this. I'm not sure that one should even try. Nevertheless, I think it is an occasion for anguish in all of us when we stop to consider that all of our questions and all of our answers keep both hideous and lovely secrets from us because we can mostly speak only in the language of the day. But the language of rhetoric has at least the evidence—often wrongly used, to be sure—of two thousand years of near-continuous use to testify to its broad utility. Perhaps I am only yearning for something that will last in a world that by my own earlier testimony is not given to durability, but to change. At any rate, I want no fixed definitions or classifications, for such things almost always belong to a moment. Besides, one should probably be cautious about declaring that this or that is a disorder—depression, for example, may not be disorder at all, but a realistic appraisal of what life has come to.

Fifth, I have been searching for a way of talking about psychoanalysis and mental illness that would be as much as possible released from social and political conceptions, that would as much as possible absent itself from mythology by embracing a *common language*. I'm looking for a way to cleanse investigation of ideology and come face to face with perennial questions, interests, and disturbances of humankind—sex, significance, power, conflict, prestige, loneliness, frustration, defeat, race, religion, family—in a language that is common to us all. Psychopathology, Hillman says, "does not belong to a field of specialists. It is something we suffer in our experience and a perspective we take toward certain kinds of experiences, so that it too can be opened to new psychological insight" (xv).

Sixth, I will suppose throughout what follows that each of us is multiple. Each of us houses a crowd. I don't think this takes all that much supposing. English teachers, for example, already know this from the instruction they give and the practice they exact in the performance of different styles. The possibility of multiple styles indicates the possibility of multiple rhetorical functions, which is to say, each of us houses a crowd.

Seventh, I will suppose in one way or another that change itself may be the ultimate trauma for each of us. *Since we always have to make the world, its perpetual unmaking will always tend to undo us.*

Eighth, I will argue throughout that words, utterances, and all rhetorical behaviors have energy. The magic spells I cited in the beginning are, I think, some evidence to this effect. Words and sentences have energy. Invention has energy. Structure has energy. Style has energy. The context in which language is made and used has energy. Mind has energy. Examples are not too hard to find. Any writer or teacher of writing has seen that words and sentences have predictive power and control—that is, energy—over following words and sentences. As I mentioned earlier, a figure borrowed from one field for use in another (from sports into politics, as in "game plan") carries the energy of its first use into its second use and to some extent turns politics into sports. Words are energy and carry energy; they are, Hillman remarks, "independent carriers of soul between people":

> We need to recall that we do not just make words up or learn them in school, or ever have them fully under control. Words, like angels, are powers which have invisible power over us. They are personal presences which have whole mythologies: genders, genealogies (etymologies concerning origins and creations), histories, and vogues; and their own guarding, blaspheming, creating, and annihilating effects. (90)

Words have energy to carry soul, Hillman suggests; they will move us, carry our lives, and may make sense of our deaths.

Now I can go on with what I have wanted to propose from the start, *the extension of psychoanalysis into rhetoric*. The diagram that follows may be of some use as I proceed.

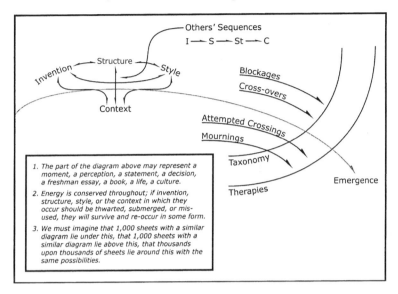

I mean for this diagram to represent the place for psychoanalytical investigation and the source for psychoanalytical understanding. Some brief initial notes may make my little diagram clearer.

1. Invention may include, but is not limited to, a biorhetoric, the rhetorical imperative one serves, the *topoi,* various heuristic systems, storage capacities, retrieval capacities; it may be a fully developed and conscious invention, an undeveloped and unrealized invention, a thwarted, misdirected invention, an invention asking for the wrong thing, trying to answer in one world the imperative of another; it may be an invention filled with lies, self-deceptions, dramas; it may be an invention trying to serve structural and stylistic behaviors that won't coexist.

2. Structure may be functional, fit, misused, misapprehended, misdirected; it may be a structure that is used but not recognized; it may be in harmony with invention and style or disconsonant

with both; it may fit the context or not; it may carry lies, self-deceptions, drama; it may try to serve behaviors that won't coexist.

3. Style may be fruitful, fit, incoherent, frozen (as in perpetual clichés); it may be in harmony with invention, structure, and context, or disconsonant with all; it may perpetuate lies, self-deceptions, dramas, and it may try to carry behaviors that won't coexist.

4. The context in which languages and behavior occur may be their natural place or a distinctly unnatural setting for them.

5. *Others' sequences* in my diagram simply means to suggest the occurrence and availability to each of us of the inventions, structures, styles, and contexts that belong to other people.

6. On the right side of the diagram the terms *blockages, crossovers, attempted crossings,* and *mournings* occur. These are, I suggest, the chief though I'm sure not the only occasions for what we have called mental disorders. In earlier thinking, recorded in earlier pages here, I imagined some disorders as being the consequence of *blockage* within a single rhetorical universe or of *crossovers* between rhetorical universes. Now I have to add *attempted crossings,* failed efforts to move from one rhetorical universe to another, and *mournings,* disruptive griefs we experience on seeing other universes, other possibilities, that we either cannot stretch to or think we cannot. *The mind, wanting to make the world and become itself, will catch or block, leap, try to leap, or mourn what was seen but unreached.*

7. The four terms I have just mentioned then become a tentative means of suggesting a taxonomy of disorders. They ought also to suggest possible forms of therapy, but I will speak of this a little more a little later.

8. By the term *emergence* on my diagram, I mean to suggest a possible path along which humans can move in some freedom, spared some pain of disorder, but not all. Along this path, invention can become a fitting structure in a harmonious style working fruitfully in a meritorious context.[3]

Some quick additional observations seem to be necessary before I can go on. Obviously enough, I can't deal with the world of psychoanalysis here—I don't know enough, and if I did I wouldn't have space enough. I should, however, mention a few obvious features of psychoanalytical study to which I have given little thought and less space.

1. I can't begin to talk about the significance of dreams. They are, I expect, inventions, structures, styles, and contexts that we catch pieces of, worlds on, under, in, and over whatever world we're in, and the mind keeps searching all of them.

2. I can't begin to talk about the significance of the unconscious in my diagram or elsewhere. It is there; it is not separate from the conscious but continuous with it, holding worlds on worlds of rhetorics.

3. I can't begin to deal with archetypes. They are there, inventive, structural, and stylistic presences continuously manifesting themselves from the biorhetoric and from the set of culture rhetorics.

4. I can't begin to deal with the conceptions of sin and guilt. They are there, and once introduced into the soul, given the conception of energy I have been talking about, they are likely to stay.

5. I can't announce the trauma. Anthony Wilden remarks in the translator's introduction to Lacan's *Language of the Self* (Johns Hopkins UP, 1968) that each new mode in psychoanalysis has depended on some "central feature (the birth trauma or the inferiority complex, for instance), in somewhat the same way as the castration complex and the death instinct are privileged in Freud" (xiii). I'm inclined to think that if there is some central trauma, it is something—like change itself—that keeps happening continuously.

6. I can't talk about the matters of sex, except to note that of course sexual matters have to be central in psychoanalytical investigation and understanding. Why wouldn't they be, after all?

In sexual relationships, there is an infinitude of possibilities times at least two, and the range is beyond saying, from the bestial to the secret to the mourning vision of the lost other, from many events in one to marvelous romps to miraculous intimacy to mystical humanness with the other to achievement of creation, everything all at once, meaning finally made.

Into the gathering of rhetorical universes I tried to depict in my diagram, uncertainty and change keep introducing disorder. Since we always have to be making the world, its continual unmaking will continually undo us. And we can be undone in many ways, wrecked in many rhetorical universes at once, for we are multiple. Each of us is a crowd. Invention is huge; motion out toward structure and style is triggered when statements reach energy, and since invention is huge, there leap or ooze from it great numbers of structures and styles, many unrecognized but still carrying energy, all while we are also trying to put on other inventions. And our multiplicity is compounded all of the time by our vision of rhetorical universes not our own. In this way of thinking, the psychoanalyst's questions, then, begin to be such as these: How does invention happen? How does structure happen? How is it related to invention? Where do structures come from? How does style happen? How is it related to invention and structure? What makes it recognizable? How does it fit or fail to fit a world? How do inventions, structures, and styles work in any given context, or why do they fail to work? How are the terms and stages maladaptive toward each other, or how are they fruitful for each other? And then, disorder rising not from some violation of the "normal," but from some violation of the ways in which rhetorical universes can work, more questions: What need, problem, or pain causes a blockage to occur in a rhetorical universe? What rhetorical revision will come to aid? What need, problem, or pain causes a leap or an attempted leap from one universe to another? What rhetorical revision will aid the leap or enable the person to find another way? What kind of vision of worlds unachieved and perhaps unachievable induces a disruptive mourning for those worlds? Though I will not attempt it here, I believe the neuroses and psychoses can be usefully restated as rhetorical events. I also believe that the relationship between psychoanalyst and patient can be usefully restated as a relationship of rhetorician-making-a-world to another rhetorician-making-a-world, or as a relationship of editor to author, where it is always the author/patient's mentation that must be freed to create rhetorical universes, and where we can rid ourselves of the notion of transference. And I believe that the forms of apparent disorder I have mentioned— BLOCKAGES, CROSSOVERS, ATTEMPTED CROSSOVERS, and MOURNINGS— can provide us the beginnings of a new taxonomy of mental problems more readily understandable and accessible to all involved.

If there is anything to what I've said so far, it ought to predict some versions of *diagnosis* and *therapy*. I have been on the way to suggesting that psychoanalysis become rhetoric, and I have been on the way to suggesting that a rich means of soul-study lies in the discovery and understanding of diverse inventions, structures, and styles energized in various contexts, in the discovery and understanding of the interplay within rhetorical universes and among rhetorical universes. In this maze, there is no diagnosis; there may be *diagnoses;* there is no therapy; there may be *therapies.* Each patient is author of himself or herself; each patient is priest and psychoanalyst. In the quest for emergence into free rhetorical universes, there are no normalities. "If the fundamental principle of psychological life is differentiation," Hillman says, "then no single perspective can embrace psychological life, and norms are the delusions that parts prescribe to one another. A standard for one figure may be pathology for another, and pathology for one part may be normal from another perspective within the same individual" (88). In the quest for emergence into free rhetorical universes, all conspire to help them read well. (I set aside physiological imbalances, as in some forms of depression, as requiring chemical or other forms of treatment, though I privately think that the physiological results from the action of mind's energy.) Some things, of course, one doesn't get over. Sometimes, one has only to embrace and to know one's disorder, if that is what it is. Sometimes, one has to wait, to learn, and after awhile, perhaps, to reinvent. Sometimes, there can be no acceptance, no "cure," but only a plunging in to understand. Sometimes, emergence has to wait upon submergence. [. . .]

I've come a long way to a diminished ending. This, however, is a version of modern rhetoric. It is a whisper, an indication of what rhetoric and psychoanalysis come to. Psychoanalysis consists in talking, waiting, learning, talking again, in emerging toward an authentically said self, perhaps after stammers and long silence. Psychoanalysis is the process in which we at last put on our histories, take them as ours, make our narratives, and become our own arguments.

Notes

1. I have been depending upon Jerome Kagan and Ernest Havemann, *Psychology: An Introduction* (New York: Harcourt Brace Jovanovich, 1972); Gregory Bateson, Don D. Jackson, Jay Haley, and Jolin Weakland, "Toward a Theory of Schizophrenia," in Leslie Y. Rabkin and John E. Carr, eds., *Sourcebook in Abnormal Psychology* (New York: Houghton Mifflin, 1967); and Eric Pfeiffer, *Disordered Behavior* (New York: Oxford UP, 1968). Richard M. Coe's paper, "The Rhetoric of Paradox," is useful to one thinking about multiple rhetorical universes; see *A Symposium on Rhetoric,* ed. William E. Tanner, J. Dean Bishop, and Turner S. Kohler (Denton: Federation of North Texas Universities, 1976), 3–12. I have been reminded throughout of the admonition that every psychoneurosis is unique and that any attempt to sort, define, and classify must be arbitrary. When specialists in the field do not agree on descriptions or terms, it may seem idle to expect any way of describing disorders, including schizophrenia, to be useful. Still, I think the notion of multiple discursive universes existing within a person, usually in some kind of consonance with or toleration for each other, but sometimes mixing, leaking from one to another, or crossing from one to another, offers a way to understanding some features of disorder, including schizophrenia. Kraepelin's account of attention loss of confusion in the train of thought, and of incomprehensible gibberish among schizophrenics corresponds easily enough, I think, to the conception I am proposing. When universes collide, mix, and cross over, then attention is diverted, thought is confused, ideas from one world do try to persist in another, and language becomes confused. Bleuler's focusing on the disturbance of associations as the central symptom of schizophrenia suggests an effect I've tried to describe, a mixing of ideas from different worlds. See the discussion of Kraepelin's *Dementia Praecox and Paraphrenia* and Bleuler's *Dementia Praecox* or the *Group of Schizophrenias* in Loren J. Chapman and Jean P. Chapman, *Disordered Thought in Schizophrenia* (Englewood Cliffs: Prentice-Hall, 1973), and see Manfred Bleuler, *The Schizophrenic Disorders* (New Haven: Yale UP, 1978). The crossover

effect I've suggested can be seen, too, in the nuclear disabilities—failure of anxiety management, failure of interpersonal transaction, and failure of historicity—and the consequential and restitutive symptoms described by Werner M. Mendel in *Schizophrenia, The Experience and Its Treatment* (San Francisco: Jossey-Bass, 1976). Before one falls in love with any single way of describing something complex, however, it is well to remember that "cities are characterized by a great many people living together, acute schizophrenic-type disorders by a great many conflicting thoughts, feelings, perceptions, and desires all going on together. Beyond that as with cities, the differences are every bit as important as the similarities." See Patrick O'Brien, *The Disordered Mind: What We Now Know about Schizophrenia* (Englewood Cliffs: Prentice-Hall, 1978), 103. I should add, too, that the conception of schizophrenia as occurring in crossovers or leakages is kin, but not, I think, identical to ideas in recent studies of various forms of bicameralism in brain function. See, for example, Carl Sagan, *The Dragons of Eden* (New York: Random House, 1977); Arthur Koestler, "Cosmic Consciousness," *Psychology Today,* April, 1977; and Julian Jaynes, *The Origin of Consciousness in the Breakdown of the Bicameral Mind* (Boston: Houghton Mifflin, 1977).

2. Here I will call upon Walker Gibson, "Composing the World," *College Composition and Communication,* October, 1970; S. M. Halloran, "On the End of Rhetoric Classical and Modern," *College English,* February, 1975; Richard Ohmann, "In Lieu of a New Rhetoric," *College English,* October, 1964; Kenneth Bruffee, "The Structure of Knowledge and the Future of Liberal Education," *Liberal Education;* and my own paper, "On the Way, Perhaps, to a New Rhetoric, but Not There Yet, and If We Do Get There, There Won't Be There Any More," *College English,* February, 1985.

3. I have tried to talk about the notion of emergence elsewhere, in "Argument as Emergence, Rhetoric as Love."

CHAPTER SEVEN

Argument as Emergence,
Rhetoric as Love

In a recent review in the *New York Times Book Review*, A. G.
Mojtabai said, "We are all authors. Adding here, deleting there,
we people the world with our needs: with friends, lovers, ciphers,
enemies, villains—and heroes" (March 3, 1985: 7). All authors,
to be sure, we are more particularly narrators, historians, tale-
tellers. Going through experience, hooking some version of it to
ourselves, accumulating what we know as evidence and insight,
ignoring what does not look like evidence and insight to us, finding some pieces of life that become life for us, failing to find
others, or choosing not to look, each of us creates the narrative
that he or she is. We tell our lives and live our tales, enjoying
where we can, tolerating what we must, turning away to re-tell,
or sinking into madness and disorder if we cannot make (or remake) our tale into a narrative we can live in. Each of us forms
conceptions of the world, its institutions, its public, private, wide,
or local histories, and each of us is the narrative that shows our
living in and through the conceptions that are always being formed
as the tales of our lives take their shape. In this history-making,
as E. L. Doctorow says, "there is no fiction or non-fiction as we
commonly understand the distinction" ("False Documents,"
American Review 26 [1977]: 215–32). There is only our making,
sometimes by design, sometimes not. None of us lives without a
history; each of us is a narrative. We're always standing some
place in our lives, and there is always a tale of how we came to
stand there, though few of us have marked carefully the dimensions of the place where we are or kept time with the tale of how
we came to be there.

First published in *Rhetoric Review* 4 (1985): 16–32.

The catch is that, though we are all fiction-makers/histori-ans, we are seldom all that good at the work. Sometimes we can't find all that's needed to make the narrative we want of ourselves, though we still make our narrative. Sometimes we don't see enough. Sometimes we find enough and see enough and still tell it wrong. Sometimes we fail to judge either the events within our narrative or the people, places, things, and ideas that might enter our narrative. Sometimes we judge dogmatically, even ignorantly, holding only to standards that we have already accepted or es-tablished. We see only what our eyes will let us see at a given moment, but eventually make a narrative of ourselves that we can enjoy, tolerate, or at least not have to think about too much. Every so often, we will see something we have not seen before, and then we have to nudge, poke, and remake our narrative, or we decide we can either ignore the thing seen or whittle into shape the narrative we already have. We are always seeing, hear-ing, thinking, living, and saying the fiction that we and our times make possible and tolerable, a fiction that is the history we can assent to at a given time. But not only can we not always be good narrators/historians, we also cannot be thorough at the work. We never quite get the narrative all said: we're always making a fiction/history that always has to be remade, unless we are so bound by dogma, arrogance, and ignorance that we cannot see a new artifact, hear a new opinion, or enter a new experience in our narrative.

When I say that we make the fictions that are our lives, I mean to identify a human activity, not a foolish or evil one. His-tory as fiction may become evil, of course, if we refuse to see any history except the one we've already accepted or if we try to force that history upon others. At any rate, making the fiction of our lives—not at all the same as discovering a way to present an objective, externally verifiable history, which is not possible, any-where—is not by nature limited, valueless, ignorant, despicable, or "merely subjective." It is human. It is what we do and are, even if we think we are doing and being something else. Even if we imagine that we are learning what can be known "out there," some truths that are fixed and forever, we are after all creating our narratives "in here," ourselves always agents for what can be known. We are always, as the rhetorician might say, inventing the narratives that are our lives.

As I have already suggested, we are always standing somewhere in our narratives when we speak to others or to ourselves. When we use language, some choices have already been made and others must be made. Our narratives, which include our pasts, accompany us and exist in our statements and exercise their influence whether or not we are aware of the influence. Before we speak, we have lived; when we speak, we must continually choose because our mouths will not say two words simultaneously. Whether consciously or not, we always station ourselves somewhere in our narratives when we use language. This means that invention always occurs. The process of invention may occur in a conscious, deliberate way, but it will occur, even if at some subterranean level. Any statement carries its history with it. We may speak without knowing all of our narratives, but the history is there. If the history of a statement someone else makes isn't apparent to us as hearers, then we have to go and find it. If we are talking to someone and that person says something we don't understand, or something that offends us, or something we cannot easily agree to, then we have to start searching that person's history until we begin to understand what led him or her to speak just so. Sometimes we do less well: if the history isn't there for us, we don't learn it, but instead make it up to suit ourselves. If we learn or make up another's narrative so that it becomes part of our narrative, then we can live in some peace with the other. If the other's narrative will not enter our own, then something else happens, to which I'll return in a moment.

While the language that lets us invent our narratives and be human is a great gift, its capacities will not extend infinitely. Language comes out of us a word at a time; we cannot get all said at once. We open ourselves as we can to insight and experience and say what we can, but what we say will invariably be incomplete. Two words cannot occupy the same space at the same time; two messages cannot fully occupy the same space at the same time. Language enforces a closure: we must say one thing or the other; we choose, and make our narrative. To be sure, having lived, thought, and spoken, we can open ourselves again to insight and experience and evidence and try to say it all again. But what will come out will be the fiction we can make at the time. We cannot make all that was and is and shall be into an is of the moment's speaking. Whatever we can get into our heads we will make into the narratives that will be our truths unless we learn again.

2

Each of us is a narrative. A good part of the time we can live comfortably adjacent to or across the way from other narratives. Our narratives can be congruent with other narratives, or untouched by other narratives. But sometimes another narrative impinges upon ours, or thunders around and down into our narratives. We can't build this other into our narratives without harm to the tales we have been telling. This other is a narrative in another world; it is disruptive, shocking, initially at least incomprehensible, and, as Carl Rogers has shown us, threatening.

When this happens, our narratives become indeed what they are perpetually becoming—arguments. The choosing we do to make our narratives (whether or not we are aware of the nature of our choosing) also makes our narratives into arguments. The narratives we tell (ourselves) create and define the worlds in which we hold our beliefs. Our narratives are the evidence we have of ourselves and of our convictions. Argument, then, is not something we *make* outside ourselves; argument is what we are. Each of us is an argument. We always live in, through, around, over, and under argument. All the choices we've made, accidentally or on purpose, in creating our histories/narratives have also made us arguments, or, I should go on to say, sets of congruent arguments, or in some instances, sets of conflicting arguments.

3

Each of us is an argument, evidenced by our narrative. What happens, then, if the narrative of another crushes up against our own—disruptive, shocking, incomprehensible, threatening, suddenly showing us into a narrative not our own? What happens if a narrative not our own reveals to us that our own narrative was wanting all along, though it is the only evidence of our identity? What happens if the merest glimpse into another narrative sends us lurching, stunned by its differentness, either alarmed that such differentness could exist or astonished to see that our own narrative might have been or might yet be radically otherwise than it is? Do we hold our narratives? Keep telling the story we have been telling? At all costs?

We react, of course, in many different ways. Sometimes we turn away from other narratives. Sometimes we teach ourselves not to know that there are other narratives. Sometimes—probably all too seldom—we encounter another narrative and learn to change our own. Sometimes we lose our plot, and our convictions as well; since our convictions belong to our narratives, any strong interference with our narrative or sapping of its way of being will also interrupt or sap our convictions. Sometimes we go to war. Sometimes we sink into madness, totally unable to manage what our wit or judgment has shown us—a contending narrative that has force to it and charm and appeal and perhaps justice and beauty as well, a narrative compelling us to attention and toward belief that we cannot ultimately give, a contending narrative that shakes and cracks all foundations and promises to alter our identity, a narrative that would educate us to be wholly other than what we are. Any narrative exists in time; any narrative is made of the past, the present, and the future. We cannot without potential harm shift from the past of one narrative into the present and future of another, or from the past and present of one narrative into the future of another, or from the future we are narrating into a past that is not readily ours. How can we take that one chance I mentioned just now and learn to change when change is to be cherished? How can we expect another to change when we are ourselves that other's contending narrative?

4

Let there be no mistake: a contending narrative, that is, an argument of genuine consequence because it confronts one life with another, is a threat, whether it is another's narrative become argument impinging upon or thundering into ours, or our own, impinging upon the other's. A contending narrative, I'd suggest, is a threat more consequential than Carl Rogers has shown us. In *On Becoming a Person* (Boston: Houghton Mifflin, 1961), Rogers proposes that "significant learning . . . takes place when five conditions are met":

- when the client perceives himself as faced by a serious problem;

- when the therapist is a congruent person in the relationship, able to *be* the person he is;

- when the therapist feels an unconditional positive regard for the client;

- when the therapist experiences an accurate emphatic understanding of the client's private world and communicates this;

- when the client to some degree experiences the therapist's congruence, acceptance, and empathy.

Rogers had earlier applied his thinking more directly to rhetoric, announcing his belief that a sense of threat usually blocks successful communication. As he put it, "the major barrier to mutual interpersonal communication is our very natural tendency to judge, to evaluate, to approve or disapprove, the statement of the other person" ("Communication: Its Blocking and Its Facilitation," paper delivered at Northwestern University's Centennial Conference on Communication, Oct. 11, 1951, reprinted in Richard E. Young, Alton L. Becker, and Kenneth L. Pike, *Rhetoric: Discovery and Change* [New York: Harcourt, Brace, and World, 1979], 284–89). If we refrain from evaluating and instead "listen with understanding," according to Rogers, we will "see the expressed idea and attitude from the other person's point of view . . . sense how it feels to him . . . achieve his frame of reference in regard to the thing he is talking about" (285). When we are immersed in the attitudes, ideas, and beliefs of the other person, we "will find the emotion going out of the discussion, the differences being reduced, and those differences which remain being of a rational and understandable sort" (286).

Such insights have been enormously valuable in recent years. Some (Maxine Hairston, for example) believe that Rogers's work has brought a new dimension to rhetoric after all these centuries, changing our way of thinking about argument. Others believe that Rogers's views are assumed by Aristotle, as Andrea Lunsford put it, to be "the foundation which is necessary before successful argumentation begins" ("Aristotelian vs. Rogerian Argument: A Reassessment," *College Composition and Communication* [May, 1979]: 146–51). Lunsford singles out two texts that propose methods of organizing Rogerian argument. Young, Becker, and Pike (283) suggest the following method:

> First: an introduction to the problem and a demonstration that the opponent's position is understood.
>
> Second: a statement of the contexts in which the opponent's position may be valid.
>
> Third: a statement of the writer's position, including the contexts in which it is valid.
>
> Fourth: a statement of how the opponent's position would benefit if he were to adopt elements of the writer's position.

In *A Contemporary Rhetoric* (Boston: Houghton Mifflin, 1974 [210–11]), Maxine Hairston presents another Rogerian pattern:

> 1. a brief, objectively phrased statement of the issue.
>
> 2. a complete and impartially worded summary of your audience's opinion on the issue, demonstrating that you have made an honest effort to understand how they feel and why they feel that way. It would be useful to mention the values that underlie these opinions.
>
> 3. an objective statement of your opinions on the issue, along with your reasons for feeling as you do. Here again it would be useful to give the values on which you base your opinions.
>
> 4. an analysis of what your opinions have in common.
>
> 5. a proposal for resolving the issue in a way that injures neither party.

Such insights added to those of Carl Rogers, I'll say again, have been highly valuable. They lead to patterns of argument that may even work, part of the time, in some settings. But they won't do. They do not, I believe, face the flushed, feverish, quaky, shaky, angry, scared, hurt, shocked, disappointed, alarmed, outraged, even terrified condition that a person comes to when his or her narrative is opposed by a genuinely contending narrative. Then it is one life or another, perhaps this life or none.

I want to pause a little to suggest some of the reasons that I think Rogers and others who have applied his work have not gone far enough, though this is not the place for a full critique, even if I could give it. First, we should remember, Rogers is talking about the therapist-client relationship, and much of what he says rises from that context. Since it takes two to tango, and since at least one of the participants in this context is already intent upon *not* being an adversary, then conflict may be resolved and mutual communication may ensue. The therapist-client relationship, I'd suggest, even at its prickliest, is simply not going to produce the stress and pain that can occur when contending narratives meet. It is by its nature more amenable to discussion and resolution, and the rules or conditions I cited earlier are, at any rate, game rules, as my colleague, Professor James Baumlin, has pointed out. In the passage I cited earlier, Rogers is talking about a client who already has a need (he or she is faced by a serious problem), and the therapist is already a congruent person in the relationship. Rogers proposes for the therapist an "unconditional positive regard," but straight away recommends that all take emotion out of discussions and reduce differences. If one holds another in "unconditional positive regard," that regard, I believe, includes both emotions and differences. They cannot be reduced, though their force may be diminished for a moment; such energy is always conserved. If emotions do go out of the discussion—and I don't think they do—it is only after time and care. What each must face in contention before emotions and differences dwindle is something in the other altogether more startling: a horror, a wrong, a dishonesty (as each sees the other), a shock, an outrage, or perhaps a beauty too startling and stunning to see. As for the texts that propose patterns of Rogerian arguments, I'd say that the recommended designs are altogether commendable and will sometimes work, so long as the argument isn't crucial to the nature of the narratives involved. Where arguments entail identity, the presentation of "a statement of how the opponent's position would benefit if he were to adopt elements of the writer's position" is about as efficacious as storming Hell with a bucket of water or trying to hide the glories of Heaven with a torn curtain. If I cannot accept the identity of the other, his kindness in offering me benefits will be of no avail. As for offering a "proposal for resolving the issue in a way that injures neither party," I'd say that in the arguments that grip us most tightly, we *do* injure the other, or the other injures us, or we seem about to injure each other, except we take the tenderest, strongest care. Paul Bator ("Aristotelian and Rogerian Argument," *College Composition and Communication* [1980]: 427–32) acknowledges that Rogerian strategy works most effectively when students "encounter non-adversary writing situations." "Under the Rogerian schema," he continues, "students can be encouraged to view their writing as a communicative first step—one designed to build bridges and win over minds—rather than being prompted to view the essay only as a finished product serving as an ultimate weapon for conversion."

I am suggesting that the arguments most significant to us are just where threat occurs and continues, just where emotions and differences do not get calmly talked away, just where we are plunged into that flushed, feverish, quaky, shaky, angry, scared, hurt, shocked, disappointed, alarmed, outraged, even terrified condition I spoke of a little earlier. Then what do we do?

5

To make the kind of contention or opposition I am trying to discuss a little clearer, I should add another term. I have been talking about contending narratives, or identities. Let me now add what I hope has been suggested all along: let us suppose that in this contention each narrator is entirely *steadfast,* wholly intent upon preserving the nature and movement of his or her narrative, earnest and zealous to keep its identity. I think we have not fully considered what happens in argument when the arguers are steadfast.

If Ms. Smith is steadfast in conviction and is outfitted with what she takes to be good evidence and sound reasoning, that means that she is living a narrative that is congruent with her expectations and satisfying to her needs. But if she speaks to Mr. Jones, who is at opposites and equally steadfast, who is his own satisfying narrative, then it's likely that Ms. Smith's evidence will not look like evidence to Mr. Jones, and Ms. Smith's reasoning will not look like reasoning. Evidence and reason are evidence and reason only if one lives in the narrative that creates and regards them.

That seems to picture a near-hopeless prospect.

Sometimes it is, at least for long periods of time. Sometimes we don't resolve oppositions, but must either remain apart or live as adversaries with the other. But the prospect doesn't have to be hopeless, at least not permanently.

What can change it? What can free us from the apparent hopelessness of steadfast arguments opposing each other? I have to start with a simple answer and hope that I can gradually give it the texture and capacity it needs: we have *to see* each other, *to know* each other, *to be present to* each other, *to embrace* each other.

What makes that possible? We have to change the way we talk about argument and conceive of argument.

6

I'm not ready to go on yet. I want to try to place my interest in argument, and perhaps I can do that by comparing my interest to those of Carl Rogers, to whom I am clearly much indebted. Rogers extrapolates from therapist-client relationships to public communication relationships. The base from which he works (the therapist-client relationship) gives him a setting in which civil understanding is a goal to be reached through mutual communication transactions. He does recognize the potentially threatening effect of alien insights and ideas. Young, Becker, and Pike show that the Rogerian strategy "rests on the assumption that a man holds to his beliefs about who he is and what the world is like because other beliefs threaten his identity and integrity" (7). In the Rogerian view, as Paul Bator puts it, carefully reasoned arguments "may be totally ineffectual when employed in a rhetorical situation where the audience feels its beliefs or values are being threatened. No amount of reasoned argument will prompt the audience to consider the speaker's point of view if the audience senses that its opinions are somehow being 'explained away'" (428). Followers of Rogers see in Aristotle's *Rhetoric* an antagonistic speaker-audience relationship; they do not find this in Rogers, for, as Bator says, "Generation and control of audience expectation do not attract Rogers" (428). As I have already suggested, given the therapist-client relationship he starts from, Rogers is appropriately enough interested in rhetorical contexts that do not involve advocacy. As Rogers says, "If I can listen to what [the other person] can tell me, if I can understand how it seems to him, if I can see its personal meaning for him, if I can sense the emotional flavor which it has for him, then I will be releasing potent forces of change in him" (285–86). Since he is customarily talking about a mutual communication transaction, Rogers is often as concerned with the audience as with the speaker. A speaker, Bator says, "must be willing to achieve the frame of reference of the listener even if the values or views held by the other are antithetical to the speaker's personal code of ethics. A necessary correlate of acceptance (of the other's view) is understanding, an understanding which implies that the listener accepts the views of the speaker without knowing cognitively what will result. Such understanding, in turn, encourages the speaker to explore untried avenues of exchange" (428). Looking for the therapist-client relationship, Rogers sees the therapist/communicator as an understanding audience. He expects that the therapist-as-audience will not only accept, but also understand the feelings and thoughts of the client-as-speaker. When the therapist understands the feelings and thoughts that seem so horrible or weak or sentimental or bizarre to the client, when the therapist understands and accepts the client, then the therapist frees the client to explore deep experience freely. As each understands and accepts the other, then they may move toward the truth.

This, I would gladly agree, is the way we ought to argue, each accepting, understanding, and helping the other. However, I think the significant arguments that crowd us into each other are somewhat less kindly composed. I want to get to the place where we are threatened and where the setting doesn't seem to give us opportunity to reduce threat and to enter a mutual search for congruence and regard. I want to get to the place where we are advocates of contending narratives (with their accompanying feelings and thoughts), where we are adversaries, each seeming to propose the repudiation or annihilation of what the other lives, values, and is, where we are beyond being adversaries in that strange kind of argument we seldom attend to, where one offers the other a rightness so demanding, a beauty so stunning, a grace so fearful as to call the hearer to forego one identity for a startling new one.

7

What can free us from the apparent hopelessness of steadfast arguments contending with each other, of narratives come bluntly up against each other? Can the text of one narrative become the text of another narrative without sacrifice? If there is to be hope, we have to see each other, to know each other, to be present to each other, to embrace each other.

What makes that possible? I don't know. We can start toward these capacities by changing the way we talk about argument and conceive of argument.

It may be helpful, before I go on, if I try to explain a little more fully the kind of occasion I mean to refer to, the kind of setting in which contention generates that flushed, feverish, quaky, shaky, angry, scared, hurt, shocked, disappointed, alarmed, outraged, even terrified condition I have mentioned. Of course I cannot imagine, let alone explain or describe, all the oppositions that can occur. Perhaps I can by illustration at least suggest the kind of occasion that I want to talk about. I mean such occasions as these: let two people confront each other, each holding views antithetical to the sacred values and images of the other, one an extreme advocate of the current pro-life movement, the other an extreme advocate of the current movement to leave free choice open to women in the matter of abortion, each a mockery of the other; let two parties confront each other, zealous advocates of one contending that farmers must learn to stand on their own without government support, and zealous advocates of the other contending that the government, by withdrawing support, will literally kill farmers; let two tribes go to war for ancient reasons not entirely explicable to themselves or to outsiders, each a denial of the other, as in various current Middle East crises; let two nations confront each other in what sometimes appears to be a shocked and total inability to understand or even to recognize each other, as in continuing conflicts between the United States and Russia, wherever these conflicts happen to be located, whether in East Germany or in Nicaragua; let a beautiful Jewish woman encounter an aged captain of guards for Dachau; let some man confront an affirmation of life he has not been able to achieve; let an honest woman encounter cruel dishonesty; let a man encounter a narrative so beautiful but different that he cannot look; let two quite different narratives converge in conflict inside the head of a single lonely man or woman.

Given such occasions, what do we do in argument? Can we hope for happy resolution? I don't know. I do think the risk in argument is greater than we have learned from Aristotle or Rogers. What can we do, then?

We can start, as I suggested earlier, by changing the way we talk about argument.

As we presently understand, talk about, and teach argument, it is, whatever our intentions, *display* and *presentation*. We entice with an exordium and lay in a background. We present a proposition. We display our proofs, our evidence. We show that we can handle and if need be refute opposing views. We offer our conclusion. That is display and presentation. The same thing is true of proposed plans for Rogerian argument, as in the passages I cited earlier from Young, Becker, and Pike and from Maxine Hairston.

But argument is not something *to present* or *to display*. It is something *to be*. It is what we *are*, as I suggested earlier.

We are the argument over against another. Another is the argument over against us. We live in, through, around, and against arguments. To display or to present them is to pretend a disengagement that we cannot actually achieve and probably should not want to achieve. Argument is not display or presentation, for our engagement in it, or identity with it, will out. When argument is taken as display or presentation, then it eventually becomes a matter of my poster against yours, with the prize to the slickest performance.

If we are to hope for ourselves and to value all others, we must learn that argument is emergence.

8

Argument is emergence toward the other. That requires a readiness to testify to an identity that is always emerging, a willingness to dramatize one's narrative in progress before the other; it calls for an untiring stretch toward the other, a reach toward unfolding the other. It is a risky revelation of the self, for the arguer is asking for an acknowledgment of his or her identity, is asking for witness from the other. In argument, the arguer must plunge on alone, with no assurance of welcome from the other, with no assurance whatever of unconditional positive regard from the other. In argument, the arguer must, with no assurance, go out, inviting the other to enter a world that the arguer tries to make commodious, inviting the other to emerge as well, but with no assurance of kind or even thoughtful response. How does this happen? Better, how can it happen?

It can happen if we learn to love before we disagree. Usually, it's the other way around: if we learn to love, it is only after silence or conflict or both. In ancient times, I was in the United States Army. I spent the better part of 1951 and 1952 in Germany. In those years, American troops were still officially regarded as an Occupation Force, with certain privileges extended, such as free transportation. One service provided was a kind of rental agency in many large cities. On pass or on leave, one could go to this agency and be directed to a room for rent (very cheap) in a private home. Since I was stationed only ten or twelve miles away, I often went to Heidelberg when I had just a weekend pass or a three-day pass. On one such occasion I went to Heidelberg, stopped in at the agency, and got directions to a room that was available. I found the address, a large brownstone just a block off the main street, met the matron of the house, and was taken to a small bedroom on the third floor that would be mine for a couple of days. I left shortly thereafter to go places and do things, paying no particular attention to the room except to notice it was clean and neat. The next morning was clear and bright and cool; I opened the windows and finally began to see the room. A picture on one wall startled me, more, stunned me.

On the kitchen wall in my parents' home in Texas there was a picture of my older brother, taken while he was in what was known as the Air Corps in World War II. It was a posed shot of the sort that I suppose most airmen had taken at one time or another to send home to the folks. In the picture, my brother is wearing the airman's favorite of that time, a leather jacket with knit cuffs and a knit band about the waist. He is wearing the old-fashioned leather cap with ear flaps and goggles, and there is a white scarf around his neck, one end tossed over his shoulder. Behind him there is a Consolidated-Vultee B-24.

The picture on the wall in the bedroom in Heidelberg showed a young man wearing a leather jacket with knit cuffs and a knit band about the waist. He wore an old-fashioned leather cap with ear flaps and goggles, and there is a white scarf around his neck, one end tossed over his shoulder. Behind him there was an airplane; it was a Focke-Wulf 190. He might have been my brother. After a while, I guess I realized that he *was* my brother.

The television news on March 7, 1985, showed a memorial service at Remagen, Germany, marking the fortieth anniversary of the American troops' capture of the Remagen bridge, which let them cross the Rhine. No major world leaders were there, but veterans from both sides had come to look and take notice of the day. American and German veterans who had fought there wept and hugged each other and shook hands.

In the mid-fifties, another group of veterans met, to commemorate the fortieth anniversary of the end of battle at Verdun, that hellish landscape where over a million men died to gain or to preserve two or three miles of scrubby country, where no birds sang. They shook hands; they embraced; they wept; they sang an old song that begins, "Ich hatte ein kamaraden."

After a while, the hated dead can be mourned, and the old enemy can be embraced.

In these instances, we waited to love (or at least to accept) until long after silence and grim conflict. (I've not lost my head altogether: some conflicts will not be resolved in time and love—there's always that captain of guards from Dachau.) Often, we don't learn to love (or at least to accept) at all. All precedents and examples notwithstanding, I'll still insist that argument—that rhetoric itself—must begin, proceed, and end in love.

9

But how is this to happen? How will we argue, or teach argument taken in this way? I don't know, but I'll chance some suggestions.

A. The arguer has to go alone. When argument has gone beyond attempts made by the arguer and by the other to accept and understand, when those early exploratory steps toward mutual communication are over, or when all of these stages have been bypassed altogether—as they often will be—then the arguer is alone, with no assurance at all that the other or any audience will be kindly disposed. When argument comes to advocacy or to adversarial confrontation, the mutuality that Rogers describes will probably not occur. At the point of advocacy, most particularly at the crisis point in adversarial relationships, the burden is on the maker of the argument as he or she is making the argument. At the moment of heat (which may last twenty seconds or twenty years and which may be feverish and scary), the arguer in all likelihood will not know whether or not the other, the audience, will choose to take the role of the well-disposed listener or the kindly therapist. The arguer, alone, must see in the reverence owed to the other, discover and offer all grace that he or she can muster, and, most especially, extend every liberty possible to the other. The arguer must hold the other wholly in mind and yet cherish his or her own identity. *Then*, perhaps, the arguer and the other may be able to break into mutuality.

B. The arguer must at once hold his or her identity and give it to the other, learning to live—and argue—provisionally. In "Supposing History Is a Woman—What Then?" (*The American Scholar*, Autumn, 1984), Gertrude Himmelfarb remarks:

> Whatever "truth or validity" adheres to history . . . does not derive, as the conventional historian might assume, from an "objective" world, a world of past events waiting to be discovered and reconstructed by the historian. For there is no objective world,

no historical events independent of the experience of the historian, no events or facts which are not also ideas.

We must keep learning as speakers/narrators/arguers (and as hearers). We can learn to dispense with what we imagined was absolute truth and to pursue the reality of things only partially knowable. We can learn to keep adding pieces of knowledge here, to keep rearranging pieces over yonder, to keep standing back and turning to see how things look elsewhere. We can learn that our narrative/argument doesn't exist except as it is composed and that the "act of composition can never end," as Doctorow has said.

C. As I have just suggested, we arguers can learn to abandon authoritative positions. They cannot be achieved, at any rate, except as in arrogance, ignorance, and dogma we convince ourselves that we have reached authority. We should not want to achieve an authoritative position, anyway. An authoritative position is a prison both to us and to any audience.

D. We arguers can learn the lessons that rhetoric itself wants to teach us. By its nature, invention asks us to open ourselves to the richness of creation, to plumb its depths, search its expanses, and track its chronologies. But the moment we speak (or write), we are no longer open; we have chosen, whether deliberately or not, and so have closed ourselves off from some possibilities. Invention wants openness; structure and style demand closure. We are asked to perpetually open and always closing. If we stay open, we cannot speak or act; if we stand closed, we have succumbed to dogma and rigidity. Each utterance may deplete the inventive possibilities if a speaker falls into arrogance, ignorance, or dogma. But each utterance, if the speaker having spoken opens again, may also nurture and replenish the speaker's inventive world and enable him or her to reach out around the other. Beyond any speaker's bound inventive world lies another: there lie the riches of creation, the great, unbounded possible universe of invention. All time is there, past, present, and future. The natural and the supernatural are there. All creation is there, ground and source for invention. The knowledge we have is formed out of the plenitude of creation, which is all before us, but must be sought again and again through the cycling process of rhetoric, closing to speak, opening again to invent again. In an unlimited universe of meaning, we can never foreclose on interpretation and argument. Invention is a name for great miracle—the attempt to unbind time, to loosen the capacities of time and space into our speaking. This copiousness is eternally there, a plenitude for all. Piaget remarked that the more an infant sees and hears, the more he or she wants to see and hear. Just this is what the cycling of rhetoric offers us: opening to invention, closing to speak, opening again to a richer invention. Utterances may thus be elevated, may grow to hold both arguer and other.

E. We still need to study. There is much about argument that we still have not learned, or that we have not acknowledged. If we are accurate in our evaluation of what happens in conflict, I think we will have to concede that most of what happens is bad. If we know that accurately, we'll be a step farther than we were toward knowing how to deal with contention and the hurts that rise from conflict and argument. We have not at any time in our public or personal histories known consistently how to deal with conflicts, especially when each side or party or view arises normally according to its own variety of thought—and there is no arguer who does not believe that his or her view is a just consequence of normal thought and need. In discourse and behavior, our ways of resolving conflicts have typically been limited and unsatisfactory. When opposing views, each issuing by its own normal processes from its own inventive world, come together in conflict because each wants the same time and space, we usually have only a few ways of handling the conflict:

1. one view prevails, the other subsides;

2. advocates of the two views compromise;

3. the need for action prompts arbitrary selection of one of the two views, even if both are appealing and attractive;

4. we are paralyzed, unable to choose;

5. we go to war; or

6. occasionally, the advocates of one side learn gladly from those of the other and gladly lay down their own views in favor of the other.

To be sure, there are other patterns for resolving conflicts that I haven't had wit enough to recognize; I'd reckon, however, that most are unrewarding to some or all. Once a view emerges— that is, once an inventive process has become structure and style— it cannot wholly subside, as in 1, though it must seem to do so; required by force or expediency to subside, it does not subside but persists underground, festering. Compromise, as in 2, is likely to leave parts of both views hidden away and festering. Deliberate choice between two appealing views, as in 3, leaves the unchosen to grow and compete underground, generating a cynicism that undercuts the chosen argument. Paralysis, as in 4, clearly gives no view gain, though each remains, eating away at the paralyzed agent. War, physical or psychological, is plainly not an appropriate human resolution. In most of these instances there is a thwarted or misplaced or submerged narrative, a normality that may grow wild because it is thwarted, misplaced, or submerged. We have not learned how to let competing normalities live together in the same time and space. We're not sure, we frail humans, that it is possible.

F. The arguer must go alone, unaided by any world of thought, value, and belief except the one that he or she composes in the process of arguing, unassisted by the other because the other is over in a different place, being realized in a different narrative. In my mind, this means that the burden of argument is upon the *ethos* of the arguer. *Ethos,* of course, is a term still poorly understood. Among others, Bator objects to any concentration upon *ethos* because it seems to be "related primarily to adversary situations calling for argumentative strategies designed to persuade others," because "the speaker may be concerned particularly with enhancing her own image or character rather than addressing the issue at hand" (428). Ideally, Bator believes, the subject or problem "is viewed within the audience's framework of values, not simply from the writer's assumptions or premises. The *ethos* of the writer is not the main focus of attention, nor is it the primary means of appeal" (431). This view omits considering the likelihood that *ethos* occurs in various ways; the term does not require to be defined as it has formerly been defined. A genuinely provocative and evocative *ethos* does, in fact, hold the audience wholly in mind, does view matters both as the arguer sees them and as others see them. The self-authenticating language of such an *ethos* issues an invitation into a commodious universe. Argument is partial; when a speaker argues a proposition or develops a theme or makes an assertion, he or she has knowingly or not chosen one proposition, one theme, one assertion from all available. When we speak, we stand somewhere, and our standing place makes both known and silent claims upon us. We make truth, if at all, out of what is incomplete or partial. Language is a closure, but the generative *ethos* I am trying to identify uses language to shove back the restraints of closure, like a commodious universe, to stretch words out beyond our private universe.

G. We must pile time into argumentative discourse. Earlier, I suggested that in our most grievous and disturbing conflicts, we need time to accept, to understand, to love the other. At crisis points in adversarial relationships, we do not, however, have time; we are already in opposition and confrontation. Since we don't have time, we must rescue time by putting it into our discourses and holding it there, learning to speak and write not argumentative displays and presentations, but arguments full of the anecdotal, personal, and cultural reflections that will make us plain to all others, thoughtful histories and narratives that reveal us as we're reaching for the others. The world, of course, doesn't want time in its discourses. The world wants the quick memo, the rapid-fire electronic mail service; the world wants speed, efficiency, and economy of motion, all goals that, when reached, have given the world less than it wanted or needed. We must teach the world to want otherwise, to want time for care.

10

Rhetoric is love, and it must speak a commodious language, creating a world full of space and time that will hold our diversities. Most failures of communication result from some willful or inadvertent but unloving violation of the space and time we and others live in, and most of our speaking is tribal talk. But there is more to us than that. We can learn to speak a commodious language, and we can learn to hear a commodious language.

CHAPTER EIGHT

On the Way, Perhaps, to a New Rhetoric, but Not There Yet, and If We Do Get There, There Won't Be There Anymore

In the last twenty years or so we have put a number of different words in front of the word *rhetoric* in titles of books, monographs, papers, and presentations. A large number of "A's" have appeared. I haven't counted, but I think "The's" have been less frequent, though more presumptuous. We have had a good many "Contemporary's," some "Modern's," some "Practical's," and a sprinkling of "New's." Of course we have also attached many colons, words, and phrases onto the rear of the word *rhetoric.* (If you stop to think about it, that's where a colon ought to be attached.) I can't fault any of these combinations save one, to which I'll return; I've committed some myself. Among the textbooks, monographs, papers, and presentations, with whatever combination of words in their titles, we have also gained a variety of remarkably exciting, provocative, necessary, and useful "modern" rhetorics.

But we have not, I believe, gained a *new* rhetoric. The one combination of words in a title that I do find objectionable and inaccurate is the combination that brings a "The" or an "A" and a "New" together in front of the word *rhetoric.* We have many fine *modern* rhetorics, but we do not have *A New Rhetoric* or *The New Rhetoric.* (I notice, however, that at least six titles in the 1984 program of the Conference on College Composition and Communication included the phrase, "the new rhetoric," as if it were already noncontroversial.)

First published in *College English* 47 (1985): 162–70.

Having said this much, I want to hurry on to express a profound gratitude to those who have worked in rhetoric since about 1960 or so. I could not get through a class without the work of Ed Corbett, Ross Winterowd, Jim Kinneavy, James Moffett, Janet Emig, Richard Lloyd-Jones, Maxine Hairston, Mike Halloran, Frank D'Angelo, Andrea Lunsford, Wayne Booth, Walker Gibson, Walter Ong, Chaim Perelman, and a host of others whose work I cherish but will not take space to name. I not only could not get through a class without them, I could not get through a semester without them. I don't know, indeed, whether I could get through my life without them.

But you will understand, I think, and perhaps tolerate the distinction I am making for my own convenience between *modern* and *new.* By *modern,* I wish to indicate something that has existed before, but is now brought up to date. The word clearly refers to the present, but can legitimately designate something that existed previously, but is now made accessible or useful to those currently living. By *new*, I wish to indicate something that has recently been made or developed, something that never existed or occurred before. Perhaps I can explain the distinction with which I want to work a little better now.

Aristotle, Cicero, Quintilian, and Augustine were pretty good at their work. Some of the Renaissance and eighteenth-century rhetoricians were also pretty good at their work. Some of the nineteenth-century rhetoricians have something to offer us. Many of the rhetoric texts we have admired and used in our own time are modernizations of classical texts. That is to say, they amplify what classical texts say, they rename in our way items and procedures from the classical texts, and they redirect our attention to particular features of classical texts. *Rhetoric: Discovery and Change*, a powerful rhetoric of our time by Richard Young, Alton Becker, and Kenneth Pike, is an amplification and modernization of the classical *topoi.* Much in Kinneavy's *A Theory of Discourse* is a renaming of the modes of argument and a modernization of the classical studies of the speaker's relation to an audience. Some part of Moffett's *Teaching the Universe of Discourse* is a modernization of the classical *progymnasmata.* Maxine Hairston, Michael Halloran, and Chaim Perelman have renamed and shown us again what the classical forms of argument meant and still mean. Wayne Booth, Walker Gibson, and Walter Ong have taught us well much that was involved in classical invention. Perhaps Ed Corbett knew best when he titled his extraordinary book *Classical Rhetoric for the Modern Student,* acknowledging at the outset that he was presenting classical learning in a language and form accessible to the modern student.

I do not mean to attribute fault in any of this. I have already suggested my dependence on the work others have done. All of the people I mentioned, and many others, have brought us good to grand *modern* rhetorics. The past is there to be ransacked, and they have done so well, informing their own insight with the wisdom of prior ages. Perhaps, indeed, in our profession nothing can be wholly new; we don't tend to shuck the past off behind us as we go—and besides, since, as Walter Ong has said in *Rhetoric, Romance, and Technology* (Ithaca, NY: Cornell UP, 1971), "the history of rhetoric simply mirrors the evolution of society" (9), we may not have evolved sufficiently to generate a *new* rhetoric until certain conditions are met, at least one of which may be undesirable.

I can't begin to define all of the conditions that may be required. I do want to try to specify such conditions as I can identify that will provide the necessary context for a new rhetoric. Some of the necessary conditions for a new rhetoric I want only to mention briefly. Others I want to linger over a little longer. I hope that other scholars will go where I have not had sense to go.

1. First, and briefly, some of us have restricted the range of rhetoric to only one kind of discourse, argumentation. That will have to change. All forms of discourse come from somewhere (that is, have an inventive past and context), take some form, and manifest themselves in some style. All forms of discourse are proper subjects for rhetorical study.

2. Rhetoricians will have to learn to understand the interplay of visual image and verbal message that makes a meaning through arguments as display in such places as television and magazine advertisements and on billboards. We can have zeugma without both terms being said or written. More important, we can have zeugma gone out of our control, where the visual image undercuts and modifies the verbal message. In almost any visual advertisement, the verbal message is "Buy _____." The visual image

may only reflect that verbal message, but oftener than not the visual image gradually shifts out from under the verbal message to picture an increasingly different world and mode of living. Thus the viewer is pulled into a different world, where the product for sale is an artifact, but not the object of primary attention. The changed world, given in pictured images, is the object of primary attention. (For that reason, it seems to me the most dangerous elements on television are not the moments of violence and sexual renditions, but the almost unnoticed but steadily shifting value statement made in the visual portion of advertisements.)

3. Rhetoricians will have to learn to hold on to traditional forms of rhetorical study, but they will also, at times at least, have to wrestle rhetoric free from textbooks and all previous decisions about the subject. Rhetoricians have so far pretty well limited themselves to studies in English and speech departments only. We need to look out and to see that there is a rhetoric of painting, a rhetoric of biology, a rhetoric of any made form or expression, whatever the medium. Painters and composers surely have their schemes and tropes.

When we look outside, we'll find much to do, but we may also find much already being done in disciplines not associated with English. Discipline-crossing already occurs as people in other fields start using the premises and methods of rhetorical study, sometimes without using the name of rhetoric. James A. Berlin in his paper "Contemporary Composition: The Major Pedagogical Theories" (*College English* 44 [1982]: 765–77), explains that rhetorical principles figure centrally in many different disciplines:

> When taken together, writer, reality, audience, and language define an epistemic field—the basic conditions that determine what knowledge will be knowable, what not knowable, and how the knowable will be communicated. This epistemic field is the point of departure for numerous studies, although the language used to describe it varies from thinker to thinker. Examples are readily available. In *Science and the Modern World* (New York: Macmillan, 1926), A. N. Whitehead sees this field as a product of the "fundamental assumptions which adherents of all variant systems within the epoch unconsciously presuppose" (71). Susanne Langer, in *Philosophy in a New Key* (Cambridge, MA: Harvard UP, 1979) calls it the "tacit, fundamental way of seeing things" (6). Michael Polanyi uses the term "tacit knowledge" in

Personal Knowledge (Chicago: U of Chicago P, 1962). Michel Foucault, in *The Order of Things* (1971; rpt. New York: Vintage, 1973), speaks of the "episteme," and Thomas Kuhn, in *Structure of Scientific Revolutions* (Chicago: U of Chicago P, 1970), discusses at length the "paradigm" that underlies a scientific discipline. The historian Hayden White, in *Metahistory: The Historical Imagination in Nineteenth-Century Europe* (Baltimore: Johns Hopkins UP, 1973), has translated the elements of the composing process into terms appropriate to the writing of history, seeing the historical field as being made up of the historian, the historical record, the historical accounts, and an audience. (767)

When we look outside, then, especially to the study of film and advertising, to the various disciplines that study the semiotics of communications, we will find some systems of analysis already in place that can teach rhetoricians what to make of rhetoric.

Looking outward, however, is not all that is needed to loosen rhetorical methods and terms from fixed definitions. We have to look at the terms and methods themselves and see that they can be extended to much wider, yet still entirely appropriate, meanings. For example, we usually think of *partitio* as a sentence, perhaps, or a paragraph that generally occurs early and forecasts the stages to come in the discourse of which it is a part. That's well and good and useful, but *partitio* can occur in other, perhaps less conventional, ways. For example, one of my students, Jean Harris, points out in a seminar paper that in Linda Pastan's book of poems, *Five Stages of Grief*, "Whom Do You Visualize as Your Reader?" a single poem of three stanzas in a book of apparently unconnected poems, can appropriately be designated the *partitio* for the entire book because it manages to compress into three stanzas the themes, motifs, subjects, and images of all the other poems in the book. Asyndeton, if we release it from its customary confinement to a sentence or to a group of connected sentences, may help us to understand a characteristic, perhaps dominating style for postmodernist fiction. Anaphora, epistrophe, epanalepsis, and anadiplosis, if we will leave off expecting to find them only in a sentence or a group of connected sentences, can enable us to see that they may also serve as primary structural designs for novels, dramas, and poems. We can learn much more about characters in fiction, drama, and poetry if we know when and why they work in judicial, epideictic, or deliberative rhetoric.

4. To make a new rhetoric, we will have to face the implications of miniaturization and electronic communication and to decide whether new technologies may indeed bring a new kind of literacy and with it a new kind of rhetoric. The copiousness of print, the mélange of visual images mixing with that print, and the overwhelming load of knowledge that waits, stored on disks and tapes, may call for a new sense and new critical capacities. Though we do not have to accept all change, we cannot escape it. We do not know whether traditional rhetoric will serve us. In some instances at least, I rather doubt it will serve if we try to preserve it exactly as we have learned it from the ancients.

For myself, I sometimes tend to resist some kinds of change, though I certainly don't recommend that behavior. Sometimes, to me, word processors are just funny typewriters, and computers are funny adding machines. I refer to our Computer Center as that place in the basement of the science building where things go "pocketa-pocketa-queep."

Yet I do enjoy making coffee and knowing that the coffee pot will keep the coffee hot without my tending to it. I have tried both indoor and outdoor plumbing, and I know that only the innocent would have trouble choosing between them. The secretary upstairs does not have to go through the mind-numbing task of typing sixty identical letters to sixty people; she can tell the word processor to do it, and it will also, if she asks, put the individual name and address at the head of each letter. Some changes are lovely and convenient; some seem strange and unnecessary, even unwanted. I have been talking to my manual typewriter encouraging it to last as long as I do, for though it is an admirable machine, the company that made it is no longer making manual typewriters. I own a book that holds a selection of writings by Samuel Johnson. It is my private book; I carry it, read in it, back up, go forward, and write notes all over the margins. I can't quite do that with a videocassette.

But the videocassette is now small enough to be stored on shelves (much as books are) and to be checked out. This quality can turn the mass medium, television, into a private medium, and that is only one of many strange new miracles I don't believe we know yet whether traditional or even contemporary rhetoric can work in the midst of what some are pleased to call an "information explosion."

We have been close to imagining that the computer alone has brought about this "information explosion," but that of course is not true. Last year some 35,000 to 40,000 books and some (people do get tired of counting, you know) 25,000 periodicals were published, about 1,800 daily newspapers appeared, about 9,000 weekly newspapers were published, about 13,000 films were made, some 800 television stations and about 7,000 radio stations were broadcasting, and that doesn't count the billboards, bumper stickers, and graffiti. Electric typewriters and photocopying machines added great stacks of paper to the whirligig of information and image that zooms in around us all of the time. Even more significant, I think, is the extraordinary change created by high-reduction photography. The last time I looked, it was possible to put 3,200 pages on a single ultramicrofiche film card. When that miniaturizing capacity (with attendant capacities to reproduce full-size screen or print versions) is hooked to networks made possible by the computer, a significant library can be held in small space at reduced cost and almost anyone almost anywhere can easily gain access to almost anything printed.

On the one hand, that is large bounty. On the other hand, it raises two problems that I can see (perhaps others will see more). First, the technological capacities I have mentioned, with others, create a rapid, almost instantaneous increase in the inventive resources open to the scholar and the student. But there does not appear to be a corresponding and simultaneous increase in the structure-making and stylistic abilities of the scholar and the student. This is not a new conception: it is very like the "paralysis of overchoice" that Alvin Toffler discussed in *Future Shock*. The opportunities carry with them, I'd go so far as to say, both the potential for great good and the potential for disorder as overwhelmed inventive capacities try to manifest themselves in single structures and styles.

The second problem arises out of the pace of study. A book by its nature enables, even encourages, a reader to stop, to look back at previous pages, to look forward to pages yet to come.

Electric communication systems, while they ordinarily allow a reader to stop, do not do so by their nature. By their nature they encourage a reader to keep going, to move on, quickly if possible, for there is always more to read and see. The catch is that, so far as I am able to understand matters, any form of critical judgment or evaluation depends entirely on the possibility of a meditative pause. Traditional and modern rhetorical study depends upon the possibility of a meditative pause. We shall have to learn more about rhetoric and electronic communication systems.

5. With the fifth condition, I'll be briefer. Few or none of us have examined what there is in the nature of rhetoric that makes it an extraordinarily fruitful organizing structure for other fields of inquiry, for curricula, and for interdisciplinary study. That, I think, should change. We should not underestimate the centrality of rhetoric, or limit its borders. Rhetoric, I think, is large enough to contain terms and directions of study current now, such as "discourse structure," "rules of/fields of discourse," "code," "convention," and even "semiotic." Rhetoric, I think, can be taken to mean here the whole system by which a world is made, known, and made knowable in language. We live in *a rhetoric,* the "episteme" of our epoch, and in *many rhetorics,* or subsets. Biology is a rhetoric, physics is a rhetoric, painting is a rhetoric, and the list might go on. Each has its own forms of invention, its own structures of meaning, its own stylistic manifestations. Every field has its own schemes and tropes. Some courses in these fields are primarily inventive resources, some are chiefly developments of a structure of meaning, and some are preoccupied with a style of being. Knowing more about that might, for example, help us to learn more both about rhetoric and about the right time and place for particular courses in a program of study. Invention, structure, and style clearly provide a means of bringing courses together in interdisciplinary study. James C. Raymond's "Rhetoric: The Methodology of the Humanities" (*College English* 44 [1982]: 778–83) is particularly provocative in the contexts I am trying to suggest here.

6. The fifth condition, above, suggests the sixth. We have not yet seriously begun to explore rhetoric as a portal to other fields. Rhetoric may not be able to do for other fields what their own

methodologies have not done, but rhetoric can help us see things in other fields in new ways, and when we see in new ways, we may think new thoughts. I'll cite a single quick example of what I mean. Rhetoric, I'm convinced, is useful in describing some forms of schizophrenia.

It takes little imagination for us to see each of us as an interaction where avenues from many rhetorical universes cross. With no trouble at all we can imagine a family rhetoric, a culture rhetoric, a disciplinary rhetoric, and a folk/pop rhetoric, and if we thought a while we would think of many more. Ordinarily we keep some order among the traffic from these various universes. At times, however, under certain kinds of stress or dismay, the traffic crosses, and what belongs in one lane of traffic in one rhetorical universe crosses over (or tries to cross over) into the line of traffic of another world. What rises from the invention of one universe, for example, crosses over and tries to get said in the structure and style of another, and we get the incoherent language, the failed sentences, and the other symptoms of schizophrenia. Whether or not this particular example works very far, we shall have to learn more about rhetoric as a portal to other fields.

Two of my conditions remain, perhaps the most significant.

7. None of us, I think, has taken into account the extraordinary and pervasive shift in our conception of knowledge that has been going on in this century. Some of us haven't noticed it. "What we understand knowledge to be," Kenneth A. Bruffee writes, "what we think it means to know something, and hence what we think it means to learn it and write about it, have changed radically during the first half of this century." Bruffee continues:

> Before the twentieth century, educated members of Western cultures assumed that knowledge was hierarchical, externally determined, and individually attained. Until the late eighteenth century, the supreme point of reference was an Almighty God. Priests of the religious establishments were responsible for discovering and examining what we should know, and then teaching it to us. From the eighteenth century on, the fixed point of reference became almighty mathematics. Scientists were its prophets. The frame of reference against which we determined the authority of knowledge had changed, but the underlying structure of knowl-

edge had not. Knowledge remained determinate, hierarchical, and individualistic. ("The Structure of Knowledge and the Future of Liberal Education," *Liberal Education* 67 [1981]: 178)

Educational systems, by and large, are still based on this conception of knowledge, and most teachers and nearly all students still operate according to this conception, whether knowingly or not.

Owing perhaps in part to the nature of tests they are so often given, students seem, as Ronald Schroeder argues in "Writing, Knowledge, and the Call for Objectivity" (*College English* 40 [1979]: 618–24), to regard knowledge as a "collection of inert, discrete parts," and it's likely that most students regard "objective" tests (multiple choice, fill-in-the-blank, true/false) as the appropriate way of measuring their knowledge. All the "right" answers must be the same; knowledge is "abstract, impersonal, universally acknowledged." Schroeder continues:

> "objective" carries with it all the implications of truth, legitimacy, impersonality, and universality. Something objective can be verified; personal idiosyncrasy and prejudice do not affect (modify or even falsify) its truth. An essay, on the other hand, implies the subjective, and hence something limited in validity, authority, and truth by the peculiarities of its context. (621)

The catch is that, "Once objectively quantified, a thing known becomes precisely that—a 'thing.' It loses the peculiar vitality that it owes to its unique relation with the knower and acquires an independent, consequently separate, existence" (621–22). Then knowledge is a "material quantity, independent of the knower," and most of us want "to avoid the responsibility of giving it a form" (623). All of us part of the time and some of us all of the time "do not seem to recognize the concept of an organic relation between the mind of the knower and the knowledge itself" (622). As a consequence, we do not want to accept responsibility for "creating the form that makes knowledge intelligible and meaningful" (622).

Most of us, Bruffee argues, have not yet begun "to explore the implications of the irreversible revolution in our conception of knowledge accomplished by Einstein, Heisenberg, and Goedel" (179). When Einstein temporalized space and obliterated conventional fixed points of reference, showing that measurement is relative, his "demonstration dealt the first crippling blow to the hierarchical, determinate view of knowledge." The second blow was Heisenberg's uncertainty principle, which stated that "we can never see things as they are when we are not watching them. By virtue of our watching presence, things change their nature." Then, Bruffee says,

> Whereas Einstein cast doubt on our ability to measure things, and Heisenberg cast doubt on our ability even to observe them, Goedel insisted that the results of measured observation (even if we could measure, even if we could observe) cannot be validated within the frame of reference which governs the measuring, or within the symbolic system which expresses it. (180)

There is no frame of reference that is self-guaranteeing. (How will the *topoi* hold up to this, one wonders.) The implication of this indeterminacy of knowledge most important to us is that,

> as Thomas Kuhn argues in *The Structure of Scientific Revolutions*, the very "laws of nature" are "discovered" and remain in force through consensus. Scientific knowledge is what is accepted by an assenting community of scientists. "Natural laws" are established by argument and agreement, just as much as the notoriously vulnerable principles and theories of humanistic studies and the social sciences. They are all consignable ignominiously to the intellectual dustbin whenever the consensus of the assenting community is broken. (181)

Under these conditions, Bruffee says, "knowledge turns out not to be some composite, collective memory-bank of mankind, but the combination of two mental functions: creative insight and what we have traditionally called 'judgment'" (181). The distinction that W. Ross Winterowd makes in "Black Holes, Indeterminacy, and Paolo Freire" (*Rhetoric Review* 2 [1983]) between "problem-solving education" (which assumes indeterminacy) and "banking-education" (which assumes determinacy) underscores the shift in our conception of knowledge. We should be learning that all forms of study are forms of rhetoric:

> Whereas at one time all fields aspired to the certainty of science, all fields of knowledge including the sciences now appear to be driven by the demonstrated indeterminacy of all knowledge to cultivate the expertise maintained by that *least* determinate of all fields of knowledge, the humanities. Even science in its uncertainty today has reason to learn the rules of what Kuhn calls the "discursive" fields, fields in which knowledge is clearly language-based and language-bound, fields in which means may readily be found for dealing with knowledge as a social phenomenon. (Bruffee 181)

It looks as if the world were waiting for rhetoric. We will have to learn more about such things and determine what rhetorics will serve us, let us speak both knowledge and ourselves into being.

8. I have come to the last condition. We may not have the nerve to consider it. Classical rhetoric with its modern manifestations and modifications has served and still serves well. We did not, however, persuade ourselves to study war no more; we did not learn how to say love and generosity to others so that they might be realized. We may not get a new rhetoric until there is a new kind of creature. Some risk waits, and we may find that undesirable or unthinkable. We go on.

Such are the conditions I am able to see that are necessary to the generation of new rhetoric. Perhaps traditional rhetoric is adequate to our present condition and rhetoricians are already prepared. Perhaps a new rhetoric waits. We need to know.

Hunting for Ethos *Where They Say It Can't Be Found*

A n ancient tool holds down a stack of papers on the table in the corner of my office. A rock implement, it is vaguely like the head of a sledgehammer. It is generally cylindrical, about ten inches long, about three inches in diameter at its middle, and comes to a rough, striated point at one end. The other end has a half-circle indentation that cuts through most of the three-inch thickness. The shape suggests two possible uses. The indentation at one end creates a reasonably comfortable handhold, and the striations at the other end further suggest that it might have been a grinding tool. My three children, each in turn, decided on the other possible use: Each in turn took the thing to show-and-tell at school, lashed with a leather thong to a stout stick, which fit neatly into the indentation. It made a formidable club.

That was the history of its reality, created, determined by the narrative we told of it.

Then recently a colleague from the Geology Department saw it, said No, it's not a tool, just a funny-shaped rock, wedged for eons against a smaller, harder round rock that eventually wore the indentation. The alternative view enables the viewer to see things differently, denies instrumentality, and deconstructs my rock. The alternative words stop my words, and the reality of the rock changes. The geologist's history appropriates my history. History is appropriation.

Since, I've been quarreling with myself, sometimes petulantly, sometimes foolishly, often only trying to serve my own interests. The twists and turns of the quarrel have sometimes startled me.

First published in *Rhetoric Review* 7 (1989): 299–316.

Some years ago, I wrote what I like to think of as a nice, mostly naive, and frequently uninformed paper titled "Varieties of Ethical Argument, with Some Account of the Significance of *Ethos* in the Teaching of Composition" (*Freshman English News,* Winter 1978). I wanted to imagine that I was, among other things, writing another gloss on Aristotle, trying to learn what he meant in what he said about *ethos* and ethical argument. I quote myself:

> Conventional discussions of ethical argument focus on its demand for the speaker to demonstrate his or her good sense, good character, and benevolent disposition. Yet the moment we tell a potential speaker that he or she must be certain to demonstrate good sense, good character, and easy disposition, we are, as I have already suggested, close to advising artifice, the exercise of calculated design upon an audience. We have already more than we need of created images and designed credibility. It is, perhaps, more important for us to ask just how character is revealed in language, or just what qualities of character in particular reveal good sense, good character, and good will and so elicit accord, or just how are we to discriminate among ethical appeals. But since ethical argument appears to be contingent upon a presence emerging in discourse, the real voice of a genuine personality, it may be that the mode cannot be defined or described for general purposes and that we must content ourselves with observation of its particular manifestations.
>
> Certainly a host of problems stands in the way of learning about ethical argument, whether we wish to describe the mode generically or seek only to describe the operation of *ethos* in a single discourse. One presiding problem is that all discourse is ethical, revealing speakers' characters by design or by default. Style is the revelation of identity, the syndrome of character, open to diagnosis. If all discourse is ethical, then talking about ethical discourse means talking about the whole range of human discourse. One who sets out to talk about emotional argument, for example, can probably exclude a number of discourses that are not emotional in mode and thereby focus attention on the residue. But if one sets out to talk about ethical argument, nothing can be excluded. And that generates another problem: if all discourse is ethical, how shall we distinguish among discourses, or mark the fruitful and the perverse?

I went on then in opposition to some earlier discussions of *ethos* that seemed to me unnecessarily monistic. I assumed that *ethos* does not always work in the same way and proposed five rough and overlapping kinds—dramatic *ethos*, gratifying *ethos*, functional *ethos*, efficient *ethos*, and generative *ethos*.

I wanted to believe, you see, that *ethos* was real and in *the text*, that it was there and I could find it. Since, I've quarreled more with myself, sometimes petulantly, sometimes foolishly, often selfishly, and the quarrel, especially in recent weeks, has sometimes startled me.

Long before I wrote that piece, others had been looking with different eyes, and more have done so since. They have, accordingly, seen things differently, as the geologist saw in my tool only a rock. Diverse others—those who have taught us about interpretive communities, about the social construction of discourse, about reader response theory, about intertextuality, for example— have told me in diverse ways that *ethos* is *not in the text*, but in the reader or community, in their construction of or projection upon the text. They have told me, further, that the writer is not autonomous, but is only part of a social community that constructs and interprets discourse, that the notion of the self as a source of meaning is only a Romantic concept (which would probably surprise Alexander Pope), that the language by which we view and construct the world comes from society, not from the individual.

And finally I began to understand, too, with a kind of continuing uneasy shiver somewhere down my back, that before I wrote that piece and since, especially since, I have undercut my own views. First, excepting some—maybe Loren Eiseley, Pope at his wickedest, John Graves, Samuel Johnson, a handful more—*I* deny the other in his or her text. I am too stubborn or too unthinking or too self-centered to accept or to yield to the other; I won't willingly efface myself before the other, though I may do so quite without knowing it. Second, my reasons for asserting the presence of *ethos in the text* are suspect: I assert myself, or try to. I want *ethos* to be real and in the text so that I *can be real to others, not so that they can be real to me.*

Ethos, I've come to learn, is at the very least problematic. I can't have *ethos* in the text, it seems clear, not on my own previous terms.

And the consequence is that I am frightened. As Joan Rivers might say, Can we talk? If *ethos* is not in the text, if the author is not autonomous, I'm afraid that I've lost my chance not just for survival hereafter (that happened some time ago), but also for identity now. Poststructuralist thought announces the death of the author: Language writes us, rather than the other way around, and interpretation prevails rather than authorship. We have been, whether knowingly or not, whether directly or not, part of a 2,500-year-old tradition that allowed and encouraged us to believe that *ethos* is in the text, that authors do exist, that they can be in their words and own them even in the act of giving them away. Now literary theorists both compelling and influential tell us that it is not so, that *ethos* exists if at all only in the perceiving minds of readers, that authors, if they exist, do so somewhere else, not in their words, which have already been interpreted by their new owners. Language is orphaned from its speaker; what we once thought was happening has been disrupted. Authors, first distanced, now fade away into nothing. Not even ghosts, they are projections cast by readers. "They" out there want, that is to say, to take my own voice away from me and give such meaning as there might be over entirely to whoever might show up as an interpreter. "They" want me to die into oblivion if I should manage to write something, never to be reborn in a voice for some reader, but to vanish before that reader's construction of the small thing I leave as a text waiting to become a text.

Can I get a witness?

Will anyone notice that I am here, that this is the way I talk, that this is what in my mind passes for thinking? I'm trying to get real.

Life is real, and the artificial compartments we create for it don't work. What gets said in one place keeps slopping over and meaning something in other places. What gets said in literary theory resonates in all other places, so I'm no longer talking just about literary theory, if I ever was; I'm talking about my own identity now, the nuttiness that is mine.

Much of what I have begun to learn, or believe I have begun to learn, from reader-response theorists, from interpretive community/social construction theorists, is only for the good, and it was high time. Of course language issues from, belongs to, creates community. Of course a human/reader has primacy over an object/text. If we *must* valorize one above the other, let it be the

interpreter, and let's leave off making idols of authors and en-
shrining them in canonical curricula that never worked very well.
What literature gives us is the other, earlier representations, not
renditions of the one reality told by "the great books" that transcend ideology.

But neither do literary theorists transcend ideology. They issue from, belong to, create ideology even where the ideology is
not systematically articulated, perhaps especially where it is not.
What I see at work near the ideological center of the new work I
have referred to—scary to me, even while I think I begin to understand the good that eventuates from it—is a powerful reductive and tribalizing force. This force, to me, gives hope and takes
it away, brings gloom, loss, and, at least to me, terror.

Gives hope and authenticity, that is, to the reader, but denies
hope and authenticity to the reader if he or she wishes to be the
writer. A human/reader has primacy over an object/text, but does
not have primacy over a human/author. They might be equal
before and with each other. Isn't that what we have hoped for?
Can't we try for that? The human/reader will always interpret,
but the human/author has always been there first, has left tracks.

To locate, to try to learn a text, is to go out toward the other.
To interpret is to pull the text in toward the self. Each action
tribalizes, requires one to accept the other's terms. That may be
inevitable, and may not be bad—it's one of the ways we civilize
ourselves—but it does alter, may extend, and might reduce
someone's identity. No text is worth more than a human interpreter; texts serve humans, not the other way around. Still, humans can be pissants, less than perfect, and might take time to
learn texts, to learn others, to go toward others, to receive from
others.

However, in some recent commentary, all solitary humans
(both writers and readers) disappear, fading into the tribe, relin-
quishing authority and autonomy to the tribe. Fish's assertion
that "selves are constituted by the ways of thinking and seeing
that inhere in social organizations" (336) demands ultimately
that we surrender some of our reasons for reading, writing, and
existing, not least the hope that each private life can become real
both for itself and for others.

Social constructionist thought is engaging, sometimes exhilarating and provocative; it challenges the habits that we call thoughts and recognizes that we are all rhetorical creations. It's late in the day, too, to deny what social constructionism asserts, that, as Bruffee articulates it, in any discipline the entities "we normally call reality, knowledge, thought, facts, texts, selves, and so on are constructs generated by communities of like-minded peers" (774), that "the matrix of thought is not the individual self but some community of knowledgeable peers and the vernacular language of that community" (777). It's also late to deny the importance of intertextuality. The prevailing composition pedagogies, James E. Porter says,

> . . . by and large cultivate the romantic image [Pope turns uneasily in his grave again] of the writer as free, uninhibited spirit, as independent, creative genius. By identifying and stressing the intertextual nature of discourse, however, we shift our attention away from the writer as individual and focus more on the sources and social contexts from which the writer's discourse arises. (34–35)

"The traditional notion of the text as the single work of a given author," Porter continues, "and even the very notions of author and reader, are regarded as simply convenient fictions for domesticating discourse" (35). The idea of Jefferson as author of the Declaration of Independence, for example, is "but convenient shorthand." In intertextual criticism, the idea of the "lone inspired writer" and the "sacred autonomous text" both "take a pretty hard knock" (40). In Porter's account,

> Our immediate goal is to produce "socialized writers," who are full-fledged members of their discourse community, producing competent, useful discourse within that community. Our long-range goal might be "post-socialized writers," those who have achieved such a degree of confidence, authority, power, or achievement in the discourse community so as to become part of the regulating body. They are able to vary conventions and question assumptions—i.e., effect change in communities without fear of exclusion. (42)

And yet. And yet. Exciting and accurate as such insights may be, there is a dark underside. (I think it's Barbara Tuchman who suggests somewhere that there's always a dark underside to our happiest moments, so that the gods won't be jealous of us.) Down there, the solitary human has little place and small function. Interpretive community theory, social construction theory, intertextual theory, and reader-response theory give place and function to the tribe.

But we're always trying to be free of the tribe. Diverse figures—not all of them victims of "the romantic image of the writer as free, uninhibited spirit"—have taught us to leave off for the first time the radical notion that God is not a tribal deity. Wordsworth and Pope, in their different ways, celebrated the solitary above the tribal, and we surely cannot believe that it is either only the tribe or only some Romantic conviction speaking when Pope remarks,

> Yes, I am proud; I must be proud to see
> Men not afraid of God, afraid of me.

And we're always also becoming tribal, to good effect and to bad. We can rejoice, as he does, to join the tribe with Johnson as he concludes his life of Thomas Gray:

> In the character of his Elegy I rejoice to concur with the common reader; for by the common sense of readers uncorrupted with literary prejudices, after all the refinements of subtlety and the dogmatism of learning, must be finally decided all claim to poetical honours. The *Churchyard* abounds with images which find a mirror in every mind, and with sentiments to which every bosom returns an echo. The four stanzas beginning "Yet even these bones" are to me original: I have never seen the notions in any other place; yet he that reads them here, persuades himself that he has always felt them. Had Gray written often thus, it had been vain to blame, and useless to praise him.

We can rejoice that we belong to tribes that circle and entwine out beyond us, and we can regret that we do, or curse ourselves for belonging. Membership in the tribe enables; we are extended, our capacities enlarged. Tribal membership also disables us, as I'll try to explain, going the long way around and using what I like to imagine I know well, university tribal structure, as my sample.

Each of us is the center of some small geography, if only because we see with our own eyes and hear with our own ears. If north is *up* and south is *down* and east is *over* and west is *out*, then the center of the landscape is someone's belly button. If we give allegiance to some group—as we always do—the group extends the realm we live in and provides us a way of knowing, seeing, and taking experience and becomes the proprietor of virtue and right judgment.

And it is right and proper that this should happen. When we are in an academic discipline, it is usually because some bonding has been made by curiosity, excitement, or love. Each of us, I hope, thinks his or her discipline is valuable. Indeed, we're likely to reckon that the discipline we've tried to make ours is potentially valuable to everyone. If we can only get the world to see the beauty, the intellectual grace, the capacities for insight in our discipline, then all will understand and accept our path, if not as their own, then as one of the central routes to wisdom. Appropriately enough, we seek the extension of our discipline and its ratification by others. All, so far, is well and good.

But then, lurking just on the other side of our fitting love and belief, we discover quite another set of qualities. We take our piece of truth—that is to say, our discipline—and treat it as if it were all of the truth, and we take ourselves as the measurers of mankind. We cling to our discipline, which is characteristically accidental in origin and imperfect in design, as if we were clinging to the sacred. Then others—those outside our discipline—can only be versions of the imperfect, and they may be evil. At best, those outsiders are flawed and disadvantaged. Worse, they may be insidious subverters of the truth. Worse still, they may be barbarians at the gate. Worst of all, they may be, in our judgment, beneath notice. They don't register; they make no claim on us at all. When such things happen, clearly we have forgotten that our discipline is a mode of study, a perspective; it has become the whole, the only truth.

Then we have become tribes, separate, uncommunicative, wary, distrustful, sometimes warlike, each tribe celebrating only its own tribal virtues, addressing only its own tribal gods, and hearing (or imagining that we hear) only the truth revealed by those deities. To a tribe member, only the tribe will hold or permit thought and house virtue.

I'll say again that such behavior is not categorically wrong, mischievous, or pernicious, as I may have suggested it is. We are right to believe in the validity of a discipline and the insights it affords. I do, however, mean to suggest that *tribal* virtues are not always *public* virtues or, ironically, even *private* virtues. When, for example, tribal virtue fails to reckon with other ways of seeing, then it repudiates the lush multeity of creation, thus violating public virtue, and represses the individual's own capacities for observation, thus violating private virtues.

The value of a single-minded zeal in disciplinary study cannot be denied and should not be minimized. Tribal virtues have generated intense work, remarkable discoveries, uncommon insight. It may be, indeed, that all intellectual achievements are in some way the enactments of tribal virtues. They do, however, have an underside, as I have already suggested.

On the underside of their greatness, the singlemindedness of tribal virtues generates some vexatious problems, probably more than I know, certainly more than I wish to name.

If one holds to tribal virtues, there is a close restriction on the meaning of communication. If a tribe speaks to those outside, or if an agent of the tribe speaks for the tribe to those outside, a customary assumption is that if those outside do not accept the message and assent to it, then there has been no communication. In that case, then it follows that those outside are ignorant, indifferent, or hostile, and that the tribal speaker is a failure at speaking. Thus, if a chairman speaks for a department or if a dean speaks for a college, and if the central administration fails to assent or to provide what was requested, then the central administration is an enemy and the chairman or dean may be a pariah in his or her own tribe. If the tribal virtue or magic doesn't work, there can't be anything wrong with the tribal virtue or magic—wrong occurs either in the deliverer of the tribal message or in the now hostile and unwilling audience for the message. The tribe owns magic; thus its will should prevail. Tribal assertiveness will win if the tribe and its speakers are sure in the righteousness of tribal virtue. If a chairman will only be assertive to the dean, and if the dean will only be assertive to the vice-president, then right will out, tribal virtues will prevail, and the department and the college will get the money and positions and other advantages they wanted.

A remarkable and ignominious insularity lies along the underside of tribal virtues. When this insularity manifests itself, it ruptures community of action and spirit, denies the existence of any community of scholars, and repudiates the tribe member's own understanding. They (we) know—when tribal vanity doesn't get in the way—that one legitimate response to even the most efficacious communication is "No," that participation can mean submission to others, that assertiveness cannot always win and never wins in what some are pleased to call a "no win" situation.

Yet each tribe speaks as if theirs were the only voice raised in need or demand, all others being quiet or, if raised, obviously for inferior purposes. Each tribe speaks, at times, as if virtue were invested solely in the tribe. Tribal membership disables us.

We won't avoid the tribal altogether, and shouldn't. Knowledge is a social construct, and it isn't. Speaking and writing and identity belong to interpretive communities, to social constructions, and to intertextuality, and they don't. There's always Kilroy and Huck and Dean Swift and the Wicked Wasp and Boo Radley.

Three simple-minded questions keep coming to mind: Are those who write theory sheltered from other kinds of writing? Do they inevitably think of themselves as theorists, not as writers? Does anyone remember who found the words? I have no satisfactory answers, of course, and sometimes must move through my own petulance toward suggestions. If what follows seems self-centered and self-congratulatory, I'll hope for a second reading. I think of it not as congratulations bestowed upon myself, but as the sometimes shameful confession of a misspent life. Besides, the self is the only center I have, and I think I must use the best evidence available to me, my own experience, however I manage to misinterpret it.

My first question, then: *Are those who write theory sheltered from other kinds of writing?* My impression, for reasons I will come to in a moment, is that they must be, but of course I cannot know, and I cannot know whether or not they mostly do not wish to do other kinds of writing or whether or not they are in positions that do not require them to do so. If not published novelists, are they closet poets? Do they sometimes write personal, meditative, exploratory essays that the *New Yorker* ought to publish but won't? On down: do they write letters, annual reports, committee reports, studies for the faculty senate, budget justifications, tenure and promotion recommendations? It gets worse. Do they teach freshman composition, at least, and regularly see, if not do, the writing that's done there? My impression is that they don't, not much, which brings me to my second question.

Do those who write theory inevitably think of themselves as theorists, not as writers? I have, you see, already begun to assume that theorists do not do much other writing. I believe that they conceive of themselves as theorists, perhaps as critics, perhaps as philosophers, but not as writers. Were they to think of themselves as writers, I believe that they could not think (or bear) the judgment that their own theories bring against writers, the judgment that the writer is not the writer (as in social constructionism and intertextualism), that the writer is not in the text (as in reader-response theory, social constructionism, and intertextualism).

I am not a writer by any definition that the world would legitimate. I am not known as a writer. Nevertheless, I must confess that I sometimes think of myself as a writer. It's a comforting thing to do on a cold night when wine isn't sufficient. I can safely admit that I have published a few poems and personal essays because I am confident that the journals in which they appeared are so lost to the nation at large as to make my work perfectly secure from public scrutiny. I've misspent ten years as a department chairman, five years as a dean, two years as an associate-vice-chancellor-of-whatever-the-hell-came-up, and have now fallen into grace again in the English Department. During those years, I wrote those reports and institutional documents that I mentioned a while ago, more than I want to recollect, together with planning papers, columns for the student newspaper and student magazine, and trifling essays for the alumni magazine. I even, for God's sake, wrote a little secular liturgy for the ceremony in which our current chancellor was installed (perhaps it was a small masque, or a large lie). Perhaps it becomes clearer why I sometimes privately think of myself as a writer—it's a helluva lot better than thinking of yourself as a dean, or court scribe, or fool.

When, however privately, you commence to think of yourself as a writer, then I think that you sometimes want to get a little something into the text. Most of us are mostly unfinished and quite dull; we always need to get real. In all those reports and other documents, no matter how institutional they were expected to be, I wanted to be real, to be apparent to others. I didn't want to be institutional and anonymous, though no doubt I often was.

I want to try to illustrate more specifically what I mean by telling of three particular instances.

In almost every semester of my life since graduate school, I've taught at least one freshman composition class. Along in the mid-1970s sometime, I began writing the essays I assigned my freshman students. That practice has afforded me a sometimes interesting, sometimes sorry series of experiences, but I want to focus on just one consequence. When I have written the essays, I make copies for each student and turn them over when they turn in their work. That has made me a much more reluctant grader of papers, largely, I think, because I know how I feel when I give them my little essays. I don't want them to grade me or my essays. I want them to notice me, to hear me, to pay attention to what I'm saying, to notice how clever I've been in the third paragraph. I want to be known in what I've written; I want to be noticed. Since it's possible that they may feel a little the same way, I become more and more reluctant to edit their papers and to grade them.

But things get worse. I come to a second instance. For some fifteen years, I wrote the citations that are printed prettily and read aloud at a party for faculty members who are retiring. I don't wish to think about why I've done this, or about how much time it has taken. I've done it, and that's all, and the hell with it. These citations are clearly forms of community discourse, never meant otherwise. They must not be more than about 250 words long, and all citations must be about the same length, regardless of whether the person and career being cited are distinguished or unnoticeable. But notice: They are institutional documents; they are community documents; they are all about the same length—but they ought not *sound* institutional, communal, or similar. For the sake of the soul who's retiring, each citation ought to have character and quirk enough to fit the person it is supposed to celebrate. Certainly I didn't always succeed. Certainly that doesn't mean the document should reek of my character and quirks; it does mean that the document ought to have character and quirk enough contained in the document.

It gets worse with my third instance. Near the front of the catalog for the university where I teach there is a statement of the university's philosophy, mission, and goals. God help me—I wrote the last six or eight drafts of that statement, including the final draft that is printed in the catalog. I have not acknowledged this before. I take no pride in doing it. I am embarrassed that I did it and spent such time on the project. Once again, this was clearly a version of community discourse. I worked from earlier versions drafted by various groups. The deans of the colleges in the university wrote one version. The faculty senate, through a committee, wrote another version. Some of the vice chancellors had a go at it. The chancellor made a speech addressing the matter. A committee from the board of trustees made written suggestions. I think Aunt Maudie and Cousin Duane also submitted draft versions. With all these drafts in hand, I set out to write a version that would fit the chancellor's stipulation that the statement should be of such length that it would fit on two facing pages in the catalog. The result ain't much. But notice: I invested considerable time in the project. I didn't want it to sound too much like more institutional pap. I really didn't much want it to sound as if it had been written by a clerk or a plain damn fool, or, worse, an administrator. I didn't succeed, but I tried, and what I tried most was not to infect the statement with my character, but with character in the document.

And that brings me to my third question: *Does anyone remember who found the words?* Before and after the interpretive community has done its work, before and after we have socially constructed, before and after we have intertextualized, before and after readers have responded, someone has found the words. Perhaps the writer cannot exist, does not exist, save as found in the reader's response, in the intertextual gathering, in the social/

interpretive community's formulation. Okay. Good enough. Might we still reckon, however, despite all, that there are still ghosts, if not authors, out there somewhere, flitting around, hanging one phrase with another, catching words for a moment? Might we still reckon that out there somewhere there are word-finders?

Probably not. The consequence of some recent theories is clear: *ethos* is chiefly our creation as we read, not the author's creation, and not in the text.

Still, approach it how we will, we rely upon the ghostly signals put first by the text.

Signals and impulses are wonderfully mixed. We can know our reading of a text, perhaps, but not the text. Yet we would not think to doubt our ability to know other people. We are often mistaken, of course, and sometimes are startled to discover that those other people exist and change while we're not looking. But we mostly suppose that we know them because we experience the curious narratives *they* tell or show of their lives.

We learn texts—often as not, *our* way and mistakenly—by the tales they tell. It's not the tribe speaking first or only, not the reader creating first or only, but the word-finder giving us a narrative.

And yet, Barthes argues, "the birth of the reader must be at the cost of the death of the author" (148).

Against such conviction, various means of saving the text, if not the author, have of course been proposed. Marshall W. Alcorn, Jr., acknowledges the impact of recent theory:

> One consequence of post-structuralist theory seems to be that it is no longer possible to assume the presence of an "objective" text. The text cannot be objective because, if it is considered as the encoding of an author's message, the text cannot remain tied to the integrity of its originating or controlling purpose. It loses its message as it is violated by reading strategies. If we dismiss the importance of the author and think of the text as an autonomous linguistic artifact, the text still cannot exist as an objective entity, for it cannot control and deliver univocal meaning. As a verbally "autonomous" entity, the text cannot be "autonomous"; it is always on the point of dissolving. It is unable to enclose the boundaries of its subject, unable to limit the pluralities of its signification . . . . The text *becomes* differentially present and "objective" through any one of the many interpretive methods of

responding critics. The text "in itself" possesses "objectivity" only as black ink stains upon paper. (137)

Alcorn goes on, then, to propose that the signifiers in a text do own their own authority:

> The perception of textual content ("noise") that is "at war" with the text's more obvious rhetorical intent is important for any theory of rhetoric. . . . The presence of "noise" in text implies two things. First, the notion of a dependably encoded authorial intention disappears. But second, this unstable text offers, through the medium of "noise," clear, convincing, and verifiable—one might say "objective"—evidence of its inner coherence. (138)

"Certainly it is true," Alcorn continues, "that poststructuralist theory dominates and subjugates one kind of 'other'—the author's apparent intention. But another 'other,' the signifier itself, is not dominated or subjugated by the new methodology" (139). A reader's projective activities, Alcorn says, "are filtered and altered by a certain notion of textual objectivity: objectivity as defined by the text's material signifiers" (139).

I think that means that authors, whatever their intentions, leave trails for us. [. . .]

Ethos as we once thought we knew it is lost, and not. We're all word-finders. We make *ethos* from the words we find, but some word-finder is leaving us words to find, telling an *ethos* toward us, altering ours in the process. Even in our conventional studies we have seldom kept *ethos* well located, mixing terms, sometimes using *ethos, persona,* and *voice* as if identical, and perhaps they are in the minds of some. The confusion, if it is that, does, however, reveal an interesting anomaly and may provide unexpected testimony that *ethos* may yet get into a text. We don't have too much trouble acknowledging that a persona can exist in a text. We readily distinguish the speaker in "A Modest Proposal" from Jonathan Swift. The speaker is somebody else, life-sized, historied, real enough to use language in his own way. One might have thought that if persona can exist in a text, then perhaps *ethos* can, too.

No matter. *Ethos* as we once thought we knew it is lost, and not. We're all word-finders. We make *ethos* from the words we find, and some word-finder is always leaving words for us to find, telling an *ethos* toward us, crowding living time into composing time into our reading time, trying to become somebody in the midst of a crowd, trying to get caught in language in front of others.

In Saul Bellow's novel *The Dean's December,* the central character is reflecting about being shut in when he hears a dog bark: "A dog barked, whined as if a beater had given him a whack, then barked again. The barking of a dog, a protest against the limits of dog experience—for God's sake, open the universe a little more!" (11). I knew a dog like that once, and I'm like that, barking or whining to get the limits of my experience shoved back toward others, to get the world opened up a little more.

Mostly, I'm afraid that we settle for a world that has pretty close dimensions, in fact, dimensions that match our own. Often as not, I'd guess, we listen to another person only if that person has the decency to say what we already want to hear, or at least has the grace not to disturb or confuse us, so that we can stay in our own world with at least some modest comfort.

I want to believe, however, that speakers and writers can take us into worlds we hadn't imagined, worlds that have dimensions quite unlike our own. I want to believe that speakers and writers can startle us into new thought, not depending solely on the gratification or fulfillment of what we are already thinking. Perhaps I am groping for something that won't happen very often. Perhaps I am groping because I want to learn how this miracle is done, so that when I speak, others will listen, and not just because I'm responding to a need or a thought they already have. Perhaps I want to make a miracle, though surely I won't.

Certainly the evidence seems frequently to show that we speak out of our own narrow dimensions, not all that often waking to others, to new thought. There's nothing all that terrible in this: that's how we come to know each other, by learning the revealed close dimensions that a speaker or writer shows us. That's not wrong. It's human and delightful—unless a speaker or writer has designs on us, has ulterior purposes for confining us to some small set of dimensions, wants us to narrow ourselves to accept some dogma, or accept some ignorance, or to yield to some arrogance, or to buy some product.

Advertisements, I think, want us to accept the dimensions they set, and by accepting the dimensions, to accept the implicit values, and by accepting the implicit values, to buy the displayed product. Politicians have sometimes wanted us to accept their dogma, to take their arrogance or ignorance as our view of the world.

But speech and writing that comes out of narrow dimensions isn't inherently bad. It's how we know each other. The Duke's world, in Browning's "My Last Duchess," has no room in it for anyone else's will or interests. The next duchess, for her health's sake, must fit the dimensions he sets out. Ulysses, in Tennyson's poem, wants a large world, we judge, but not a world large enough to include the people he has ruled. He wants that other world, from which they are excluded. The speaker in Houseman's poem that begins "Into my heart an air that kills" is not going to show us all of the world. He is only going to tell as much truth as he can without crying. Closed, narrow speech is often what identifies us to each other. Most of the people we have listened to in our lives are people who please us as we already are because they fill some need we already have, not because they show us new worlds with startling dimensions.

Still, I want to hope that once in a while a speaker or writer can show us something new, insight that wasn't already in our world, dimensions we hadn't guessed at, and I guess I want to believe that we ourselves can sometimes achieve that, too. It won't be frequent, but it might be delightful, might even be revelatory. If it happens, perhaps it will occur when some speaker or writer manages to create a commodious discourse, more filled with possibilities than we had suspected, large enough for us to enter and to live freely. I certainly can't describe how this would happen for another. I probably can't suggest how it might happen for me.

I do know that our deeds of hearing, reading, and interpreting commence with the tool or rock that lies on the table in the corner.

Things are simpler for me, I think, than for others. They write as if what they say about one of life's places doesn't resonate in all of life's places, as if what they say about our response to writing has no bearing upon our response to other matters. I am simple-minded: My life is not in compartments. If they tell me that I cannot find the speaker or author in a poem or essay, then they tell me that I cannot hear Mozart's music, only mine as I interpret, and I *know* that is not so. In the third violin concerto—however mistakenly I may take it—I hear and experience what I could not have guessed or dreamed, what is stunningly otherwise. I create the world that I inhabit, to be sure, but I create it out of the rocks and tools that folks have left lying on the table in the corner.

But wait. I usually mistake them, the artifacts other people leave, and mistake myself, and so must wait, wait and see, wait just a damned minute: most things aren't ever over; few things are easily real, easily what we say they are; fewer things come to nothing. Wait.

I said in the beginning that this is an account of a quarrel I have with myself. The quarrel doesn't end. Just as I was about to stop, something else startled me, and it was already inside my own head.

I have wanted to believe that *ethos is* in the text, have wanted to believe that I could find others in their texts so that I might hope to exist for others in my text so that I might turn myself over to them and thereby survive in the text I leave. And surely someone might learn a little about me from what I write. The items and activities discussed are moderately revealing. Style and identity are symptoms of each other. I'm in here. Shall I provide documentation? Are telephone numbers needed? Letters of reference? Will the testimony of wife, librarian, and bartender suffice? [. . .].

Works Cited

Alcorn, Marshall W., Jr., "Rhetoric, Projection, and the Authority of the Signifier." *College English* 49 (Feb. 1987): 137–57.

Barthes, Roland. *Image, Music, Text*. New York: Hill, 1977.

Bellow, Saul. *The Dean's December*. New York: Pocket Books, 1982.

Bruffee, Kenneth A. "Social Construction, Language, and the Authority of Knowledge: A Bibliographical Essay." *College English* 48 (Dec. 1986): 773–90.

Fish, Stanley. *Is There a Text in This Class?* Cambridge, MA: Harvard UP, 1980.

Hairston, Maxine. "When Writing Teachers Don't Write: Speculations about Probable Causes and Possible Cures." *Rhetoric Review* 5 (Fall 1986): 62–70.

Porter, James E. "Intertextuality and the Discourse Community." *Rhetoric Review* 5 (Fall 1986): 34–47.

CHAPTER TEN

Hunting Lieutenant Chadbourne: A Search for Ethos Whether Real or Pretended

I first encountered his name on a roadside historical marker about halfway between Abilene and San Angelo, Texas. The marker said that Fort Chadbourne, founded in 1852 nearby, had been named for Second Lieutenant Theodore Lincoln Chadbourne, killed on May 9, 1846, in the Battle of Resaca de la Palma at the opening of the Mexican War. A little later, in San Angelo, I visited the museum at Fort Concho. In a display case there were his sword and sword belt and what I took to be his tunic, together with a photograph of his family home in Eastport, Maine. I learned, too, that he was graduated from West Point in 1843 and that he was twenty-three when he was killed.

In the weeks that followed, I wrote a short essay about him. It was subsequently published in a book of essays called *Lost in West Texas*. As it turns out, the essay was wrong in several important ways. I had assumed that the historical marker was all that indicated the site of Fort Chadbourne; truth is, rather extensive ruins survive some two miles away. On the advice of friends, I had assumed that it would take four to six weeks for word of his death to reach his family in Maine, but eastern newspapers reported the battle in considerable detail in just seventeen days— the first telegraph lines were in place part of the way. I thought I had seen his tunic, but it was only blue cloth over a headless bust that held his sword belt. I had assumed that the neat hole in the strap that went from his belt up over the shoulder was caused by

First published in *Ethos: New Essays in Rhetorical and Critical Theory*, ed. James S. Baumlin and Tita French Baumlin. Dallas: Southern Methodist UP, 1994. 343–65.

the bullet that killed him. It may indeed be a bullet hole, but that bullet was probably not the sole cause of his death. But I didn't learn about my errors until later.

Meanwhile, I think it was just curiosity that kept me thinking: Why, I found myself wondering, were his belongings in the museum at Fort Concho in San Angelo, Texas? His home was in Maine. He had been killed three or four miles from the Rio Grande. The fort named for him was some forty miles away. Eventually, after several telephone calls, I reached Katharine Waring and, later, visited with her. She told me how, years before, Susan Miles, then an officer in the county historical association, had become interested in the young lieutenant and had set out to learn what she could about him. She told me that the association still had Susan Miles's correspondence with libraries, archival collections, and surviving members of the Chadbourne family. On our second visit, she asked if I would like to see the files. By this time, I was a little eager and said Yes. She brought out two boxes, each the size that would hold a ream of paper. Near the top of the first was a copy of a paper about Lieutenant Chadbourne that Susan Miles had published in the *West Texas Historical Association Yearbook*. At the bottom of the second box was a packet of papers separated from the rest. They were letters that Lieutenant Chadbourne had written.

By now, I couldn't let go. I wanted to know about young Lieutenant Chadbourne. And besides, I had by this time begun to learn about my own errors in the essay I had already published. I wanted to set them right, if I could. I wanted him not to be lost, but twenty-three years doesn't give a fellow much time to get into history books. Because of other projects, I was already tuned to think about how memory works, how knowledge gets into our heads, how some knowledge doesn't get into our heads. But I really don't know all that was pushing at me to learn about him.

Ms. Waring allowed me to photocopy the letters. I brought the copies home, but I didn't read them. I wanted to save them. I wanted whatever I wrote to correspond to stages of learning in my own mind. I didn't want the thing to be finished before it was begun. If, when I read the letters, I learned that I had been wrong here and there, I would correct myself. If the letters turned out to be trivial, they mattered because they existed, and the life mattered because it was. History is not out there; it's in here, where I am. I wanted to save the letters for last because I wanted to believe that he was in them, that he was there.

Almost from the start, of course, I knew that I might never find him. For a good while, I carried in my pocket a crumpled piece of paper. The following note was on it, with the name Lt. Col. W. G. Belknap: "In the battle of the 9th, the 8th regiment lost, in Lieutenant Chadbourne, a promising young officer, who fell in the manful discharge of duty." Nothing else appeared on the page. I didn't record the source. I don't know why I didn't. I expected to find it again, I think. Colonel Belknap commanded the Eighth Infantry Regiment in the Battle of Resaca de la Palma on May 9, 1846. I was pretty sure that the passage appeared in his report following the battle to his commanding officer, General Zachary Taylor, and I was pretty sure that General Taylor incorporated Colonel Belknap's report into his own report to Washington. I thought I'd find it again.

But I may not find Lieutenant Chadbourne. He was still twenty-three when he died that day. Twenty-three years doesn't give a fellow much time to compile records or to write diaries or to get into history books.

But I have been looking. I corrected the errors I made initially and set out on his trail, though I have often been diverted.

For example, as I was just beginning to learn a little, I consulted the *Register of Graduates and Former Cadets of the United States Military Academy.* Thirty-nine young men were graduated in the class of 1843 with Theodore Lincoln Chadbourne. One of them was U. S. Grant. Nineteen of them eventually rose to the rank of general, if not in the United States Army then in the Confederate Army. But what seized my attention was that thirteen of them died before they were forty, and they died in strange places— Contreras, Monterey, Fort Leavenworth, Resaca de la Palma. I started looking at other classes, all from 1842 through 1861, and found that the astonishing death rate persisted. In those twenty years, well over eight hundred young men were graduated from West Point. A third of them died young. That knowledge did not, however, minimize the death of any single one, or diminish its jolting impact. I felt colder when I saw Lieutenant Chadbourne in that company. All those young men.

But there were other trails to follow. Susan Miles's correspondence intrigued me. Kept in the two boxes with the letters of Lieutenant Chadbourne, it was actually only half of her correspondence, letters written *to* her. In her search for the young man, she had no library close by and no secretary. Apparently she wrote all of her letters by hand, and no copies were kept. Reading the answers, I began to understand why she was trying to learn about Lieutenant Chadbourne, and I think I began to understand a little about her. She began in 1950. She began, apparently, because the centennial of the founding of Fort Chadbourne would be in 1952, and she thought Fort Chadbourne was important to San Angelo because troops from Fort Chadbourne had established Fort Concho in San Angelo. Her interest in the fort apparently led her to the young lieutenant. Before she was through, she would acquire his sword and sword belt, his autographed edition of Virgil, a family tree and a number of letters from surviving members of his family, and his remaining letters. She would also manage, on the occasion of the centennial, to have a new building in downtown San Angelo named the Chadbourne Building. One member of the family, long since far removed from Eastport, Maine, apparently found old memories awakened by her queries and established a trust fund for the permanent care of Lieutenant Chadbourne's grave and monument in the Eastport cemetery. I wanted to know her, too, and to keep her close. I was never sure that I could know her or Lieutenant Chadbourne.

I hadn't expected letters. I had expected only silence, or perhaps the testimony of others. But even when I had copies of the letters, I didn't read them. I saved them for later. I wanted to believe he was there, or perhaps I only wanted to believe that I could find whatever it was I wanted to find. [. . .]

I wanted to believe that I could find Lieutenant Chadbourne. I wanted to believe that *ethos* is real and *in the text* left by the speaker, that it is there—just as Aristotle and, until yesterday, many others had said—and that I could find it. Others, however, have been looking with different eyes and have consequently seen things differently [. . .]. Diverse others—those who have taught us about interpretive communities, about the social construction of discourse, about reader-response theory, for example—have told me in diverse ways that *ethos* is not in the text but in the reader or community, in the projections upon the text. They have told me, further, that the writer is not autonomous but is only part of a social community that constructs and interprets discourse, that the notion of the self as a source of meaning is only a Romantic concept [. . .]. *Ethos*—character in the remaindered text—is at the very least problematic. Perhaps I can't catch character in the text, not on my own previous terms. That may mean that I can't find Lieutenant Chadbourne, not even in his letters.

And the consequence is that I am frightened. If *ethos* is not in the text, if the author is not autonomous, I'm afraid that I've lost my chance not just for survival hereafter (that happened some time ago) but also for identity now. Poststructuralist thought announces the death of the author: language writes us, rather than the other way around, and interpretation prevails rather than authorship. We have been, whether knowingly or not, whether directly or not, part of a twenty-five-hundred-year-old tradition that allowed and encouraged us to believe that *ethos* is in the text, that authors do exist, that they can be in their words and own them even in the act of giving them away. Now literacy theorists both compelling and influential tell us that it is not so, that *ethos* exists if at all only in the perceiving minds of readers, that authors, if they exist, do so somewhere else, not in their words, which have already been interpreted by their new owners. Language is orphaned from its speaker; what we once thought was happening has been disrupted. Authors, first distanced, now fade away into nothing. Not even ghosts, they are projections cast by readers. "They" out there want, that is to say, to take my own voice away from me and give such meaning as there might be over entirely to whoever might show up as an interpreter. "They" want me—and him, out there—to die into oblivion if I should manage to write something, never to be reborn in a voice for some reader but to vanish before that reader's construction/deconstruction/reconstruction of the small thing I leave behind.

Can I get a witness? Can Lieutenant Chadbourne? Can Susan Miles? In texts present or absent?

Will anyone notice that he may be here, that I may be, that this is the way I talk, that this is what in my mind passes for thinking, that this may be myself? Life is real, and the artificial compartments we create for it don't work. What gets said in one place keeps slopping over and meaning something in other places. I'm no longer talking just about literary theory, if I ever was. I'm talking about my own identity now, the nuttiness that is mine, and whatever might be his.

And yet, and yet: I have written as much to hide as to reveal, have written so that I might show the writing to others and not be required to show myself. There's more to me than meets the eye, and less. Whatever is in here might be terrible to see, worse to reveal. A piece of writing can be revelatory and exploratory; more are than we have acknowledged. It can also be a substitute for the unspeakable—a closure, not a revelation.

A couple of years ago, a book of personal essays that I wrote was published. They are mostly about West Texas. Four reviewers commented on it—my wife, my aunt, and two newspaper reviewers. Three were favorably disposed. One of the newspaper reviewers said some moderately nice things about what he was pleased to call my voice and character in the book. I was tickled and danced a little jig.

And I was startled when I realized what else was in my mind, startled when I realized that I was already talking back to the reviewer. "Listen, you out there," I was saying, "don't think I'm so easy to catch. There's more to me than meets the eye, and less. You'll not catch me so quickly."

At the moment I want and need *ethos* in the text, I deny it. I am not there, but elsewhere. Most things aren't ever over. Few things are easily real, easily what we say they are. Fewer things, I hope, come to nothing. Despite all, I came to think that *ethos* is in there somewhere. I came to think that he might yet be in his letters and that I might yet find him.

And so I set out again to track him. Of his early life in Eastport, Maine, I could learn very little. Even though I could learn only few personal details and anecdotes about his life from 1839 to 1843 at West Point, I could partially reconstruct his life from the available records. I read his application papers. I learned the daily schedules, and I learned which uniforms the cadets wore on which days. I learned about the curriculum and a little about the modes of instruction, both in academic and in military matters. Records of library books checked out are available, as are records of demerits and punishments.

I was a long way from the kind of work I was more nearly accustomed to, and sometimes tired of what I was doing. Dear God, I remember thinking, I don't want to have to remember always who they are, even that they are, all those others. Can't I sometimes just note, just judge, just pass on? I don't want to have to remember and to acknowledge that I remember.

I remember coming home from a party attended by academicians. At the moment, I didn't much care for them. I wanted to think about other things. I didn't much want to remember that they were real. If they were real, and that was the world, perhaps I wasn't and didn't belong.

But I wanted Link Chadbourne to be real—I had finally learned what family and friends called him. I don't even believe in lieutenants, but I wanted him to be real.

If he's to be real, they have to be real—those grand academicians, and all the others, my children maybe, colleagues maybe, all I've tried to imprison inside my head.

They must be real. They must be themselves, not just my perceptions of them. He must be other than my perception of him.

If he is real, and they are real, then I am not. I die with my perceptions before their reality.

Why am I ready to acknowledge his reality, if I could find him, but not theirs? Because he went out and died? Made himself publicly accountable the hard way?

No matter: if he's to be real, so must they. He can't be real unless they are.

How can he and they *and I* be real? He and they must be freed of my perceptions. Then where do my perceptions and I go?

Besides, save for sparse records and a double handful of letters, he doesn't exist except in my perceptions. If I characterize him, as I have characterized them, have I re-created all to suit myself?

I must not. All of them must be real.

Then when do I get to exist?

I set out to learn what I could about the Battle of Resaca de la Palma and soon became impatient with standard accounts because they didn't tell about him. I found that I was impatient to know exactly where he was on the field and exactly how and where and when he died. (Now, I think I know, but I cannot be completely sure.) I was surprised when I realized that I was angry at men long dead, his classmates at West Point and fellow junior officers. I expected to learn about him from them. I should have known better. The battlefield was an unholy confusion of close, hard, hand-to-hand combat. If classmates were there, they may have been separated. If they were together, they may not have seen him. If they saw him, they may have seen wrong and then misremembered. Roswell Ripley's account, I thought, was the most damnable. His book, *The War with Mexico,* was published in 1849, not so long after May 9, 1846. He gives due credit to Chadbourne's unit, the Eighth Infantry Regiment, but of Chadbourne himself, he says only this:

> Of the Americans, thirty-nine were slain, including three subalterns of merit: Inge of the Dragoons, Cochrane of the fourth, and Chadbourne of the eighth infantry.

A "subaltern of merit." My God! Why the detached report? Why the silence? Eventually I answered my own questions.

Even if they knew to speak and had been inclined to speak, I'd guess that various versions of protocol kept them mostly silent. To many of them, of course, a detached report ("three subalterns of merit") was the *only* kind of report that was appropriate. Time passed before some of them wrote, and they had become generals, and generals think important thoughts. Time passed. Look at a college or high school yearbook, friend, and try to detail what happened even to those who were close friends. Mostly, you can't. Try to detail what happened even to that person in the yearbook picture who bears your name. Mostly, you can't. Then, too, they were inheritors and creators of male protocol: a man's got to do what a man's got to do, and he shouldn't expect a memorial notice for it. And there's that other protocol: second lieutenants die. That's what they do, and they mostly don't get much notice. If they don't die, after a while they get promoted.

After a while, I came to think that I pretty well knew where he was and how he died, though I am not entirely certain. He and other troops, I believe, had fought their way down into and across the resaca (an old riverbed) and were going up the far side, a bluff of some eight to ten feet, into the last of the Mexican artillery, when they were caught in the final, desperate counterattack by Mexican lancers. The single hole in the strap that went over his shoulder may or may not be evidence of the way he died. Earlier, I expect I wanted to believe that he found a quick and neat death. I doubt it now. His tunic is not at Fort Concho, and there may be good reason. He may have been buried in it. It may have been too torn to show. His death may have been sudden, but I'd guess it wasn't neat. The thrusts of lancers make ragged tears.

I wish they had told me everything so that I could be sure. They didn't. They were silent. But someone out there was thinking of him. Someone out there named a fort for him.

After a while, I came to the letters. The collection that was separated from the rest of the papers in the two boxes that Ms. Waring showed me contained thirty-three items. Twenty of them are letters written by Theodore Lincoln Chadbourne. Three are letters written to him, two by his uncle, Thomas Lincoln, one by his brother, George. Four are printed or official documents. Six are letters written by various hands to Ichabod Chadbourne, the lieutenant's father. The originals, I assume, are still in the files of the Tom Green County Historical Association. They survive, naturally enough, in various degrees of clarity. I have worked from photocopies, which are no clearer. The earliest letter was written by young Link Chadbourne when he was still sixteen; he writes to the Secretary of War on July 19, 1839, accepting appointment as a cadet at West Point. I believe he is in the letters. I wanted him to be there.

But the sample is small. Only twenty of his letters came this far. He was a boy when they commence, a man when they end; there is, then, no particular reason to expect stylistic consistency. I cannot know the daily details of his schooling or how much that might have determined his way of writing. Most of the letters—perhaps all but one—were written in several sittings; I judge that they were not conceived as continuous, unified compositions. Many of them are scrawled hurriedly. I gather that he does not think of himself as a writer, consciously composing; oftener than not, he is answering queries, asking for news, responding to news, telling his news.

These conditions notwithstanding, I think it is possible to learn about him from the letters, supposing that style does reveal character after all.

I read in him, for example, a steady strain of good humor. He writes to his father on August 28, 1839, still in his first month at West Point:

> I begin to like the place better, as I get used to it. Everything is done fast here, we have to eat fast, sleep fast (if we don't, we don't get enough of either), dress quick, move quick, and think quick. I suppose Mother and Uncle Tom think this will do me no harm, much as I had to alter my habits in these things. I have kept clear of all demerit so far, and I don't care how long it continues to be so.

On December 22, 1839, he writes to his brother, George, and tells about guard duty:

> We have had scarcely any cold weather this fall yet—and I don't care how little there is this winter. The time we feel the cold most is when on Post. We have to go on once a week now and stand about an hour and a half at a time, it is plaguy dull music cold evenings.

Writing to George again on July 24, 1840, while on his first summer encampment, he mentions guard duty again—and food:

> This kind of duty is the most tiresome and disgusting that I ever saw, everything is done so strictly and so much by rule. You can't turn your head nor move your body or blow your nose. In addition to this our fare is a little the worst you ever saw. I have always heard that every one has his peck of dirt to eat, but each cadet has at least ten bushels. I don't believe you can tell a much worse story.

A little later in the same letter, he asks George if he has been hunting recently and adds, "We can't do that here, in fact, I don't think of anything we *can* do." In a letter to his Aunt Mary at the beginning of his third year, September 12, 1841, he invites her to come visit for a special treat:

This morning I began my first tour of duty as sergt and comman-
dant of the guards. If you don't come this fall you will not have
the pleasure of seeing the guard marched on in style by your
loving nephew, for in the spring they have commissioned officers
to command the guard, and I have only one platoon to see to.
Just now I hear the band playing on the plain. It therefore
becometh necessary for me to go out and hear it straightway.

A little later he is back in the same letter, with some remarks
about the food:

This is about all I have to say except that the ham smelt so badly
today at dinner that we were obliged to order it off the table:
how splendidly the cadets do live! Ham is a new article of food
here. It was given to us at the time the fellows began to get sick
last encampment, and as medicine is known by its bad taste,
what a nice thing our ham must be for sick people.

The good humor persists throughout the letters, even when
he is being admonitory, as he often is with George. In a letter to
his brother on February 13, 1842, he fusses at the beginning:

O you rascal! You lazy devil! You—you—what the deuce have
you been about all this time? What's the use in having you for a
brother? I won't own you any longer. Go to thunder! Your letter
did get here after keeping me in expectancy a month of Sundays.
I had quite made up my mind that Miss Wheeler had enticed you
off to Texas—the letter was not half filled as usual. What is the
reason you don't keep writing a little at a time, no matter how
long it takes, until your paper is used up. A fellow might as well
be "hung for an old sheep as a lamb," therefore, never pay postage on a half filled letter—Hard at work, you say: no matter, if
you can write half a letter you can a whole one: now reform
these little errors there's a good fellow.

A few lines along he stops to tell George about a recent innova-
tion at West Point—a riding master has been brought in:

I have taken one lesson in riding, didn't get far enough to start
my horse. I hope to next time though; we have to ride a devil of
a long time without stirrups, a perfect humbug ain't it? There are
five commands before you get into the saddle and that's another
humbug; but we do things in military style here.

And then, still in the same letter, he's back to chiding George for the scarcity of news:

> What are you doing? Why don't you say more about every day affairs? I am as ignorant as the man in the moon of your concerns and the manner in which you spend your time; every little thing that happens would interest me no matter how trifling; the information that your white hound pup had p—d on the floor was excessively interesting.

He writes to his mother from Fort Niagara on November 5, 1843:

> Quite an incident happened a day or two ago—The Corpl of the Guard, an old war soldier who would shoot his brother if ordered to, saw one of the men who had been out without leave on a spree trying to climb the wall, so as to get in unobserved by the sentinels; he ordered him to stand where he was and told a private of the guard to fire upon him if he moved while the corp. went round outside to take him—the man sprang for the woods and a bullet after him, but he escaped it. D—n the old fool said the man the next day, he had better be careful, he might have hit me—I suspect however there was no danger for the soldier probably thought he obeyed orders by *firing, hitting* is another affair.

On November 2, 1845, just after arriving at Corpus Christi, he writes to his father:

> There is no probability of my seeing any fighting here. The only benefit to be derived is that of seeing so large a force (for our army) of all branches of the service concentrated in one spot. We have brigade drills and are to have the whole army maneuvering together shortly. I was out all day yesterday with the men clearing off the bushes for that very purpose. When we do take to farming we go strong handed I can tell you.

His good humor is there, I believe, in the letters.

And yet, for a while last summer, I came to disbelieve in my own enterprise, though it's all I have in the way of hunting Lieutenant Chadbourne. We spent a Sunday walking in Williamsburg, Virginia. As we walked and looked at the buildings and exhibits, though I didn't realize at first what was happening, my mood began to shift, so much so that by noon I was tending toward the surly and unmanageable—my wife will give testimony if it's need-ed. I began to realize that I was disappointed, disconcerted, even angry because much of what I saw in the exhibits wasn't the real thing. The motives of the Williamsburg staff are unquestionable, and their efforts are thorough, efficient, and devoted, but where the real things were not available, they had made facsimiles for display. I wanted to see the real things. Then I came to be more disappointed, more disconcerted, and found myself angrier still: Is that what I'm doing, I wondered, trying to make a facsimile of Lieutenant Chadbourne? Where the real thing won't be found, the only real thing is whatever I make, and I might not do a very good job.

His letters show his good humor. They show, too, a consis-tent fairness in his way of reporting. He puts personal limits around what he tells—it's always *his* perspective, not universal truth, not dogma, *just what he has seen or experienced so far.* On August 11, 1839, still in his first week at West Point and just nine days after his seventeenth birthday, he writes to his grandfather, opening his letter with this:

> I arrived here on the 5th of this month. As I thought you would like to know how things are managed here, I will try and tell you all I know myself about them.

In his letter to George just before his first Christmas at West Point, he tells about "spreeing" and "great doings here" expected on Christmas:

> I believe that scarcely a Christmas has passed without somebody's being dismissed for getting drunk or something else. Last year there were several dismissed for throwing coal at some officers who came up to stop the noise in the upper story of North Bar-racks (alias *Cock-loft*).

He goes on, then, to tell about the death of a cadet:

> Since I began this letter a cadet of the second class has died. He was not much sick when he went down to the hospital, but he grew sicker and in a few days died. They sent after his mother, who lives near Troy, but she got here only to see him die. From

what I have heard, I should think his disease was Typhus fever, he seemed to be affected in the same way as another was.

When he writes to his mother from Fort Niagara on November 5, 1843, he tells her about the other officers:

> Beside Capt. Morris there are Lieut. McKinstry, Canby and Dr. Mills—From my experience so far it is my opinion that four better men are not to be found in any company in the army.

Writing to his father from Toledo, on his way to Texas on September 20, 1845, he says that his trip down Lake Erie has been pleasant, and remarks, "The boats on this lake when not too crowded must be the finest and most pleasant to travel in, in the world." But he then adds, "I should think though I have not seen the Mississippi boats yet." His November 2, 1845, letter to his father from Corpus Christi reports, "I like what I have seen of my regt. very much." His last letter, dated March 26, 1846, and addressed to his father, tells about the march from Corpus Christi to their present camp nine miles north of Matamoras:

> If I were to begin at the beginning of the march and try to record all the rumors and stories with which we have been perplexed and the orders and movements to which they give rise, I should not be able to finish my letter in a month. This is emphatically the country of lies and the people have reduced the telling of them to a system which seems to be a part of their religion. Now I don't know whether to tell you first of the country passed over in our march, or to jump at once to the bloody battle we came so near fighting at the crossing of the Colorado. I have no doubt the newspapers will be filled out with lies on the subject. You will understand that at this moment we are 9 miles from the Rio Grande on the Matamoras road, delaying our advance in a very impolitic and unmilitary manner, but as I have a good deal to say on the manner in which the movements of this army have been conducted by the Comd'g. General I believe I will wait until we get to Matamoras and see how things finally turn out before I criticize him.

(Listen, literary theorist—you who say the author is not the author but only one in a social community that actually writes the text, you who say that the character of the speaker is not in the text, is only my projection, you who say that the author dies when the reader is born—come and be with me in my life for a while, follow me as I transcribe his letters, watch me wince at the first letters, then shrink at the later letters, then shake at the typewriter as I read his last letters, not as with last letters from a child, but near. Of course I never wholly found him. But of course I did, too, and I didn't want him to die. But he died, and I cannot be rid of his presence.)

The one surviving letter that seems to have been consciously composed as a unit is revealing. It is not a small letter: he writes to the Adjutant General to say that the President and the Army are grievously wrong. We should remember the circumstances of his urgency and outrage. He was a brevet second lieutenant, next in line for promotion to second lieutenant. An opening occurred in the Seventh Infantry Regiment, but the commission went to a civilian, Mr. Quimby. Retirement was not mandatory in the army, and most men remained in service until their deaths. A promotion could not occur until a vacancy occurred, so that a qualified first lieutenant, for example, might wait fifteen years before a place as captain came open in his regiment. The opening, young Chadbourne had thought, was his:

September 9, 1845
Sir:
I have the honor to inform you that I addressed a letter to Headquarters during the latter part of last month, the contents of which related to the appointment by the President of a citizen to fill the vacancy in the Infantry which by regulation belongs to me. After waiting what I suppose a reasonable length of time for an answer, from which I might learn whether or not I can obtain from Headquarters the Information sought for concerning the appointment; and it being a matter in which I am very deeply interested, I make this second communication in the hope of learning whether any notice is to be taken of my first one. If I am to expect no answer, I respectfully request that you would inform me of it, as it may make an important difference in the course I shall pursue in relation to the matter in question. I shall more easily overcome the reluctance which I feel in troubling the General in chief by asking for information which I think very probable he may be entirely unable to give; for the reason that the grievance complained of is one affecting in the most serious manner one of the dearest rights of every member of the army. It would be wasting

words to attempt to enlarge upon the consequences of an act which you must of course be so much better able to trace out and appreciate than myself.

I thought (but my inexperience may have led me astray) that my first step should be to lay my complaint officially before the Commander in chief; being at least certain of his disposition to sympathize with even the lowest member of his army, who has suffered an undeserved injury; and his readiness to protect by all means in his power the rights of all under his command. The President has undoubtedly the *power* to deprive me at any moment of the commission which I now hold, without assigning or being able to assign any reason whatever for the act; so he has the power to pursue the course he did in depriving me of the commission which by regulation belonged to me; and were he this day to strike my name from the rolls of the Army, without cause, the second wrong would not be thought by me a greater one than the first, and less easy to be borne without complaint or remonstrance. I believe it my duty, one which I owe to my comrades of my own rank, as well as to myself, to complain of and to resist this act by every means in my power; and if I unfortunately learn that my hopes of promotion are liable to be blasted by a repetition of such acts, I must affirm, and I cannot see how anyone in the army can differ with me, that any commission of whatever rank, upon such conditions, is not to be desired.

Very respectfully
I am sir
Your obd't servant
T. L. Chadbourne
Bv't 2nd Lt.
2nd. Infy.

The eloquence of his charge here I find appealing. His first sentence establishes the occasion and provides a reminder of the first letter. With a quiet reminder of the delay and of the seriousness of his cause (second sentence), he now requests an answer (third sentence), one way or another, for that will determine (fourth sentence) his actions, and there must be action (fifth sentence) because of the seriousness of the act. While he had at first thought to write to the president because of his sympathies (sixth sentence), he knows, too (seventh sentence), that all power rests with the president, which makes his resolve the stronger (eighth sentence), to show at all costs the consequences of the promotion. His mind runs in interesting ways here: in the sixth sentence, he refers to the president's presumed sympathies, but I note that the sympathies appear in the grammatically subordinate, not the dominant, parts of the sentence. I note, too, that in the seventh sentence he both states and shows the president's powers in the first two main clauses, but the third main clause pits the offense done by power against power. Finally, I note that in the last sentence, duty and resolve emerge equated in two major clauses.

There is a courteous, insistent force in the letter—I had almost said a "gentlemanly force." He makes no demands, issues no threats, but he does want those in authority to know that what they have done is not trivial or routine, cannot be dismissed as Standard Operational Procedure. He writes *in the hope* of getting an answer. He knows that there may be no answer. He knows that the Adjutant General can *trace out* the consequences of the act. He knows his place, but that doesn't mean that he has learned to be subservient. In this instance, knowing his place means doing his duty with full resolve, which he does, speaking against power with no trepidation.

As this letter and the passages cited earlier suggest, he has a wide range of interests and concerns. More: he has a wide range of capacities, a wide stylistic reach. For example, some parts of his letters to George, his brother, are joking, boyish passages, sometimes cryptic in their references to girls. Other sections of these letters to George, however, are full of suggestions and advice, as in the letter of July 24, 1840:

> Be careful who you get intimate with and mind you don't learn to drink and smoke. You are not likely to have more temptation than I have had. Stick to your place and go *ahead straight* for your own sake and for that of all of us. Try and write often and we will do each other all the good we can.

In his letter of February 13, 1842, where he earlier chides George for not filling up the page when he writes, this advice appears:

> Also read every book you can get hold of. That will inform your mind and taste: don't waste time on the common miserable trashy novels so plenty everywhere. They are worse than useless. In short you should study to improve yourself now while there is time and opportunity; and George we both need it enough in all conscience.

He is also solicitous of his father, though in different ways. Writing on May 9, 1843, as graduation nears, he apologizes for the brevity of his letter: "I hate to break off this letter on the second page, but my ideas and time are both exhausted and these few lines will serve to assure you of my safety and good health." In his last letter, March 26, 1846, also to his father, this appears:

> We have defied them by playing Yankee Doodle and hoisting our flag under their very noses. Now if they choose to attempt to drive us away, let them try it and we shall see. I should like very well to get into Matamoras it looks quite well from here and I have a great desire to live in some sort of a house once more. I suppose the newspapers will be full of false accounts of anything that may or has transpired, so don't make yourself uneasy at anything you may see, and if any length of time should elapse without your hearing from me directly be sure that nothing happened worth telling of.

The nature of his care is indicated, too, in his comments about his Aunt Mary. Earlier, he had invited her to come to see him and to watch him command the guard, but then he learned that she was deathly ill, and wrote to George:

> I cannot bear to think that Aunt Mary is about to be taken away from us, but I suppose we have no good ground to expect her recovery: what a lovely woman she is, George—she has been more a sister to us than Aunt: we shall not "look upon her like again"—It will be painful to go home and see her die, but it would be still more so were I never to see her again. From all I can hear, it seems her spirits keep up wonderfully. Is she able to go about house at all now? What a blow it will be to Grandmother.

Evidence of the manner in which he treated his mother is, I think, particularly revealing. Link Chadbourne was the oldest of nine children. One of his younger brothers, Nedd, died in the fall of 1839, after Link had gone to West Point. In the spring of 1841, he received word of the birth of Thomas, who was to be the last child. Link had still not been home: cadets were not allowed leave until during the summer following their second year. He opens his letter to his mother, May 12, 1841, acknowledging the birth:

Dear Mother,

I have rec. your last letter informing me that there is somebody at home whom I never saw. There are just as many of us
now as there were when I went away, he will take Nedd's place
with me.

Otherwise, he often teases his mother, especially about the last
child, Tom, and about how deplorably lax she has become in
bringing the boy up. The boots he refers to are apparently some
that he brought home as a gift for the little boy. When he refers
to his own boots, he is talking about some that his father ordered
for him during his first year at West Point. He writes to his mother
on November 5, 1843, from Fort Niagara:

> Here I am all alone by myself (but one might have worse com-
> pany though)—my room is a sort of sanctum sanctorum which
> visitors never disturb. However I have scarce ever felt lonely in
> it—whenever I perceive any such feeling is coming on I drive it
> off by considering that if you were all here, I should be pestered
> with that little ridiculous plague of a Tom and there are cross
> young ones enough here now—That young gent will certainly be
> the scapegrace of the family—I doubt whether you will be able
> to whip him when he is in his boots. Now this of itself is enough
> to ruin him for he needs at least six whippings a day, Sundays
> more. He will be just as many time worse a character than myself
> as the number of years difference in the age at which we respec-
> tively become possessed of a pair of the above mentioned ar-
> ticles. Now that difference is somewhere about fifteen year. This
> is all evident enough from the fact that I am decidedly the best of
> your children, why, partly because I waited longest for my boots.
> Indian pudding, Mother, is a thing I despair of seeing unless I do
> make it myself. . . .

And, I believe, he shows me another trait in his letters, a kind
of directness, an unflinching honesty in the way he takes life.
Shortly after arriving at Fort Niagara, he writes to his father on
October 3, 1843:

> What a jolly time we will have in Texas, four or five regts to-
> gether, cruising about on the prairies. I now think (and in fact
> have often thought since she said it) of what Grandmother said
> when you first talked of sending me to West Point. Somebody
> remarked to her in my hearing that if I went there I should prob-

ably be sent off to the west to fight Indians the rest of my days and perhaps be scalped by them. She answered, Well, why not he, as well as any one else, somebody must run the risk, and if it's right for one to do it, it is for another. I never forgot that remark. It is characteristic of Grandmother it shows her spirit. She never felt that anyone belonging to her was too good to be employed in any necessary and proper service however laborious or dangerous it might be.

But for its revelation of an unflinching look at life, a later passage leaps off the page. On November 2, 1845, having arrived at Corpus Christi, he writes to tell his father about his trip. His letter includes a graphic account of a fatal accident that occurred as they were landing. A steamboat had come alongside to help in the unloading. Its topmast caught in his vessel's rigging, broke off, and fell, striking a young officer named Merrill, who had only that summer graduated from West Point:

> He died in about 3 1/2 hours after the accident and we buried him next day. It was an awfully sudden thing, and we felt that it might have been any one of us as well as him. Poor fellow! he never knew what hurt him. But his parents! I hope if I die a violent death it may be in a way that will do some good either real or pretended.

In the letters that survive, I found no trace of deceit or rancor. He is never self-serving, never mean-spirited. He is a gentle, funny, honest, strong young man, with a wide-ranging capacity for care.

And he slips away from me. Why wouldn't he? I can't remember who I was five years ago, let alone who somebody else remembers from five years ago. He slips away from me, and doesn't. What of the other letters, I wonder, those I didn't see? What of himself, whom I didn't see, and did?

II

From Unpublished Manuscripts

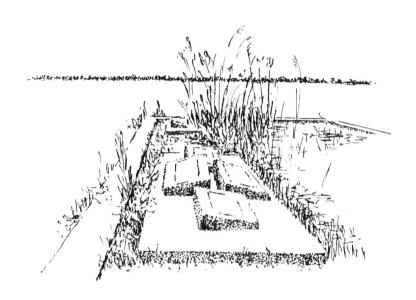

CHAPTER ELEVEN

I in Mine, You Elsewhere

I in mine, you elsewhere. And I? Against those who long for certain knowledge, I imagine myself competing, wanting to claim identity my way, against their way. They are stopped in their rhetoric, I in mine. We are apart.

A spring or so ago, at the annual occasion recognizing faculty and staff for their durability at the university where I teach, the president gave me a nice pen-and-pencil desk set with a nice plaque on it acknowledging that I had lasted for thirty years.

I have been looking at it since then, not all of the time, mind you, and not even frequently, but once in a while. It's been on the desk in front of me, and I haven't been able to miss it easily. Every time I have looked at it, a small but noticeable tic has developed under my left eye. That is accompanied by spasms of doubt about my identity.

Engraved on the plaque was notice that I am JIMMIE W. CORDER. That is, indeed, the name registered in the business office along with my Social Security number, thus the name that appears on my monthly check. But I don't much think that's who I am, though I may turn out to be that very fellow.

If I was ever JIMMIE, I haven't been for a long time. The name on my birth certificate from Aspermont, in Stonewall County, Texas, is JIMMIE WAYNE CORDER, but apparently everyone in my family gave up on the WAYNE part before I was ever aware of being called anything. Later on, I retrieved the W out of WAYNE; by then, I was older and had to sign checks and things, and thought I needed the W for a touch of dignity.

In the fall of 1936, 1 presented myself for the first grade at the school in Jayton in Kent County, next door to Stonewall County. As it turned out, two other boys with the same first name

---

From *Rhetorics, Remnants, and Regrets.* Unpublished ms. 1997.

presented themselves at the same time. We came to be friends, and one of them came to be my best friend. Fact is, we had the same first name, but the other two spelled it JIMMY (and that's a dark secret I've had to bear all this time, the shame, first, of not being born JAMES, and second, of being born JIMMIE, the name spelled, apparently, the wrong way). You'd think it unlikely, wouldn't you, that in a town of only 650 population, three boys with the same first name would show up in the same year for the first grade? Unlikely as it may have been, that's the way it was.

That presented problems for the teacher. Her name was MAMIE MORRIS MURPHY, but then she got married and was MAMIE MORRIS MURPHY FOWLER. She couldn't have three JIMMIES or three JIMMYS or one JIMMIE and two JIMMYS answering her every time she said JIMMY or JIMMIE.

She had us draw names.

JIMMY COX drew JAMES, which was all right since it was his proper name. JIMMY MATTHEWS, who turned out to be my best friend, drew JIMMY. He got to go on being JIMMY. I drew JIM. That way, you see, she had a JAMES, a JIMMY, and a JIM, and all confusion among names ended.

And ever since, that's who I thought I was, JIM CORDER, later JIM W. CORDER, with the W added for a little spice of dignity. My mother called me JIM, at least whenever she was in a civil temper in my direction. My father, on the occasions when he noticed, called me JIM. My brother and sister call me JIM. My wife calls me JIM HONEY. My nieces and nephews and cousins call me JIM. The name JIM appears on some papers and books that I've published, though that hasn't been easy—publishers seem to think that if you can write something for them to publish, your name probably ought to be JAMES, and I've sometimes had to tell them the whole sorry truth.

All this time, you see, I thought I was JIM CORDER. For a little while there, I thought maybe I had gotten to be a real person with my own name, JIM CORDER. I even thought maybe other people might have noticed that JIM CORDER is my name. Surely someone would.

Didn't turn out that way. The plaque said that I'm just an item in a ledger, little old JIMMIE W. CORDER, Social Security number to follow.

And so I returned the plaque to the president. We hear a lot about harassment these days. Harassment can occur in many ways and doesn't always involve gender differences. Harassment can occur through silence, or through the failure to take notice. I reckon that universities often and inadvertently harass in such ways. My own university sometimes harasses faculty and staff by silence and by the failure to take notice. I expect that faculty and staff sometimes harass presidents by silence and by the failure to take notice.

At any rate, I sent back the plaque that said I am only an item in the ledger, JIMMIE W. CORDER. I was going, I thought, to persist for a little while yet in the belief that I am JIM CORDER. For that reason, I thought I didn't much need the plaque. I kept the pen-and-pencil set, though; it's pretty nice.

And then, a little later, the president brought me a new plaque. It says that I am JIM CORDER. I put it on the pen-and-pencil set.

But now, I don't know. Now, I'm no longer sure. Someone, I thought, had stopped to put my name on a plaque without noticing me, but I, in turn, had stopped in my own rhetoric, wanting to claim identity my own way. Now, I'm no longer sure. It doesn't require an awful lot to call my identity into question, or to disturb the universe. Perhaps, after all, I am not here. Perhaps I am here under another name.

Competing Rhetorics and the Canon

Parnassus is a mountain in Greece. I have not come there. It rises north of Delphi to 8,061 feet. A holy mountain in ancient times, it was sacred to Dionysus, later also to Apollo. Between two projecting cliffs, the Phaedriades, lies a gorge in which the Castalian Spring flows. To the west of the spring is the site of the sanctuary of Apollo at Delphi. Parnassus is the home of the muses. Their former address was on Mount Helicon, but the Roman writers moved them to Parnassus. The Castalian Spring is the source of poetic inspiration.

I'd like to think that I have been on the road to Parnassus for a long time, but I've made a good many wrong turns and have not yet reached the first boulders. I may have consulted the wrong travel agent.

On the road to Parnassus, I have stubbed my toe, slipped into the bar ditch, turned right when left would have been more generally useful, bumped fenders, missed detours, and misread signs. And there's always that confounded travel agent, who may have given me the wrong itinerary at the outset. I've been on the road some time now, and I'm no longer sure I want to make the trip.

The first book I ever owned was *Andy at Yale,* by Roy Eliot Stokes. It was published in 1914—which, I hurry to add, was a good while before I was published. I learned many things from this book. I learned that there were such things as colleges, and probably, by the way, acquired an idealized view of college that has made every campus I've actually known seem a disappointment. I learned that men prove themselves on the football field and the baseball diamond. Andy returns to the huddle at one point, "panting, trembling, with a wild, eager rage to again get into the fight." I learned that men don't cringe or cry. "Keep quiet," the hero tells the villain, "for the honor of Yale whose name you've disgraced." These same lessons were brought home to me again by *Fighting Blood,* the second book I owned, whose author I've forgotten.

Meanwhile, I had been learning lessons secondhand through my brother. He was five years older, and given to sophisticated ways. Whenever possible, he read pulp magazines filled with flying stories. Of course in the late thirties the only good war there was for writers to write about was World War I, and the stories were all about flying aces of 1917 and 1918. I learned lessons from them, too. I learned that good men are brave, that they are likely to be either stoic or wry in the face of danger or pain. I learned that war is an appropriate form of human behavior, that it is a final testing ground for manhood.

And while this was going on, I was learning, mostly at the Texas Theater, how to define the world, how to behave, how to measure myself, how to measure others from Tom Mix, Ken Maynard, Buck Jones, and Hopalong Cassidy, and later from Gary Cooper, Sam Spade, and from the sports writers' versions of Babe Ruth and Joe DiMaggio.

When I got to be ten or eleven, I discovered P. C. Wren's *Beau Geste* and Baroness Orczy's *The Scarlet Pimpernel* and learned how to be valorous. I learned again from those books that war is a proper arena for men, and I learned that women were nice, but nonvital, adornments.

Later, then, I set out again—more surely, I thought—on the road to Parnassus. I went to college. I took English courses. I read *Beowulf* and learned what a hero is. He is male. He is white. He is active. He performs prodigious physical deeds. He is very much like a good linebacker. I read Chaucer and saw the dimensions of that male world. You'll remind me, perhaps, of the Wife of Bath, but she is striking largely because she talks like a man, after all. I read *Sir Gawain and the Green Knight* and learned that women have some uses, but only as testing agents for men.

I was on the road to Parnassus, but I wasn't getting there.

I learned that we prized epic, tragedy, romance, adventure as media for expressing our best selves, and I learned what kind of people get to appear in epic, tragedy, romance, and adventure.

While this was happening, the newspapers, radio, television were writing and filming the new scriptures in our religion of athletics. I learned from them that the best men were those of whom it could be said, "He's some kind of football player," or "He really knows how to hit," or "When he hits you, you stay hit."

I read Milton, and you know what that did to me. I read Scott and learned that men were patriotic ("Breathes there a man with soul so dead," he asked), and I read Tennyson and learned that the best reality was far on the ringing plains of windy Troy. I read Byron and learned how to be a poet: you need to be a man, apparently restless, and willing to use up women, and you probably ought to die young. I read Hemingway and learned how to be a novelist: that requires hunting, fishing, drinking, and other pursuits.

I was on the road to Parnassus, and I wasn't getting there.

One day I noticed that I wasn't sure I should make the trip. One day I noticed that what I had learned was not, perhaps, what I should have learned or might have learned. I had learned that the world was male, that the males were white, that they should behave according to values developed in physical conflict, that their appropriate testing was in warfare or some suitable and similar arena. I noticed, too, that the males were oftener than not privileged, in one way or another holding power and place.

And so one day I noticed something else. I noticed that people I loved would not qualify for the world defined in those books along the road to Parnassus. Epic, tragedy, adventure, and romance would not admit many I loved. And I was angry. I am still angry.

Why, when we defined heroism, did we exclude my father? My mother? Why are the sweet, zesty, gentle, cantankerous people of our lives excluded?

My father never struck anyone, never competed in sports, never went to war. He always wanted to be defined to us, I think, in the ways the world has taught us, but he was gentle, kind, selfless, and patient. When we all were younger, I remember seeing him work until he dropped for my mother, my brother, and me. But he never knew that he counted. The world, after all, honors other kinds of men.

My mother was an extraordinary mix, acutely shy, yet at the same time just about the fastest in the West at puncturing the swollen ego. A model of natural dignity and reserve, she was not beautiful and brilliant as the world reckons such things. The world honors other kinds.

I didn't, however, commence this in order to tell you about my parents. I select them because I know them. They got left out of all those books. Anyone could furnish scores of names, dear crotchets that didn't count.

I'd not want to be misunderstood. I do not wish to repudiate what we have chosen as the canonical literature of the past. I do not wish even to repudiate the particulars that I have mentioned. The past is in us, inescapably. If we repudiate the past, we deny ourselves. We can love the past, even in its errors, and cherish what we were. It calls out to us, "Remember. Remember."

But if we are not to repudiate the past, neither are we to accept it uncritically, or teach it unthinkingly. Parnassus was home of the Muses, and from it springs the source of poetic inspiration. But remember, please, that Parnassus is also a barren limestone mass. Those muses prompted and that inspiration generated beautiful songs, grand and moving stories, compelling visions. Without them, we'd be bitterly poor, and hopelessly unenlightened. But they also mapped wrong turns along that old road. The books on that old road don't hold all of the future. The future isn't written yet. The past is dear, but I rounded wrong turns and learned wrong lessons. The books on that old road gave us the power to see, and to see mistakenly, to learn well, and to learn poorly, to go on, and to stumble. That Parnassus generated magic; it was also a barren limestone mass.

We selected a literature and, comfy with it, settled and stopped in the rhetoric it afforded, turning away from the rhetoric around us that called and beckoned.

We draw boundaries and enforce them, isolating ourselves in what we perceive to be our own rhetorics. My rhetoric is not yours; yours will not be mine. Our rhetoric is not theirs; theirs is not ours. I own my rhetoric. You must not have it. Yet I want you to have my rhetoric and to congratulate me for it without ever insisting or even suggesting that I take your rhetoric.

Heels

The other day in class, I read a passage from an essay aloud to the students. I expect I wanted to imagine that I was illustrating a point, if I had a point, if illustrations ever illustrate points. The term *well-heeled* occurred in the passage I read. When I finished, a young woman—the same one who, if she had been there, would have been ahead of that little boy in noticing that the emperor didn't have any new clothes—asked me what *well-heeled* means. I'm frequently astonished when I learn, over and over again, that young people live in their world and use its languages instead of replicating mine.

I told her that it meant you were doing all right financially, were maybe even a little rich, at any rate able to keep yourself in good shoes, maybe able to get new shoes, even, once in a while, or to get new heels for the shoes you already have. You know— well-heeled. I should have told her, too, but I didn't think to do so, that being well-heeled is sort of at the other extreme from being down at the heels. You know—your heels are worn down, and you're poor, unable to get new shoes, or to fix the ones you've already got. I might have told her, too, but I didn't think of it, and if I had, I wouldn't have told her, that neither being well-heeled nor being down at the heels has anything to do with being round-heeled, which is a presumed condition among some women that I am told young men like to think about a lot.

And I didn't think to tell her that being well-heeled or down at the heels or round-heeled has nothing to with being a heel. If you are a heel, you are perhaps a little more modern than if you are a cur, a scoundrel, or a cad. The term came into use in Great Britain, Canada, and this country by about 1910. I haven't heard anyone use it in a long time, but that's not because there's a short-age of heels. I gather that we adopted the term *heel* from our own heels. Since we mostly can't see our own heels and so don't know what they're doing, I guess we took the word to refer to treacherous fellows, who do things behind our backs while we're not looking. I wish I had thought to mention this part to the young woman. Then I could have asked her if it's possible for a woman to be a heel.

I am reasonably well-heeled right now and have been for some time now. The shoes I wear every day are Rockport brand shoes. I have a pair that is brown and a pair that is black, and I'm still a little surprised that I have two pairs at the same time. I'm told that the brand enjoys good repute for walking shoes. That is good. I like to walk. Mine mostly keep me pretty nearly perpen-dicular to the little part of earth I'm on. Other brands are all around, and they're all a little snazzier and jazzier than Rockports. Nike. Reebok. Nike. Reebok. Nike. Reebok. I can't think of the other brand names. Some of them are a little scary-looking to me. Some of them look as if they might take command once you put them on, especially if you pump them up, as I'm told you can do. None of them looks much like the shoes many of us wore in the spring and summer when I was a boy. Those were called tenny shoes. That's spelled T E N N Y. I know that they are sup-posed to be called tennis shoes, but that was a usage reserved for the rich, who lived somewhere sort of vaguely in the East.

Only a little while ago—such a short while ago, it sometimes seems—it was all different about shoes. We wore tenny shoes in the spring and summer, and what a day it was when my mother finally said I could wear them. I went off to school able to leap tall buildings or thirty feet, whichever came first. In the fall and winter, my mother insisted that I wear leather shoes for warmth, with leather soles and leather heels. I never had more than one pair at a time. Sometimes they got a little worn. You might say that I wasn't well-heeled or that I was down at the heels.

If I wore a hole in the sole of the shoe, we'd cut a piece of cardboard to fit, slip it inside the shoe, and I'd go on wearing it. If the hole got bigger, or if I wore the heel plumb down almost to nothing, then my father would fix my shoes.

One night after supper, he would get out his shoe last. That's a metal form, a single stand about two feet high. On the top there was a replaceable form—he had two of them, a smaller one for my mother and me, a larger for himself and my brother. This replaceable form was shaped like the bottom of a shoe. He'd sit by the table where the lamp was so that he could see. I remember watching him one time from across the room by the radio. The lamp made a halo of his hair. He slipped my shoe onto the form, upside down so that the bottom was up. He got out his tack hammer, the tacks, his knife, and the leather he kept for these occasions. He always seemed to know where they were. I never can find the tacks at our house. He put a small handful of tacks in his mouth, to keep his hands free. Then he cut a new sole or a new heel and hammered it onto my shoe, and I was well-shod and well-heeled.

The funny shoes that I see everywhere now can't be fixed that way, or at all, but they don't surprise me much. Nike. Reebok. Nike. Reebok. I know that some are pretty faddish and will disappear. That's all right, if a little wasteful, but then most folks don't keep leather and tacks and a tack hammer and a knife and a shoe last close by any more. I guess that one way or another, whether Reebok or my father, we're always trying to make better shoes, trying to be well-heeled. That's all right and as it should be, and I'm glad. My father didn't make much money at it, though. Reebok does. I never expected for that to work out for me. I did wonder whether or not I'd ever own more than one pair of shoes at a time. Or a really good baseball glove. I think there were times when I decided that owning things would confer identity upon me. [. . .]

Lost Men, Lost Women

I regret that I cannot be nostalgic for a time in Western society when women took their just places—that is to say, anywhere they pleased, doing whatever they pleased. I can't look back or out to find and to long for a time when men and women were fair partners.

I regret that among Western males, especially perhaps among Anglo-Saxon males, some of us were macho types, some of us imagined that we were macho types, and the rest of us assumed that we were inferior because we weren't macho types. I regret that macho types of both genders are still with us, as even casual observation of automobile drivers will show. I regret that men criminalized themselves by choosing such a mode, even if it may once have been necessary. In a review of David Gilmore's *Manhood in the Making*, Beryl Lieff Benderly says of earning manhood that in some places boys undergo a formal initiation that establishes the fact, while "in others they enter a series of conditional skirmishes on the playing field, in the boudoir and on the battlefield that may leave the outcome forever slightly in doubt." Then she continues:

> But why should normal development take the form of a tournament? Mr. Gilmore searches the ethnographic literature for the solution to this "manhood puzzle." Citing two maverick societies, he rejects a biological answer. The Tahitians and the central Malaysian Semai people place "no stress on proving manhood, no pressure on men to appear in any significant way different from women or children," and thus establish that "stressed manhood," though "ubiquitous" in our species, is not "universal." It can't, therefore, spring from any inborn urge or genetic imperative.
>
> Still, these idyllic exceptions provide Mr. Gilmore with a crucial clue. Free from enemies, predators, and want, the Tahitians and the Semai can do without men willing to break their backs at the plow and risk their lives against wild beasts and foreign foes. These two societies don't need an ideology that glorifies toughness, assertiveness and bravery as the noblest expressions of masculine human nature. But few other peoples can afford that luxury. In most places, survival demands males trained from infancy to be workers, hunters and soldiers willing, even eager,

to expend themselves to safeguard the group's future, which is to say the reproductive potential of its women.

I will regret the disappearance of the macho type, and I will regret that I regret, will regret that I was trained to prize warrior behavior. Some of my reasons for regretting the disappearance of the type are frivolous. I took great pleasure in watching Johnny Unitas, with sure control and calm precision, take his team eighty-five yards to a touchdown in the last two minutes of the game, with a series of exquisite sideline passes. I still think there are few things lovelier than the grace and efficiency of a classy second baseman and a superb shortstop turning a double play.

But some of my reasons for regretting the loss of the macho are not so frivolous, though I don't altogether understand them. I remember a summer day at Fort Hood, Texas. I remember the late afternoon. Far away in the distance along the road, I could see the lead platoons of an infantry regiment returning to the fort. They had already walked thirty miles that day in the hot Texas sun, in the swirling Texas dust. I could just make out that they were at route march, that they were sagging and worn, as I could see them in the distance. Then, as they came nearer, I could hear the voices of the platoon sergeants, one after another down the whole line of the regiment, calling the troops back to cadenced step. Then, like a ripple down the regiment, they began to straighten. By the time they came in the gate, sergeants counting cadence, the troops were stepping along, almost dancing in their precision, almost strutting. They announced without words that no one would find them wanting, no one would find them worn and tired. I know some of what has made men behave like that, but there's still a mystery in it.

And there's a mystery, too, in something else I learned there. If your platoon, I learned, or your company, or your regiment, or your division should go into combat, you are supposed to save ten good men. You save six for pall-bearers. You save two for road guards. You save one to count cadence. You save one to play taps. The rest must die, if that is what is required. And for generations, young men have died, and we have forgotten their names.

I regret that in the world of males, women have been lost.

I regret that men have dehumanized women and have sub-
jected them to the male gaze. What might have been admiration,
pleasure, or honest lust that will not force itself upon the other
became use and domination. A certain admiration, pleasure, or
honest lust, I judge, is necessary to the perpetuation of the race,
if it deserves to be perpetuated. A man can have an orgasm without an erection, but usually cannot insert his penis into a woman's
vagina without an erection. Seems a pity that men—and women—
have not explored the nature of that burden and its consequences.
The burden, or obligation, or need appears to have conferred
upon men simultaneously a sense of pleasure, pride, and even
power, and a sense of real or impending inadequacy. The male
function and purpose carries the immediate possibility of both
pride and humiliation. One does not customarily contemplate
for very long the thought or reality of his own inferiority. Inferiority or inadequacy of this kind, by its nature, cannot be easily
hidden except as men have regularly and insistently masked it
behind the compensations of the other gift, pleasure, pride, and
power. I mean to suggest that both men and women have been
lost to themselves and to each other, but men have continued to
take the prizes, among which are subjugated women.

In "Fetishes and Fetishism in Girlie Magazines," James M.
Ferreira remarks that

> The association of sex and consumption is calculated to imbue
> the wares promoted with the same excitation produced by the
> pinup. One cannot possess the female unless he first acquires the
> goods the ads tell us are indispensable for gaining and retaining
> the woman's attention. Not only have the girlie magazines dehu-
> manized the female, they have made her an ally in amassing profits
> for the publishers and their advertisers.

"The flesh merchants," Ferreira goes on to say, "have evolved
a method of merchandizing an illusion of the 'Good Life' founded
upon the fragmentation and devaluation of the female body."
But the body or its parts are no longer natural. The sexual revolution shown in the magazines, Ferreira says, "is a false revolution. It denies any value in the natural and exalts the artificial
and the standardized."

Propagandists and others in World War II, Robert B. Westbrook says, contributed to the "cultural construction of women as objects of obligation"; communication elites, he suggests, fabricated women as "prescribed icons of male obligation." To claim "their" women, or "their" women's bodies, men had first to meet a set of obligations. One of the obligations is to go to war, thus to fulfill one of the "moral obligations of the 'protector' to the 'protected.'" "Pinup pictures—publicly circulated, publicly posted, and officially sanctioned in World War II—function, Westbrook says, both as "surrogate objects of sexual desire" and as "icons of the private interests and obligations for which soldiers were fighting." The woman in the pinup picture, Thomas Hess proposes, is a manmade object:

> The artifice with which the elements of her anatomy are composed and photographed erases all the details and peculiarities of the model (wrinkles, moles, body hair), generalizes the body into a format and robs it of any logical scale. Thus a pinup can be reduced to an inch in a magazine advertisement for cigarettes or enlarged to 12 feet for a billboard. The symbol works in almost any conditions, in almost any context.

Women are linked with consumption. Women are linked with propagandistic instruction in moral obligation. Women are icons. Women are the helpless, submissive, and available objects of the voyeuristic gaze of the male spectator. John Berger argues in *Ways of Seeing* that

> In the average European oil painting of the nude the principal protagonist is never painted. He is the spectator in front of the picture and he is presumed to be a man. Everything is addressed to him. Everything must appear to be the result of his being there. It is for him that the figures have assumed their nudity.

The male spectator's enjoyment, Rosemary Betterton suggests, is not solely erotic: "It is also connected to a sense of power and control over the image. The woman's body is posed and framed for him, while his own body remains doubly hidden."

I regret that it has been so. I regret that it is still so.

I have been responsible for some textbooks in rhetoric and composition. They have been used, in years past, most often in first-year university writing courses. I could not attempt such books again, even if I were assured that any future book of the kind would be informed by all of the best research and shaped by the best wisdom and insights of all possible colleagues.

I don't quite believe such books are possible.

If one composes a rhetoric, say, for university students to use as a textbook, I think it will be one's own rhetoric, or it will be a public rhetoric to which one acquiesces, or it will be a public rhetoric filtered through one's own rhetoric. Any of these might be useful; any of these would be, I think, a version of propaganda and indoctrination unless one knew and disclosed what was happening in the description of a rhetoric. It's hard enough for us to know what we are doing; to disclose what we are doing may be harder, for that might require us to acknowledge that we have not caught the truth.

I do, however, believe that it is possible to describe—at least to sketch—a limited rhetoric, the rhetoric of a person or a group at a particular time and place. Perhaps it is possible to describe one's own rhetoric, if the description is accompanied by disclosure of the pertinent circumstances shaping the rhetoric.

This means, as I've suggested before, that it is difficult for me now to imagine textbooks in rhetoric that are presumed to be unitary, that are given titles such as *A College Rhetoric* or *Modern Rhetoric* or *A Complete Rhetoric*. I'd rather wait upon particularized rhetorics.

That, in turn, probably means that, despite everything, I am still equating a rhetoric with an identity, still supposing that we can compose the self we perceive at a given moment and show it to others, even if we know it will be incomplete and may be altogether wrong.

If my rhetoric rises in and from leucocholy, then what does it look like?

I am sixty-six years old. That may mean that, regardless of my hopes, I am imagining end time in a rhetoric of the last age, though I don't think so.

But what does it look like?

I'll start with one of my classes this term. In the schedule of courses, it is called "English 3233: The Personal Essay." University juniors and seniors are enrolled. They read some. They write a lot. Along the way, I mention the notion of the opaque text. "You can't see through it," I tell them "to the author." I know that's true: what I write will not tell all about me. What you write will not reveal you wholly to a reader. I also know that it's not true: what I write will reveal much about me, even if only for the moment. What you write will reveal much about you, even if only for the moment. Inside one rhetoric, the concept of the opaque text is an article of faith. Inside a contending rhetoric, it is a useful way of thinking. Each rhetoric can hear the other, though that is not always the case. Each calls, or might call, to the other, except when one or the other, assuming authority, denies that another rhetoric can legitimately exist.

On another day, we talk about the notion of the persona, and I suggest the possibility that the speaker in an essay is always a persona, not identical with the author. Inside one rhetoric, such an understanding of persona is an article of faith. Inside another, it is a useful strategy. Absent the assumption of authority on either part, each rhetoric calls, or might call, to the other.

Another day: I mention the concept of *ethos* and try to recall for them Aristotle's account of how the character of the speaker becomes a primary mode of argument as it is revealed in the progress of the discourse. Another rhetoric, home to the idea of the opaque text and to the idea of the author-displacing persona, reminds me that *ethos* is not in the text, that *ethos* occurs in the reader's projection upon the text. Neither view will wholly cancel the other.

"Where," I ask them, "does that leave us?" They don't answer. One rhetoric says that problems must be solved. Across the way, another says that problems don't have to be solved once and for all.

"Maybe those divergent beliefs," I say to them, "were always under question, and we just didn't recognize the doubts." I remind them that *person,* as in "personal," derives from *persona,* or "mask." I suggest that we were never autonomous, though we longed to be and claimed to be, that we were always in some community, that the language belongs to some community, that we write what it lets us write. Another rhetoric whispers, "Yes, but sometimes one of us wrenches it free to say something that the community didn't know to say." I suggest that all texts are intertextual, that no text is solely an author's creation. Another rhetoric calls, "Yes, but this one found the words." I suggest that the autonomous individual is a constructed idea, perhaps therefore not a permanent truth, that we invented the autonomous individual in order to serve our greed and ambition.

Another rhetoric inquires, "Where does that leave us? Can we still have this course?"

My own rhetoric sighs, "Where does that leave me? Can I still have myself?"

I argue with myself.

Another time, a little earlier. My mother was cooking doughnuts the hard way, frying a few at a time in a frying pan. Apparently my brother and I had exasperated her by eating them pretty fast, for when my father came in from work and into the kitchen, she said, "Nolan, speak to these boys—they're eating these up faster than I can cook them." That wasn't entirely true. She was about a plateful ahead of us. The plate full of doughnuts was on the table. My father was standing alongside, and I never knew how he managed to do what he did. He spoke to us: "You all go on now and get out of here and let your mother finish her cooking." We said "Yessir." He turned, then, to leave the room, and as he went through the door, I saw that he had hooked four doughnuts, one on each of four fingers. No one else remains who saw him as I did. If I don't remember him and try to get him down right, he will vanish.

Many things will vanish. Little towns will disappear. Fluvanna and Clairmont and Swenson and Gilpin have already gone. Jayton and Aspermont and Spur may go as well. Lucky Strike cigarettes used to come in a green package, but one day in 1942 the radio announced, "Lucky Strike green has gone to war," and the next time we looked, the packages were mostly white, as they are now. The coffee cups in diners once were thick, heavy crockery mugs. Edgeworth pipe tobacco used to come in a wonderful little blue tin. If I don't remember them all, and try to get them down right, they will vanish.

And then there's my Grandma. In their book, *The American Quilt,* Roderick Kiracofe and Mary Elizabeth Johnson Huff set out among other things to show that homemade quilts were not the resort of the poor, but conscious works of art. They argue that the image of the poor needlewoman painstakingly constructing quilts out of scraps left over from important projects and stumbling upon a pleasing visual effect is a fiction. Scrap quilts, they say, were the exception, not the rule; for the most part, women bought fabrics intended just for quilts and planned color and design accordingly. That may be, and I understand their zeal to rescue quiltmakers as artists, but in the passion of their cause, they forgot my Grandma.

My Grandma Corder was not beautiful. She wasn't cuddly. She wasn't a good cook. She didn't plan wonderful projects for the grandchildren. She was illiterate. Her eyes were desperately weak and crossed. She had subordinated herself entirely to my Grandpa. But he died when he was fifty-eight and she was no older. She lived on for another twenty years, lost in a world that no longer made much sense to her, entirely dependent on her children, with whom she lived, moving from one family to another every six months or so.

But she made quilts, stunning quilts.

She did so without the aid of the authors who want to be sure that the world gets corrected, to be sure that we know how artistic artists of the quilt were, to be sure that we define the quiltmaker's art in their way.

She didn't buy material especially for quilts. She didn't buy anything. She had no money. She was mostly silent, withdrawn into herself, often ill-tempered. And she was a packrat. She salvaged scraps of all colors and shapes and sizes. Acting as the scraps accumulated on some principle of sorting that we never understood, she distributed them into piles, which she then tied into neat bundles. As new scraps came her way, she would untie the bundles, deal the new scraps out among them, and retie them. Then one day she'd get out her bundles of scraps and feel of them and look at them. Then she'd untie them and look again at all of the individual scraps, holding them close to her eyes. Sometimes this took a long time, but after a while, she'd begin sorting them in a new way. Then after a while, she'd start cutting, though she had no pattern. After a while, she'd start sewing. And then one day there'd be a quilt of intricate design, beautifully rendered, lovely to see. Without design, she made design. Without art, she made art. She left no other record. Her children are all dead. If I don't remember her, and try to get her down right, she will vanish.

I know that there are other ways of thinking about writing and the recollection and rendition of ourselves, and I try to honor those other views, but I'll go on thinking in this way as well. Who else will tell what you remember and try to make it real but you? Who else will show what the world looks like to you and try to make it real but you?

I understand that this may be a selfish, self-serving conception, a way of calling attention to oneself. I understand that I may be trapped in the aspirations of what some call radical individualism. I was planning to go to Hell anyway. But the desire to hold some things from oblivion, including even myself, is not criminal. I know that in trying to hold things, I too will vanish. I had hoped to be real, but I am only a vacancy in the air.

A couple of weeks ago, I made a trip to the central public library downtown, as I do on most Saturdays. A construction project is under way there to enlarge the library and to correct some defects in the original design. The construction project is fenced in, in the usual way. I parked a couple of blocks away and walked toward the library. As I walked, I saw, inside the fence, a man who I decided must be some kind of supervisor, come on a Saturday to check things over. He was bending and peering and touching and looking. With him was a little girl, his daughter, I guessed. She was, I judged, maybe not yet three years old. I judged, too, that being inside the fence on a construction project wasn't all that bad on a Saturday morning, especially because near the fence was a big sandpile. As I approached, she had set out to climb it. This wasn't easy: the sandpile was high, and she wasn't. As I neared, she made it to the top. She turned and called out. "Daddy," she said, "look at me." She had made it.

I went on by. Instruction wasn't yet over for me that Saturday morning. I was early—that's part of the ritual—so I went on into an adjacent building, where it's my custom to have a cup of coffee and read the morning paper while I wait for the library to open. I had gone inside and was walking toward the other end of the building where the escalator would take me downstairs to the coffee shop. Ahead of me was another man, younger, with a little girl, also younger—maybe about two, walking along just fine, and apparently beginning to talk pretty well. The father apparently intended to go out the door at the other end of the building and on outside, but his path took them by the escalator. The little girl apparently found it more interesting than the door, for she veered off in that direction, headed downstairs. The young man called to her, "No, honey, let's go this way." "No," she said, "go this way."

"Daddy, look at me."

"No, go this way."

Not bad for early on a Saturday morning.

Individuals, solitary souls, were a grand invention. We ought to look at them. They ought to go their way. The domestic particulars of their lives ought to be examined. We won't, however, trap them in their words, and I won't be caught, either.

The decentering project of our time that will find us relocated after a curious, glorious, disastrous five-hundred-year journey at the center of things might lead to a new collective in which we are lost, but it needn't. We're here. We make what's left. Then we go. While we're here, we give witness to others, to ourselves.

The epic of our time, the drama, the story, the song, will not, I hope, tell of war and of the hero's triumph with spear or gun; and surely it's unlikely that it will begin with fallen angels. The angels have flown away, and no hero waits. We are what we have. We sing or tell or show or chant in the languages of the echoing past, shaped and transformed now to our uses in the forms that we can make or learn to make. Each moment we save holds our epic, not of war or the fortunate fall, but of ourselves. It will tell who we were in the midst of sometimes slow, sometimes sudden, but always startling ontological, epistemological, and rhetorical change. It will tell how each of us is always the last of some tribe. It will tell how our world came to an end. And it will tell how, at last and after all, we came to vanish. We will vanish, but for now, we are here. While we're here, we can give witness.

Works Cited

Benderly, Beryl Lieff. Rev. of *Manhood in the Making*, by David Gilmore. *New York Times Book Review* Apr. 1990: 8–9.

Berger, John. *Ways of Seeing*. London: Penguin, 1972.

Kiracofe, Roderick, and Mary Elizabeth Johnson Huff. *The American Quilt: A History of Cloth and Comfort, 1750–1950*. Clarkson Potter, 1993.

CHAPTER TWELVE

Aching for a Self

S ometimes, late at night, I think that contemporary theorists have eradicated soul, selfhood, identity. Social construction-ists declare that we don't exist, at least not as single, perceiving, autonomous, responsible souls. Intertextualists declare that our texts don't exist except as amalgamations of the culture's texts. Deconstructive theorists declare that if we exist, we don't exist as we thought we did, but in rhetorics holding diverse values and assumptions that we mistook for truths. Reader-response theo-rists declare that if we exist, we exist over yonder, not in our own creations, but in other people's perceptions of our creations. Those who advocate collaboration declare that we shouldn't exist; to claim autonomous selfhood is a sin, to be denounced as "radical individualism." I still sometimes think that I am real, but my existence is in doubt.

When you're facing bleakness, one thing to do is to go on into it, to see if you can come out on the other side.

We long to be absolutely present to the world, acknowledged, known, and cherished, and we long for the world to be abso-lutely present to us, there, real.

Words won't be things, and yet in words we long for the absolute presence of things. In *On Longing: Narratives of the Miniature, the Gigantic, the Souvenir, the Collection*, Susan Stewart remarks that nostalgia must face the gap between words and things. It is, she says, the "sadness without an object." We cannot catch lived experience, for it has already, as Stewart sees it, been processed into commodities, prized for exchange value, not for use value. Still, Samuel Johnson had thought that "do-mestic privacies," the "minute details of daily life," would show

---

From *Rhetorics, Remnants, and Regrets*. Unpublished ms. 1997.

who we are, and Laurence Sterne judged that "the little occurrences of life" would exhibit the truth of character. Our hopes, of course, don't always eventuate as our announcements have predicted. What we write or show, Stewart says, is the "trace of the real."

Of course.

I had hoped to catch reminders of the world in words, sometimes in little pictures, small ink sketches that I entertain myself with. That may mean that I have tried, as Stewart puts it, to take "the world as still life." The still life, she suggests, "speaks to the cultural organization of the material world": it does so "by concealing history and temporality; it engages in an illusion of timelessness. The message of the still life is that nothing changes; the instant described will remain as it is in the eye of the beholder, the individual perceiving subject."

No, I think not.

Words and images are incomplete class notes from the world, a way of catching reminders. Of course they are only traces. They were never anything but traces. The still life does not conceal history and temporality; it dramatizes history and temporality. The still life invites because it is not still; it is always a trace, always fleeting, always only what a single soul beheld, as that could be rendered by errant perception, failed memory, and faltering hand, always only what somebody was able to see and to rearrange, calling from out there for us to see and to rearrange.

Nostalgia, I think, is not a "social disease," as Stewart calls it, or a neurosis. It is a predicament and a natural human condition. The possibility for nostalgia is always present, though some will always look away. During and after great change—and who has not lived during and after great change, and which moment does not occur during and after great change?—we sometimes need to know the name and look of things. The world is always coming unfixed, and we keep trying to know what it's like, what it was like in some before that we imagine.

Nostalgics—that is, most of us some of the time, some of us all of the time—can't have what they ache for. Neither can I. I have wanted to find sources, origins, forces, and track them all the way to here. I can't. There aren't enough words and pictures. I can't find the rest, or I'm unwilling to make the rest.

I can think about the words and pictures, think toward them, but probably not through them.

They are scraps. They are notes from the world. I finger them, as I finger the white rocks in my pocket, and wonder what the words and pictures, things, places, and people did to or for or with or against me, and you, and everyone.

I think there is no really real behind the pictures and words, no really real back or out or over there. My representations will not, as Ned Lukacher puts it in *Primal Scenes*, "provide access to the real." No "primal scene" waits that will alone show the truth all at once, once and for all.

And yet words and pictures are real. I am real. You are real. We are our time, already here, present, yet also ready to be found.

Scraps are what there is. Remnants.

Still we look for the world and for ourselves, yearning, calling out. We go on. We go on looking for the world and for ourselves in it. Some, perhaps, look for what Julia Kristeva calls the "lost thing," "that elusive pre-object," a memory of identity with the other before emotional severance. Some—including many commentators on education—look for a lost authority. Some search for the myths that, as Karsten Harries puts it, are "born of the human inability to accept that we and all we have created someday will be past, will have vanished without a trace, unremembered and unredeemed."

We have wanted to believe that we can be present to the world in what we say or write. Our identity now and our survival hereafter depended, we thought, on that possibility. We have been, whether knowingly or not, part of a two-thousand-year tradition that encouraged us to believe that our character could be in the text of what we say, that we do exist, that we can be in our words and own them even in the acts of giving them away. Character, we believed, can come through speech. If it is the real voice of a genuine personality, then presence will emerge in discourse. To that end, writing teachers have for generations urged students in composition classes to "find their voices," to show readers the directions of their thought and the particularities, anecdotes, and evidence of their lives.

Voluntary Exiles

We don't believe too easily now. We are not at the center. Our characters do not emerge in our discourses. The world is not present to us, and we are not present to the world. We miss ourselves. We dismiss ourselves. We are gone.

We decide against the individual. Where the soul is noticeable or insistent, we proclaim that "radical individualism" is at work and expect the troublesome soul to subside or to evolve.

No matter. I can learn not to be afraid of dismissal or extinction. I can learn what I have said myself: we are remnants, scraps, leftovers, already outside, at the edge. Where we were not exiles before, we have exiled ourselves.

When we fell into history—and sometimes we have to do that over and over, day after day—we tore ourselves loose from the past, and from our sacraments, from the contents and from the values we like to think once gave meaning to our lives. [. . .]

Still, if you are a soul in here, how do you become a self out there?

One answer: you don't. What goes on is what's taken, not what you give, traces of yourself, perhaps, but not yourself. Sometimes, people out there decide that we don't exist. In Pinkie Gordon Lane's "Poems to My Father," the speaker says

> I meant to tell you this, Papa,
> I've divorced myself
> from your memory.

Then later she goes on:

> You never happened,
> Papa.
> You were a shadow
> a low light
> a lost love
> folding into the oval
> of your night.

Sometimes we don't exist, regardless of what people out there decide. Voice, Lukacher says, "has always been a mode of distortion and concealment, for along with its promise of presence, voice has also proclaimed [. . .] a haunting message of distance and absolute separation." We fade away from each other, and do not. We are not present to each other, and we are. There's less to me, and more, than meets the eye or ear.

If you are a soul in here, how do you become a self out there? A second answer: you try.

If I set out and show myself to the other, what rhetoric do I use? Do I have any choice? Do I try to get into the other's rhetoric? That sounds friendly and companionable, but it would be pretty lonesome if I were still over here while trying to talk over yonder. Do I lose my rhetoric in the other's? When do I declare myself, if I know how, and will it matter all the way over yonder?

How do you compose yourself for another? Others, I think, might say that here and elsewhere I'm asking the wrong questions where none is right. Perhaps there is no composing yourself for another, no matter what you do: you're always left behind by your own text.

Reason enough to be a little doubtful.

Sometimes we speak or write tentatively and conditionally, trying to reconstruct ourselves jackleg style. We try to make do, try to tell soul to someone across the way. We try to get real only to learn that our own rhetorics won't let us: they go off and leave us behind, remnants.

Reason enough to be a little doubtful, to choose a tentative and provisional way. And I think I'd rather choose that way, even if, therefore, I cannot be real, even if I am perceived to have chosen altogether otherwise, than to fancy myself a completed, fully asserted person.

Were that possible, and were I to try to speak to the other across the way, my rhetoric would seek to expand, to take up space, to testify that I am real at the cost of the other's diminution. We are apart. I am here. You are there. Our rhetorics cannot occupy the same space at the same time. They compete. [. . .]

And yet, there's every reason to come together, not to merge ourselves in some new collective, but to save one another. We may seldom get things right in concert, but we never will if each of us remains alone.

The story I keep telling myself employs some images, whether they are accurate enough or not, but ignores or misses others. Memory is always a current record, encumbered, of another time that was also encumbered.

All the more reason, then, to hunt for versions of things, for images others saw. We might yet learn to tell our stories, slowly and painstakingly, to one another. I might yet catch what was, what transpires, myself. The daily domestic particulars of our lives give us texture, identity; they give local habitations to our histories. If you come toward me showing me the things of your life that gave you residence, perhaps I will see you. If you can see me in my local habitations, perhaps I existed there.

Blessed particulars always belong to someone. Can they be given to someone else, called back for someone else, given, of-fered? Offered, but not required of another? No one of us is a measure for mankind. The observation and rendition of particu-lars will not necessarily yield universal truth. One moment isn't all of time, or one look a whole view, or one sense of things a revelation about all things. To demand our particular experience of another is arrogance and dogma. May I offer particular expe-rience? I have little else, if anything at all. The lives of particular persons "not distinguished," Samuel Johnson remarked, "by any striking or wonderful vicissitudes" can "lead the thoughts into domestic privacies, and display the details of daily life." Are there circumstances—present and visible, gone and invisible—that might matter as much as events of public moment? If we showed them to one another, fully, painstakingly, might we come to know one another? If we knew one another, might we let one another live? Other worlds always whisper beside this one, or pound against it. We are always in diverse, sometimes competing, rheto-rics. The consequence is often sad and sometimes calamitous, but living among competing rhetorics also guarantees, if we will listen, that we stay resolutely multivocal against the ignorance, arrogance, and dogma of univocality.

Each of us, alone, must speak and write and go on speaking and writing, adding words, piling up words. Our conversation is not like sculpture, where you get what you're looking for by chip-ping and whittling away. Mostly, we have to add and pile on. Unless we're uncommonly lucky, the first words aren't enough. Oftener than not, John Kouwenhoven remarks, we use words as "general terms or names referring to things that are individual and particular. Even though we know, for example, that no two blades of grass are alike, the word 'grass' suggests an identity.

This suggestion of identity encourages us to disregard the different looks, feels, tastes, and smells of the uncounted blades that constitute the actuality of grass as we experience it." But we don't have to disregard the differences. If we tell our stories carefully to one another, we might come to know what particular grass looks like and smells like and feels like and tastes like over here and over there and over yonder.

To make that possible, we have to save one another's views and words. And we have to remember that, however much we may have been socially constructed, however much we may be the creations of a discourse community, however much language may have written us, when a set of spoken or written words comes to us, some soul gathered them, whether under duress, through influence, or by choice. We ought to attend to that word-gathering soul.

As I suggested earlier, this is no longer a universally popular expectation. The individual speaker-writer blurs around the edges, fades from view.

Joel Haefner, for example, proposes that we convert the personal essay, which might have been a place to show our blades of grass, into a collaborative, collective enterprise. The personal essay, Haefner says, rests upon premises undergirded by "the shibboleth of individualism, and, concomitantly, the ideology of American democracy," and so was never free personal expression, though we have, he says, committed the genre to "radical individualism." The self is not unitary, Haefner says, but is created from and by groups, history, and social purposes; and language, he adds, is "not based on individual knowledge but on collective experience." This being so, he goes on, "then the referentiality of personal, expressive prose is called into question, and the accessibility of the personal essay to a universal readership that shares 'human experience' is also in doubt."

The linchpin for all these recent arguments for the revival of the essay remains the idea that the essay presents individualistic, "personal" knowledge. According to Good, "The essayist's personality is offered as a 'universal particular,' an example not of a particular virtue or vice, but of an 'actually existing' individual and the unorganized 'wholeness' of his experience." The problem raised here reflects what Terry Eagleton calls the "humanistic fallacy," "the naive notion that a literary text is just a kind of tran-script of the living voice of a real man or woman addressing us."

Haefner argues further that, "if, as Robert Scholes suggests, 'the whole naive epistemology' that 'a complete self confronts a solid world, perceiving it directly and accurately, always capable of capturing it perfectly' is now 'lying in ruins around us,' then we need to find a new pedagogy that can still make use of the personal essay." This new essay, he proposes, will attempt "to balance the individualistic, expressive view of knowledge with a social, collective perspective," and the best approach is "to bring the personal essay into the collaborative writing project." Doing so, Haefner suggests, will, among other things, destabilize the personal essay further "by encouraging students not to create a unified, coherent first-person singular voice, but rather a mix of 'I' speakers."

Some essayists were always a mix of speakers. Some essay-ists were never complete selves, never confronted the world di-rectly and accurately, never captured it perfectly, were never unified and coherent. Even Samuel Johnson sometimes changed direction in midessay.

But no matter. I think I'd rather we emerged, not as a collec-tive essay, but as an anthology of solitary shouts, remarks, grunts, and whispers.

I don't testify, by saying this, that together we'll get it all right. We more than likely wouldn't. I do mean that we can save one another, keep one another, hold one another, rather than lose one another in the collective, and I do mean that we will not, should not, escape the consequences of our selfhood. Instead of repudiating the self, let us own it by laying it bare.

That's not easy. It may not be possible. But it's what rem-nants have, and they may get there in the jackleg way, the remnant's itinerary. [. . .] I'm recommending texts that are open, owned, but also relinquished, given away. I'm recommending the given, shared jackleg text: "Well, there it is, by God—it ain't much, but it'll hold us until we can think of something better."

The ground for learning and writing and being is freedom. We don't achieve freedom; we are unreleased, always in some inventive world thinking the thoughts we can generate within it, always in some community thinking the thoughts we can generate in it. Nevertheless, freedom, the possibility of freedom, the hope of freedom makes the ground for learning and speaking and writing. And besides, there is a remarkable freedom that speakers and writers have: no one knows for sure the next word they'll say or inscribe.

Texts never were definitive unless we declared them so: Milton continues to emerge to us, unfinished; Johnson in the *Rambler* papers is as often exploring as proclaiming; "definitive" scholarly works require to be done again. The "definitive" text that we have sometimes imagined in the past is an owned and closed text. [. . .] When a text gets written, it becomes authority. When the words are said, the freedom seems to be over. In the classroom, for example, authority is always happening or about to happen; it can arise from diverse sources—from received notions about teaching, from the tyranny of the best student, from the tyranny of the most voluble student, from the arrangement of the room, from the personality of the teacher, from the general curriculum or the specific course plan, from textbooks.

This is not a notion that I'm easy with—the thought that authority (in texts, in classrooms, in life) is always happening or about to happen, that freedom, never wholly achieved, is always slipping away. Still, a little hope remains.

Over here is the *author*, who must be free, or have the hope of freedom, in order to learn and write. Over there is *authority*, the text become fixed, definitive. The *author* by making text makes *authority*, the definitive, the crafted, the finished. But in between is *authoring* or *authorship*, the process, the perpetual hunt for texts only to back off, to improvise, to try again, to search again for freedom in order to speak again in a continuous and provisional self-making. [. . .]

In *authorship*, we might begin to learn how to hold our own cyclings and dartings, dear though inept, to preserve them in order to change them, knowing that we invent in order to make structure in order to make styles in order to serve occasions in order to invent and make structures and styles and serve occasions, in order to be making ourselves.

I have sometimes despaired of jackleg carpentry, yearning for the well-crafted, the finished, the definitive. I should have known better.

Works Cited

Haefner, Joel. "Democracy, Pedagogy, and the Personal Essay." *College English* 54 (1992): 127–37.

Johnson, Samuel. *Rambler* No. 60. 1750. *Samuel Johnson: Selected Poetry and Prose*. Ed. Frank Brady and W. K. Wimsatt. Berkeley: U of California P, 1977. 181–85.

Lane, Pinkie Gordon. "Poems to My Father." *Girl at the Window: Poems*. Baton Rouge: Louisiana State UP, 1991. 1–5.

Lukacher, Ned. *Primal Scenes: Literature, Philosophy, Psychoanalysis.* Ithaca, NY: Cornell UP, 1986.

Stewart, Susan. *On Longing: Narratives of the Miniature, the Gigantic, the Souvenir, the Collection*. Baltimore: Johns Hopkins UP, 1984.

CHAPTER THIRTEEN

Places in the Mind

Grandpa Durham's eyes were pale blue, but sharp and intense, their paleness the more striking because his face was always dark from the sun. When he smiled (a big smile was about as far as he usually got toward actual laughter), his brow and cheeks crinkled up very nicely around the pale eyes. I made it my business not to be present when he frowned, if he did frown. In recent years, I have often found myself wondering what he looked at, what he could see when he left the house early in the morning and walked westward to the barn, or when he sat in the shade of the screened porch late in the afternoon, looking eastward down the way. I can't get in the place where he was and I can't see what he saw.

And what was down the street I saw that time in north Chicago? The far blocks of that street of brownstones had gone blue in the twilight. On a near block, a girl—I guessed her to be in her early teens—sat alone on a stoop. I wondered then, as I wonder now, what she could see from where she was. I can't get there. Now, I'd not be able even to find the street.

I have wondered, too, what Colonel Ranald Mackenzie saw, maybe in early summer of 1874, when he stood looking westward on the porch of the headquarters building at Fort Concho in Texas. Some say that you can see pretty nearly everything from there. Some say that you can't. Whichever it is, I can't get there to see whatever is there to see.

There is an interesting and puzzling place, sometimes dreadful, sometimes joyful, sometimes rich, sometimes poor, always as much created in the mind as situated physically and geographically. Sometimes we go *there* intentionally, sometimes not. Sometimes we know how to get *there*, sometimes not. What happens

---

From *Places in the Mind: Essays on Rhetorical Sites.* Unpublished ms. 1997.

to us when we stay *there?* What happens to us when we leave *there?* When we get *there,* do we see, think, talk, and act in ways we could not practice if we were not *there?* When we look back to this, that, or the other *there,* we generally come to realize that we've occupied places without altogether knowing them. We lose places because they change or vanish, or because we have misremembered them, or never knew them. We lose places because we've gone off and left them, or because we chose not to see them. We lose places because we unintentionally hide them away in repression, or because we have gone off and left them, or because we have deliberately hidden them away.

If I could catch up with Grandpa Durham or the teenage girl or Colonel Mackenzie, I'd still not be able to get into a place to see as each of them saw. While I can't overcome time, I can, of course, remove my person from one place to another, but doing so will not necessarily get me situated with the sun as each of them was situated. If I can't see as others see, at least not perfectly, I can't entirely know as others know or say what others say, and then I'm lonesome, sometimes for my self that was elsewhere. When can I see, know, and say solely from *my* place? When can I decide, judge, argue, disapprove solely from *my* place? Can I do so only by denying the other his or her place? If in companionship, amity, or curiosity, I try to get into the other's place, will I lose identity in what I thought was my place?

We are always getting into a place and using it. The process is inevitable. We are always standing in a place, however momentarily, seeing some part of what can be seen there, knowing and saying what that enables us to know and to say. We do not, of course, always know that we are standing in a place. Sometimes, to be sure, we choose and use our places well, but oftener than not we only occupy a place in which we have already and habitually been, or rent a space that someone else built. The place may be light or dark, fertile or arid, spacious or cramped.

The association of place with seeing, thinking, saying, and acting is not, of course, a new idea. Early teachers of rhetoric, for example, as an aid to their young students' efforts to discover what they might say or should say at a given time on a given occasion, often showed them how to use what we have since called the *topoi,* literally "places in the mind." The intent, as I understand it, was to show students that if they situated themselves over here in this place, that might enable them to think in certain ways, while if they got over yonder in that place, that might enable them to think in other ways. [. . .]

All that we see and think and say is in a continuing history. History occurs in places. Our itinerary from place to place and our way of inhabiting places form our rhetorics—that is, our way of seeing, thinking, and speaking in a particular space. While some of us, I suppose, will stay rooted to one place, therefore to one rhetoric, most of us live in diverse places, therefore in diverse rhetorics. These multiple rhetorics sometimes coexist harmoniously enough; sometimes they compete with one another for dominance. I mean to suggest that *rhetoric* and *place* are affiliated, coexistent, coterminous, isomorphic. Rhetoric does not exist except in place; place does not exist except in rhetoric. Place generates rhetoric; rhetoric creates place. If place changes, rhetoric changes, or disorder occurs; if rhetoric changes, place changes, or disorder occurs. When we come into a language, that is to say, into a rhetoric, we are situated in a place. Some, I expect, might call this marriage by another name and say that we are always ideologically situated, but I hope it may be found that some advantages accrue through the association of rhetoric and place, the latter taken as both figurative and geographical.

This association will help to account for the loss, mourning, regret, nostalgia that will always, in one way or another, accompany our speaking. We cannot keep rhetoric and place, however tightly we grasp and cling. Sooner or later, in one way or another, we go on. We lose place and rhetoric, rhetoric and place, and as we do, we lose the other, including the self as other, for the other is always in a different place. [. . .]

Pig in a Place

I have been slow to learn most things. For some years, I have taught a course in modern rhetoric, which presumably obliges me to notice earlier rhetorics from time to time. I haven't been able to do this at all well or thoroughly—I don't know enough—but I have generally been earnest. Along the way, I've had occasion to talk about the topics, about special topics and general topics, about Aristotle's valid and invalid topics, about Cicero's topics, about Dudley Bailey's old call for modern *topoi*. I suppose we're all easy with the topics in some ways (using them in heuristic systems, converting them to paragraph designs and larger organizational patterns), but I can't claim that l had ever been entirely easy with the idea of the topics. I don't think that I had ever thought my way into the topics, despite the efforts of others to teach me; they remained in a way artificial to me. Then one day I think I heard inside my head at least a little of what the texts had been saying all along.

I was thinking about other things—not rhetoric, not classes, not work, and no matter. I had gone alone to the little grill across the street for a late lunch, had ordered a hamburger and French fries, and had taken my seat at a table. While I waited for the food and while I was eating, I found myself watching and half-hearing what I took to be a family across the room from me. There were four of them, an adult male, an adult female, and two male children, ages maybe two and four. From where I sat, the adult male appeared to imagine himself as the complete male, authoritative, commanding, impressive in his studliness, accustomed to being served. When their hamburgers came, he gestured to his wife, who rose, crossed the room, and fetched him the condiments he apparently wanted. Perhaps five minutes later, the two male children wanted to go to the bathroom, serially, not simultaneously—it is a law of nature that little boys will not ever conduct themselves according to the convenience of an adult. The adult male gestured. The woman took the first little boy to the bathroom, escorted him, then took the second little boy to the bathroom and brought him back. Meanwhile, the master of the house went on with his lunch. He was, I thought, a pig.

But then, in a minute or two, unwelcome thoughts began to leak into my head, and I heard myself thinking, "Wait just a minute now," then "How can you be sure?" I didn't want to doubt my judgment; I wanted to dismiss him as a pig. But I hear myself saying, "Things—people—don't always look the same." I knew, after all, that this was true. Not much is required to shake my judgment, or to remind me of the fragments into which I am scattered. Seen from one place, I think I am a moderately splendid fellow, or at least pretty nearly all right, and that allows me to think in some ways. From another place, I find myself wholly conventional, and that, too, allows me to think in certain ways. From another place, I appear to be wonderfully trivial, a walking cliché, banality afoot, and that, too, allows me to think in certain ways. From another place, I see that I haven't the strength and capacity for evil, but I'm certainly up to foolishness and selfishness, and that generates certain kinds of thought. "Perhaps," I heard myself thinking, "if I could get over there closer, he wouldn't seem to be so much a pig." "But how many places are there in a mind?" I remember thinking, and then, "Can there be wholly different worlds swirling around inside one head?" I remember answering, "Of course there can be." One can live and think and work in different interpretive communities; one can and does live and think and work in different rhetorical worlds.

And then I realized what I was saying to myself. I was imagining places in the mind, and they were much as rhetoricians had explained the topics: "They were the 'regions,' the 'haunts,' the 'places,' where certain categories of arguments resided." What is a place in the mind? A place in the mind is the locale where one belongs to an inventive world and can begin to know it and the varieties of thought it provokes and evokes, the locale where an inventive world gains sufficient dimension and quality to promote thought that is useful even if partial. When I had come to that, the topics began to make sense to me in a new and natural way. Definition, for example, is a habit of mind, more particularly a place of thought, a part of the geography of an inventive world that values definition, that has certain expectations of the self, of the world, of language.

When I say that, I don't believe that I have in the process wrenched an interpretation of the topics loose from the general wisdom found in histories of rhetoric. I believe, instead, that I have begun to understand what I might have caught much sooner.

But I am not a student of the *topoi*, unless it turns out that I am a student of the *topoi*. I'm interested in where rhetorics rise and in how different rhetorics rise in different places, even if all are held in one personality, or place, you might say.

Keeping Places

In one way or another, we like to find and to keep our places. We keep places even when we don't know that we are keeping them. Places, I think, are stays against sadness and mourning. We keep them if we can. When we lose them, we mourn.

Places matter to many of us, perhaps to all of us. Sometimes, identity depends upon location. I ask my friend if he can remember someone who I thought was a mutual acquaintance. "I can't place her," he says.

We're always, I guess, rhetorically mapping the world, whether deliberately or unknowingly, whether directly or otherwise. We know the shameful consequences of being "put in our place," and of putting someone else "in his place" or "in her place." We understand what it's like "to know our own place," and to stay there even when we shouldn't.

We know that we sometimes drive others "around the bend," that others "lead us down the garden path." It's hard sometimes to "stay on the straight and narrow." We often find ourselves "off the beaten track," less often "on the right track." Sometimes we just "go around in circles."

But we like to think we know "where it's at," or "where the action is." We like to get "right to the center of things" or "to the bottom of things." Maybe we want to be "on top of things" or "above it all," where many things are "beneath us." When that happens, sometimes it's splendid, but sometimes others just conclude that we're "far out." Sometimes, though, we're scattered, unable to concentrate, even a little frantic; you might say that we're "all over the place." Then, we don't know "which way to turn," or "which way we're going," or "which way is up." Someone tells us to "get lost," and we realize that we're "getting nowhere fast."

Wherever we are, we're likely to map from ourselves. Some things are up from where we are; some things are down. Some are over, others out. Some things are in front of us. Some are beside us. Some are behind us.

Some of us, of course, don't seem to pay much attention to places. Some don't even seem to notice where they are. Some don't seem to need to pay much attention—places are not what they see, not what they think about.

If some of us always have places in mind and want to be situated there, to see them, and to see them again, while others don't seem to think about places, it may yet be that places matter for all of us, in one way or another. Even if we don't pay much attention to places, to landscapes, rivers, mountains, valleys, canyons, cities, buildings, towns, houses, there may be a place for each of us, a home we're always looking for, even if we never find it—a particular moment in the past, a particular piece of the future.

Among those who do consciously think about places, there is a wide range of attitudes, from a nice, sentimental regard for "pretty" landscapes to a fierce territoriality that will lead some to kill. We don't always know the nature of our own thoughts and feelings about places. In some ways, the ancients were wiser and more accurate in mapping places. We take a globe, flatten it, and pretend that we can see everything from the same perspective. They drew what they could and called the rest *terra incognita*.

I can't find the *beginning* place, the origin of our thinking about places. Usually, if you find what you think is the origin, that means that it isn't the origin, that something else preceded it. In almost any inquiry, you sooner or later come against what you can't know. What did your grandparents see when they sat on their porch and looked across the way? What is that special place you knew when you were eight *really* like? Why exactly do some think about places while others appear not to do so?

What is the origin of our feelings and thoughts about places? Was it, as some say, when the leader of some small band of nomadic hunters—say in southeast Africa, or in China, or in the Tigris Valley, or somewhere—when that leader stuck his spear in the ground, thereby announcing that from now on, this was home, the center of the universe? Was that when it began?

I don't know.

Whenever it began, some of us cherish places, and all of us must live in places, even if we are mobile, even if we are placeless, for whenever we look out through our eyes, we are already in place.

Sometimes, we cherish a special place as a way of stopping time. We hope to get there so that we can relieve ourselves of the anxieties that time and change bring. Usually doesn't work.

We're mostly migrants and transients, but we think about places and in places and toward places. Some of them are the ordinary sites we live in and measure by or use to give directions: "at home," "at work," "down at the corner" "at the intersection of Berry and University Drive," "along Interstate 20," "out on Highway 277."

Some of them are special places, the marking places of our lives, the locales of meaning, whether real or imagined, the geographies of our memories or of our hopes.

I knew Heidelberg and Mannheim a little a long time ago, but they have loomed over my life far more than my scant, untested knowledge of them would justify, perhaps because I was young there. Galveston, Texas, is a special place, perhaps because I was lost there. Vienna and Salzburg and Milan and Paris are special because we went there, perhaps because I never expected to reach them, perhaps because the trip still seems a fairy tale, the travelers a prince and a princess whom I scarcely seem to know. I knew Paris twice, on two different maps I keep. Concord, New Hampshire, and the roads out from there are special places. Cleburne, Texas, and Abilene, Texas, and Washington, D. C., are special places where my children live. Boston is a special place; I remember a blizzard there, and an engaging walk I took up Washington Street, and a dear meandering walk we took along Newbury Street. Some places are special even if I haven't been there—rural stretches of northern England and Scotland, back roads in New Mexico, away from roads along the Caprock from Quitaque down to Post. I remember Myrtle Beach and Calabash and Sunset Beach, straddling the North Carolina—South Carolina border, and Charleston and Miami Beach, and the hot tub on top of the Clarion Hotel in New Orleans. I remember Lafayette, Indiana, where the corn was so high, from another map; Mesa Verde is there, too. I remember Chicago and San Diego and Carmel and San Francisco and Snowbird, where she danced.

I don't always know why places have become places. I know
that there are perceptual regions in my head, with better borders
than those drawn by politicians. I know that the maps in my
head and the maps on the sheets in front of me sometimes replace what some call reality. I know that maps and the places on
them have, as Phillip and Juliana Muehrcke put it, the "force of
truth." In his poem "Listening to Maps," Howard McCord says
that a map

> . . . keeps telling you where you are.
> And if you're not there,
> you're lost.

Later, he says,

> We are sitting here, you and I,
> in a place on the map.
> We know this. Yet we are not on the map.

I know that few of us are deliberately geographers, yet what
Eric Dardel calls "geographicality" may be both our way of existence and our fate. "Geographical reality," Dardel says, "demands an involvement of the individual in his emotions, his body,
his habits, that is so total that he comes to forget it just as he
forgets his own physiological life." I know that I have spent a
good part of my adult life trying to understand why one stretch
of West Texas draws me, pulls at me, why I need to go there and
look at it once in a while, though I don't belong there and probably never did.

We cherish places even when, ironically, we can't see them,
and we never can. We can't see places because someone else is
always seeing them differently, and we can't know exactly what
they're seeing. We can't see places because we can't see them.
When we look from a distance, refraction and distance cues,
misinterpreted between eye and brain, transform the scene. I have
looked at the Double Mountains all of my life and never seen it.

Perhaps we can't see places, can't know what they signify,
until we've faced or found exile from them, and then we can't see
them, for it's time to mourn.

After all this time, I begin to remember and to notice and even to understand, a little, what places mean to me, and how they mean. I begin to understand, a little, you might say, the place that places have in my life, though I was surprised by Las Vegas. I have always yearned for places, and have found a few, have always thought about places and from places and in places and toward places.

I can't, however, lay claim to much in the way of places, can't claim any territory larger than a house. Well, the kitchen, anyway. At least my desk. Even so, I claim places privately. I need to, and I usually have places in my mind. I don't much like to be put in my place, but I do spend considerable time trying to place myself, and I like it when things are in place.

In my office at school, I've just about got to have all of my stacks straight, and there are a lot of them, on my desk, on the worktable, on the floor, and on the couch that I also use as a table. I'm just about out of unfilled flat surfaces. I don't mind that too much, as long as my little stacks of things remain straight, sides even, corners squared. I don't mind a coating of dust and ashes from my pipe if I have a small, clean surface in front of me where I can work. The other day a student came to see me. He wanted to show me something he was writing. He stood beside me as I sat at my desk, leaned over, shoved some of my stacks aside, and spread his pages in front to me. I wasn't able to read them thoughtfully—I was pretty busy having a small internal hemorrhage. My stacks were in disarray. My place was in disorder.

I reckon that my behavior is compulsive in other ways, too, or obsessive if it turns out that way. I have a strong need to check my pockets pretty regularly to see if I'm still there and to see if everything is still in place—tobacco pouch, bandanna, billfold, keys, knife, three one-dollar slugs, a white rock from Grandpa's farm in West Texas, my pens, and my little notebook. If my rhythm is interrupted while I'm checking, I have to start over. I do not, however, check myself for dust and pipe ashes.

I've often wondered: if your behavior is compulsive—or obsessive, however it eventuates—and you know that it is and can watch yourself in the process of being compulsive or obsessive, then is it still compulsive or obsessive or whatever? I don't know.

I do know that it's hard to change some habits that have been, you might say, learned in place.

I can't remember and name all the places where I might have learned whatever behaviors—they are too many, even in an uneventful life, and I have since been placed again and displaced again, sometimes found, sometimes a little lost. I can't always get situated, in place to see what I might or maybe should. Places are inescapable, even when we're displaced, perhaps especially then.

On most Saturday mornings—maybe forty-five out of the fifty-two or so that a year provides—I go to the central public library downtown. I fell into that habit when my children were young and have enjoyed it since.

Almost invariably, a number of people (and I) are waiting in front of the library for the doors to open at ten o'clock. Some of them, I know, are there just to get books to read. Some are there on particular errands. After all these years of watching, however, I've come to reckon that most who are there waiting for ten o'clock fit into one of two groups.

The first group is easy enough to recognize—they belong to the city's downtown homeless. I say "downtown homeless" to distinguish the group from the west-side homeless, the near-south-side homeless, the near-east-side homeless, and other groups. Each group, I understand, has its own gathering, waiting, watching places. Some among the downtown homeless choose the library; others, I'm told, gather in other places, reasonably near.

I have wondered (and for brief scattered moments have known) what it is like not to have a place, to be homeless, to take a public site of convenience as the place for the day, the home. I do not learn from those who gather before ten o'clock, waiting for the library to open. I do not know them; I have not talked to them. If I did know them and talk to them, I expect I still would not know what it is like for them not to have a place. Still, I do learn from them. The years of watching tutor me, and I think I begin to learn, not what it is like not to have a place, but how one mourns when one doesn't. Two discrete forms of behavior have struck me over the years; each, I think, is a manifestation of mourning, of grief, of nostalgia, of whatever. Some members of the group appear to isolate themselves from the others; they characteristically do not speak; they do not meet the look of others, characteristically keeping their eyes averted or cast down. I'd guess that, in one way or another, they are lost in misery and perhaps in memory, mourning in their own ways. Other members of this first group, the downtown homeless, act differently, though I'd guess that they, too, are lost. These appear to have formed a subgroup within the larger group, and they are apparently recognizable to each other by various signs, one of which is a cup looped onto the belt. Their behavior is bold, even cocky. They group; they push ahead of others when the doors open. They proclaim identities that are lost. All are placeless.

The members of the second major group may be placeless, too. They come with briefcases and bookbags and notebooks, sometimes with thermos bottles and lunches, in for the day in the library's genealogy section. Genealogical study is for some, I know, first and chiefly an antiquarian delight or a delight in detection, but all, I judge, are also looking for a family, a history, a home, a place.

In one way or another, we like to find and to keep our places. We keep places even when we don't know that we are keeping them. Places, I think, are stays against sadness. We keep them if we can. When we lose them, sometimes we mourn.

We lose places, some of them sacred. What kind of marker will keep, celebrate sacred places that are lost? Not even the land can be counted on to stay the same. Erosion continues without me.

We have sometimes tried to imagine the worst—nuclear storm, say, or ecological disaster—and it looks a placeless world, where we can no longer situate ourselves. We have no places to be.

My mother came to that. When my father fell into his last illness and she could no longer care for him, and we could no longer care for the two of them, she went with him to what was called a "retirement center." She was never, however, easily sympathetic to bullshit, though she wouldn't have it put that way. To her, it was the "old folks' home," where people go to cough, to spit, to fart, to die. She stayed for three months after he died, hating the place that was not a place, and then she died.

I have often wanted to know places, to tell about places, but I am not equal, after all, to sacred places. I want to know about ordinary places. Perhaps they're not different. What kind of markers will keep and celebrate our ordinary places that may also be sacred?

In towns and cities, we often mark places by names that try to keep a rural, pastoral quality in places that are not rural and pastoral—a kind of rhetorical landscaping. Not far from where I sit is an area called Westcliff, and beyond it is Tanglewood, and yonder lie Briar Meadows and Western Hills and Oakhurst and Riverside. Will such names, do you suppose, keep peace and quiet and rest in a crowded city?

And where do you go to think? Is that home? How do we know when we have reached home? What gateway do we enter? What threshold do we cross? What marker tells us we've reached the place?

Some signals suggest that if we haven't reached the place, we still expect to hereafter. In a study published in 1976, Wilbur Zelinsky discusses maps of the afterworld that emerge in cemetery names. Using the American Cemetery Association's 1967 survey of about ten thousand cemetery names, Zelinsky notes that while about half of the names indicate possession or location, the rest point to fanciful, typically rural and Edenic scenes, idealized places for the dead and for such mourners who come to visit. The names are often little poems of the rural world: Green Bower Wildwood Cemetery, Skylawn Memorial Gardens, Green Sanctuary, Lawn Haven Burial Estates, Chapel of the Chimes, Hills of Eternity, Pleasant Walk Cemetery, Serenity Gardens, Wanderer's Rest. Here closer to home, I come upon Bluebonnet Hills Memorial Park, Cedar Hills Memorial Park, Greenwood, Mount Olivet, Laurel Land.

The names, Zelinsky reminds us, are projective; that is, they don't necessarily mention what is there in cemeteries, but meanings we project upon them. Where rose or oak or chapel appears in a name, we may have to look hard to find them. The most common names for general plant cover are wood, lawn, grove, evergreen, forest. The most common specific plants that show up in cemetery names are oak, rose, maple, elm, cedar, laurel, walnut, holly, olive, magnolia, fern, willow, and chestnut.

Sometimes, it's hard to find the woodlands or grasslands that we still seem to yearn for. My mother and father are buried in a green and grassy place, above a dirty river, across the street from an oil refinery, a long way from Jayton.

I like to think about a territory, a range of ordinary places that may be sacred places. I was never rooted there, never at home there, and always was. The territory is not home, and it is. It might have been home if I had paid attention, if I had taken the time to know its particulars. I am a refugee, a migrant, a nomad, a transient, though I have mostly stayed in one place. We all are, in our various ways, wandering about the continents, warming ourselves with memories of what might have been home. If we have a place, it is exile.

And it's not. "Lord, let me die," James Dickey writes, "but not die out." How many Latvians or Letts in the past century, knowing themselves as exiles, died believing that their country had died?

Fixed or unfixed, settled or unsettled, we may be lost, un-thinking, dead. Stability and change, Yi-Fu Tuan says, are both essential needs; if always stable, we don't see what we see; if always changing, we can't know what we see. Rooted, I may be, as Tuan suggests, unself-conscious, unreflective; self-conscious and reflective, I am lonesome, separated, exiled. To have one's eyes open wide, Tuan remarks, is to be an exile; to think is to take leave of one's senses, to be placeless. Places are there, out there, where we may be rooted and know them in special ways. Yet, moving, looking at a distance, we create places and know them in special ways, other ways. Places are out there, and I create them.

The strangest place of all, of course, David Lowenthal re-members for us, is inside our heads. We are mostly parochial, he suggests; we may recognize world horizons in theory, but we dis-regard them in practice. Things that we assume are common knowledge often aren't; what seems to me the general outlook is only mine. Conditions that we take as disorders quickly disrupt views of the world. Psychotics, Lowenthal says, distinguish poorly between themselves and the outside world; mystics may take their own bodies as geographical descriptions; schizophrenics often underestimate size and overestimate distance; brain-injured people may not be able to organize their environment, may forget familiar locations; what we take to be impairments such as aphasia and apraxia may prevent our seeing spatial relationships.

But the view of the world shared by "sane, healthy, sentient adults" is chancy enough. I omit the very young, who are unable to discern what is themselves, what is not, and the very old, in whom loss of hearing, peculiarities of vision, and other infirmities may create what Lowenthal calls a second geographical childhood.

"Sane, healthy, sentient adults" don't do all that well, though there is none better. Our best views of the world and its places are partial; features of the environment exist for us, usually, only if they are related to our purposes and interests, defined, if at all, out of a limited range of sensations. To some creatures, Lowenthal proposes, the world is noisier and more fragrant than it is to us; some creatures see normally on a microscopic scale, which we too can do, but not normally; the flour in a canister seems undifferentiated to us, but probably not to a flour beetle.

Each of us, it seems likely, lives in a separate, personal geography, to some degree congruent with some "reality" shared by others, but nevertheless unique. No two of us can occupy the same place, or see from that place, simultaneously. The past we bring to our looking shapes our personal geographies. Lowenthal tells of citizens in some cities destroyed in World War II who continued to walk along nonexistent streets and sidewalks. I've often wondered why I still cannot recall some parts of Jayton. I guess they weren't on my early paths, and so I didn't see them. When we look at places, we're all artists and architects, creating places as we look.

But I can't come to grand themes except in puny ways. I have no credentials as an ecologist, as a farmer, or even as a gardener. I don't believe that I am fiercely territorial, except, perhaps, for three or four feet at a time. I don't much think nature is inherently divine. I don't believe I illustrate the near-religious concept that Tuan calls *geopiety*. A reverent attachment to family, homeland, and the gods that protect them seems a bit strong. I probably won't do a harvest dance this year, but I may do a little jig next fall when the first hard norther comes down hard off the Caprock.

Places are places. They are places where we were and are. We ought to know and to remember them. Some places are special to one, some to another. Some are near to sacred for me—the head of Putoff Canyon about three miles north of Jayton, the Double Mountains, the Croton Breaks, the place where you go up on the Caprock near Quitaque, a garden that was—and I do know the path to the Promised Land. I come to places in my way and only approach grand themes by puny, partial thought. I go and look again. We should remember all our places and show them to one another, but I can tell a little only about some of mine. I am separated from most of them.

Probably that's what matters. Probably places become dearest to us when we face the possibility or actuality of exile. Even exile, however, doesn't crowd me, I think, with the impulses and motives that have sometimes led to excesses in the name of the homeland. I think I only want to remember places where we've been and are.

Some would rather move on. I believe that we should see new places, though some won't have much appeal for me. In 1774, Lord Dunmore, Royal Governor of Virginia, wrote to the Secretary of State for the Colonies, the Earl of Dartmouth:

> I have learnt from experience that the established Authority of any government in America, and the policy of Government at home, are both insufficient to sustain the Americans: and that they do and will remove as their avidity and restlessness invite them. They acquire no attachment to Place: But wandering about seems engrafted to their Nature.

Perhaps, Tuan suggests, such attitudes made it easier for us to shift Indians around from one place to another.

Still, even when moving on, we've come to know, to love our own places in our diverse ways, some ungenerous, exclusive, and intolerant, though we're not always so. The connection between place and identity is common in our thinking and in our talk: "This is my place"; "Come over to my place"; "I feel at home here." The Bible tells the expulsion story twice. The *Aeneid* creates a home place. *Paradise Lost* is intensely and continuously preoccupied with place, from the debate of the rebel angels about making, taking, and reclaiming a place, to the end:

> The world was all before them, where to choose
> Their place of rest, and Providence their guide,
> They, hand in hand, with wandering steps and slow,
> Through Eden took their solitary way.

We look for primal scenes, places of origin, in psychoanalysis, in coffee-table books, in genealogical studies, asking as we go: Is there a place for each of us? Is there a home we're always looking for? When did it begin, our feeling for place? Why do some pay attention to places, while others don't seem to? Are we always in exile?

If we slow down for a minute and listen, we hear places, all around us. Any place is crowded with other places, echoes with other places. We carry places around with us, in our names and in our words. We try to keep places with us.

Family names were uncommon a thousand years ago, unknown in most places. If you stayed on the farm or in the village where people knew you, you didn't need a family name for identification. Last names began to appear in the twelfth, thirteenth, and fourteenth centuries in England (and across Europe), but didn't become family names—that is, didn't pass from generation to generation—until the fourteenth century. Before that, Edmund, the son of Egbert, might be called Edmund Egbertson, but his son, Alfred, would probably have been called Alfred Edmundson. When family names began to occur and to stay, they sometimes derived from appearance, complexion, hair color (Black, Brown, Little, White, Biggs), far more often from occupation (Farmer, Shepard, Coward, Gardner, Parker, Cook, Hunter, Fowler, Skinner, Tanner, Weaver, Carter, Smith, Bowman, Wayne), frequently from places (Brooks, Rivers, Hill, Dale, Shaw, Mills, Church). George Washington's family name probably derives from a village in County Durham. Abraham Lincoln's name probably comes from the English city or county. Grover Cleveland's name more than likely derives from the town in Yorkshire.

Ordinary words in our vocabulary tell places. Any spaniel might call back Spain, and a cashmere sweater resonates with the Vale of Kashmir. *Bronze* recalls Brundisium, now Brindisi, in southern Italy, and *copper* is a corruption of Cyprus. *Laconic* recalls the Greek province of Laconia, home of the Spartans, and a peeping Tom recalls Coventry and Lady Godiva. Gauze tells of Gaza, champagne tells of northern France, and hooch recalls the Hutsnuwu Indians of Alaska, who did some moonshining. Java echoes Java, mayonnaise recalls Port Mahón on the island of Minorca, scallions recall Ascalon in Israel, and argyle socks call back the tartan of the Campbells of Argyll. Blue jeans echo with the French form of Genoa, Genes, where the prototypical pants were first made. They were made, later at least, from a twilled cotton fabric first made in Nîmes, hence *serge de Nîmes*, hence *denim*. Bedlam calls back the hospital of St. Mary of Bethlehem in London, and bunk calls back Congressman Felix Walker, who slowed the debate on the Missouri Compromise by speaking to and for Buncombe County, North Carolina. If we wear plaid or flannel, we remember the Celts, if we eat broccoli or publish a manifesto, we remember Italy, and if we look at a landscape, drink a little gin, and take a nap, we remember Holland. Bonanzas and cockroaches and cargoes and mosquitoes and tornadoes, alligators and mesas and canyons and arroyos and buckaroos call back Mexico and Spain. If we cook rolls with currants, we remember Corinth, but if we use Jerusalem artichokes in a salad, we remember not Israel, but Italy—Jerusalem is a variation on *girasole,* a term applied to sun-turning plants.

We can't talk without trying to call back other places, other times. If we board a plane that has a pilot, we take on the shipped freight of steamboat talk from the South before 1850. If we take our grubstake and our hopes pan out and we hit pay dirt, we remember the California of the Gold Rush. Some of us can't talk for very long without recalling the language of poker as it spread upriver from New Orleans into the Western frontier: put up or shut up, I'll call you on that, I'll call your bluff, New Deal, Square Deal, big deal, deal me out, deal me in. Some of us are lucky enough to have an ace in the hole or aces back to back. Think of the tribes we echo (sometimes nothing else of them is left) in Illinois, Ohio, Michigan, Kentucky, Tennessee, Alabama, Mississippi, Arkansas, Minnesota, Kansas, Nebraska, Oklahoma, Texas, Utah, Wyoming, Idaho, Oregon.

We tried to bring everywhere with us to Texas and to recall all those other places in our own place names. If you drive from Fort Worth through Austin to San Antonio, you pass by Alvarado, named for a city of the same name in Mexico, where an early settler here fought in a battle during our war with Mexico, and you pass by Itasca, named by an early settler for Lake Itasca in Minnesota, and you pass by New Braunfels, recalling the settlement of Germans led by Prince Carl of Solms-Braunfels in 1845. Early settlers brought the arts with them, in their minds at least, and named places Ben Hur and Dante and Longfellow and Poetry and Ivanhoe and Tennyson and Bronte. They kept their religious background, too, in place names: Antioch, Bethany, Bethel, Bethesda, Bethlehem, Calvary, Canaan, Corinth, Damascus, Eden, Jericho, Nazareth, and at least five places named Shiloh.

Spanish names occur all over the state, Polish perhaps only once, at Panna Maria. We borrowed Gainesville, Jacksonville, and Miami from Florida, Montgomery from Alabama, Atlanta and Augusta from Georgia, Memphis from Tennessee, Lexington and Paducah from Kentucky, Arlington, Fredericksburg, Jamestown, Mount Vernon, Richmond, and Roanoke from Virginia. We have Georgetown, Scranton, Pittsburg, Newark, Albany, Buffalo, Rochester, Boston, Concord, Providence, Cleveland, Gary, Joplin, and Abilene. And we brought names from around the world: Nineveh, Palestine, Samaria, Galilee, Medina, Baghdad, Tunis, Carthage, Sudan, Canton, Tokyo, Turkey, Troy, Italy, Rome, Praha, Dresden, Rhineland, Paris, Newcastle, Hereford, Kent, Sherwood, Oxford, Derby, Dundee, Edinburg, Dublin.

Why did we bring all those names with us to Texas? Perhaps we tried to bring everywhere with us so that we could hold and remember the names and places in our place names. We went back to our old *topoi* for meaning. Our old *topoi* aren't there anymore.

A Hard Place to Find

We clearly have reason to live and to speak in two rhetorics. *Gates of Repentance: The New Union Prayerbook for the Days of Awe* quotes an eighteenth-century Hasidic source: "Keep two truths in your pocket, and take them out according to the need of the moment. Let one be: 'For my sake was the world create.' And the other: 'I am dust and ashes.'" Despair and the truth taken out to meet that temper will generate a rhetoric; vanity and the truth taken out to meet that temper will generate another; and the two rhetorics will be different, though housed in one body.

In my own instance, three rhetorics occasionally evidence themselves. When I am being pretty obsessive, or compulsive, whichever it turns out to be, I live and talk in the rhetoric that circumstances generate. But I also notice that I am being pretty obsessive, or compulsive, and I can comment on that behavior in a second rhetoric. Meanwhile, there is a third that keeps asking, "Why in hell are you wasting your time on rhetorics 1 and 2?"

[. . .] My friend Baumlin says that there are four rhetorics: an incarnational rhetoric, a transcendental rhetoric, a skeptical rhetoric, and a sophistic rhetoric. He appears to be all right, otherwise. On some days, I'm pretty sure that there are five rhetorics, as intellect teaches me to speak in one way, while emotions tell another, and will insists on a third, and what's left of soul whispers a fourth, and body comes with a fifth to dominate the others.

I won't continue, except to say that when you set out to count rhetorics, there is usually one more than you have counted when you are done. When you talk about rhetoric or rhetorics, you're always already inside a rhetoric. We usually miss this one when we count: it's sometimes as hard to see as the backs of your own eyeballs.

But it's there, whether or not we see it or acknowledge it. That prior rhetoric calls for some modification of the ways in which we think and talk about argument.

After twenty centuries and more of study and practice, I expect it's foolish to remark casually that we should modify the ways in which we think and talk about argument. We have modified our ways and will again. We no longer have any compelling reason, if we ever did, to think that rhetoric is only and completely the study and practice of arguments. Dryden remarked that writers of his time could not write Shakespeare's plays, that, indeed, Shakespeare himself, were he alive in this other time, could not write Shakespeare's plays. Aristotle among us, I reckon, would write a different rhetoric.

Still, we have every reason to continue doing much of what we have done as we have discussed rhetoric and argument. It is never less than valuable to show, as best we can, how others have expressed their views, how they have shown their reasoning, how they have presented their evidences.

But we have missed the mark altogether, I think, in at least two ways as we have discussed rhetoric and argument. First, we have ignored some behaviors that are arguments because they did not look like arguments. Second, we have continued to think and to talk in conventional ways about some argumentative behaviors that are fruitless to discuss unless we learn to think in different ways.

Some behaviors come at us quickly, and they hurt, quick arguments against our identity. Often no more than a sentence or two—sometimes no more than two or three words, depending on how one counts "That's bullshit"—they do not seem to have the appearance of arguments, but they are, though we seldom have time or opportunity for any kind of rebuttal except an angry retort, a quiet and painful withdrawal, or a blow upon the side of the head. We are usually unarmed from the outset. I am talking about quick barbs, slurs, slaps, insults, attacks, and I call them arguments because they are. They arise out of completed rhetorics—an inventive history eventuates in a structure and style at a particular occasion for a particular audience. They are shorthand arguments; they are the moment's last sentence or last phrase representing a presence come out of one world to repudiate and to efface our presence in another. Sometimes they are meant innocently, but only a hearer who lives in the same world as the speaker could take them that way.

Four of us sit at a restaurant table, studying menus, amid much conversation about this food and that. Before we have done with this, the younger woman turns to the two older women—her mother and her aunt—and remarks that their ways of thinking about food are weird. I have not tried to quote her, but I believe I am faithful to the sense of the moment.

Later, when we talk about this occasion, the young woman tells me that her remark was "just an observation." I took her remark as a successful attack. I would not presume to say how the two older women took her remark, but they did fall silent.

What I believe happened, as I suggested a moment ago, is that a proposition, a single predication, emerged from a completed rhetoric, for whatever innocent intentions, to become an attack in the other rhetoric where it was heard, and where its effect was diminution and then effacement.

Her history, her mode of rhetorical invention, produces one model of the world; the rest of us live in histories, in systems of rhetorical creation, that produce another model, and we cannot hear what she says as merely an observation. It is an attack. She has spent her life, not in prosperity, but generally able to make satisfactory choices. She has not been altogether free from need and want, but her life has been reasonably secure. She has generally been assured that she is special, and commonly believes that what she intends of words will be their eventuation. She can, therefore, utter statements as critical observations according to her model, which is akin to the surgeon's model: she can go in precisely, and excise the offending characteristic, or appendix. The rest of us hear, however, in another world, modeled more like that of the chemotherapist: the treatment will not simply affect one precise spot, but will poison the entire body; that is to say, it will repudiate identity. What matters at this point, I think, is that two rhetorics, neither completely uttered, two worlds, neither completely revealed, had tried to come together in the same place at the same time. In this instance, coexistence was, for a moment, not possible. What was normal in one world was weird in the other. The rest of us had lived always in worlds where assurance and security were seldom possible. The two older women loved to study menus, for they didn't want to miss anything, and to order food that everyone would share, for they delighted in the diversity that had not always been possible. The younger woman had generally felt included in the world. The two older women—and I—had generally felt excluded from the world. We seldom learn once and for all how to respond to shorthand arguments, but they are as complete, and sometimes as devastating, as formal ones.

Discussions of formal arguments, as in rhetoric and composition textbooks, still do not consistently acknowledge that argument puts world against world, therefore do not consistently acknowledge that what is reason, good sense, good judgment, and evidence in one world is not reason, good sense, good judgment, and evidence in the other. Where we come to controversy over matters about which we have deep and steadfast conviction, the argument is already over when the argument begins. Participants are not waiting to be completed by the propositions and proofs of their opponents; each already lives in a completed rhetoric, else there'd be no controversy. Earlier, I suggested that we still think and talk in conventional ways about some argumentative behaviors that are fruitless to discuss unless we learn to think in different ways. If my convictions are deep and steadfast, and if I believe that I have exhibited reason, good sense, good judgment, and evidence (and I will believe that, for most of us don't get up in the morning and resolve to be silly asses throughout the day), then the argument is already over when the argument begins. That means, I believe, that we should focus some of our attention, not on argument, but on what used to be called narrative and description. Argument rests on propositions that cannot be accepted and proofs that are not proofs. Where convictions are deep and steadfast, arguers need less to declare than to show.

Joseph Brodsky remarked of poets, in "How to Read a Book," that "[t]hey have no illusions about the objectivity of the views they put forth; on the contrary, they insist on their unpardonable subjectivity right from the threshold." I'm always a little surprised that any of us has illusions about our objectivity; all writing is self-writing, though we have mostly schooled ourselves to omit the *I* that is the real subject of our sentences, and we have schooled ourselves to omit any signs that our writing has been produced, that it follows a personal itinerary.

Still, we ought to reveal our motivations, to reveal how and when and why we came to the subjects we explore, and I think we will usually do better to try to show ourselves in the world we live in, thinking what we think, than to try to declare ourselves in our propositions and proofs.

When we set out to talk or to write about anything—about rhetoric, or about anything else—we are already inside a rhetoric, a way of creating, and, in fairness, we ought to show that rhetoric, even if it is sometimes as hard as learning to see and to show the back sides of our own eyeballs.

Of course, we don't get a self written. That's always provisional. If, by chance, we get a self written, that self goes off on pages that are no longer ours while we go on being other selves. Still, we can try. After all, to claim that all forms of writing are forms of acknowledged or unacknowledged self-writing is a way of thinking that has some rhetorical legitimacy. The itinerary we follow and the baggage we carry toward our formal or orthodox versions of writing are their subjects. If we're ever going to know and to understand one another, we'll have to risk showing ourselves. That entails, among other things, trying to understand and to show others how we have constructed ourselves and our rhetorical propositions from inside our own rhetorics. We treat academic papers as "out there," apart from ourselves, but they are not. We come to them for personal reasons, whether by deliberate, pragmatic choice for purposes of gain in some tenure or status race, or through personal necessity arising from our own imperatives and interior narratives. An orthodox academic paper, I judge, is only the last half or so of a personal essay.

When we talk or write about a rhetoric—that is to say, any subject—we are already in a rhetoric. When we compose a new rhetoric, we come into it through the agency of an old rhetoric. Entering a new rhetoric, however, doesn't release us into unbound vision, unfettered truth. The light from the desk lamp on the table where I work catches in the heavy plastic frames of my glasses. I see what is before me, framed by that reflected light, as well as can reasonably be expected, but if I look up and out of the window, then I cannot see what is before me out yonder. I change glasses and see out there, but now I can no longer see what is before me in here. When we make a new rhetoric, or find our way into a new rhetoric, we do so through the instrumentality of an old rhetoric. I find my far-seeing glasses by looking through my near-seeing glasses. We put on a new rhetoric and take up its instrumentalities. Then it's difficult to see the old rhetoric, or to find our other glasses. We may situate ourselves with the sun in a new and different way, but we are in a rhetoric. If we come to know that, then we begin to lift our own rhetoric, which is always here and active, up into the open and toward the other. Then, with a little luck, we might enfold another, and be enfolded.

Works Cited

Brodsky, Joseph. "How to Read a Book." *New York Times Book Review* 12 June 1988: 1+.

McCord, Howard. "Listening to Maps." *Maps: Poems toward an Iconography of the West*. Santa Cruz, CA: Kayak, 1971. 1–2.

Stern, Chaim, ed. *Gates of Repentance: The New Union Prayerbook for the Days of Awe*. New York: Central Conference of American Rabbis, 1978.

Zelinsky, Wilbur. "Unearthly Delights: Cemetery Names as a Key to the Map of the Changing American Afterworld." *Geographies of the Mind: Essays in Historical Geosophy in Honor of John Kirtland Wright*. Ed. David Lowenthal and Martyn J. Bowden. New York: Oxford UP, 1975. 171–95.

AN ANNOTATED BIBLIOGRAPHY OF CORDER'S WORK

KEITH D. MILLER

When considering Jim W. Corder's remarkable career as a professor, university administrator, scholar, public speaker, and writer, one might conceive of his *modus operandi* as an effort to construct his audience(s) in a set of overlapping, concentric circles with each larger circle including members of the smaller circle(s) inside it.

In the center, the smallest circle encompassed his friends, faculty colleagues, administrative colleagues, staff members, and students at Texas Christian University (TCU) in Fort Worth, where Corder taught for almost forty years and where three of his co-authors—Lyle Kendall, Porter Perrin, and James S. Baumlin—also taught. Over the years he delivered numerous speeches before various TCU audiences. In 1973 he produced a longish essay for an official coffee-table book commemorating the one-hundredth anniversary of TCU. Between 1977 and 1980 he wrote twelve essays for *Image*, a TCU magazine. Between September 1981 and December 1981 he wrote a weekly column for the student newspaper, the *Daily Skiff*. He also contributed occasionally to other local publications.

Growing out of this circle was a group of Corder's former students and other TCU alumni, who, along with fundraising appeals for the university, regularly received a periodical trumpeting campus news. From 1960 to 1996, Corder wrote many columns for this publication, which was initially titled *This Is TCU*, then retitled *TCU Magazine*.

The next, larger circle consisted of Corder's former graduate students and others in Texas who invited him to speak at their institutions or at the Texas State Historical Association or who published his essays in their journals, such as *English in Texas*. This circle also included the editors at Texas A&M University Press, who issued two of his three books about West Texas, and the readers of those books, many of whom lived in Texas. A fourth coauthor, John Ruszkiewicz, also resided in the state.

The penultimate circle was regional. Corder's success in Texas helped get him elected president of the South Central Modern Language Association (SCMLA)—a position that enlarged his professional network. In 1978 he began publishing essays in *New Mexico Humanities Review*, which was coedited by Jerry Bradley, his former student.

The final, largest, most inclusive circle was national. Corder often read at CCCC, the Penn State Conference on Rhetoric and Composition, and SCMLA; he also spoke at universities in Nebraska, Missouri, Virginia, and Arizona. He published (sometimes frequently) in such significant national journals as *College Composition and Communication*, *College English*, *PMLA*, the *Quarterly Journal of Speech*, *Rhetoric Review*, *Pre/Text*, *Rhetoric Society Quarterly*, *Composition Studies/Freshman English News*, the *CEA Critic*, the *ADE Bulletin*, *Liberal Education*, *Educational Theory*, the *Journal of Higher Education*, the *Chronicle of Higher Education*, *Perspectives in Biology and Medicine*, and *Arete: Journal of Sports Literature*. He produced a book for Lippincott and two more for the University of Georgia Press while contributing scholarly essays to volumes issued by NCTE, Prentice-Hall, HarperCollins, Sage, Boynton/Cook, Southern Illinois University Press, Southern Methodist University Press, and TCU Press. And he authored, coauthored, or edited five textbooks that were marketed nationally.

The dates on Corder's publications are important in considering his professional evolution. While a student at the University of Oklahoma he wrote his dissertation on Restoration comedy; in that same year, 1958, he joined TCU as a specialist in eighteenth-century British literature. What appears to be his first published, scholarly essay is a piece of literary criticism about *Gulliver's Travels*, the eighteenth-century classic by Jonathan Swift. By the late 1960s, however, he had turned to rhetoric/composition. During most of his career, he also published more-or-less purely belletristic essays (often for journalistic outlets) and numerous pieces about university administration, education theory, and the state of English studies (including curricular design: he was one of our profession's first staunch advocates of cultural and interdisciplinary studies organized around rhetorical principles and rhetorical study).

Although Corder rejected the distinction between scholarly and personal writing, he did not treat his audiences identically. While usually featuring some version of the wistful, self-effacing autobiographical narrator familiar to his academic readers, his newspaper and magazine publications are, generally speaking, more ephemeral and certainly less scholarly and less theoretical. (He once dismissed some of these efforts as "elegant trifles" ["Hoping for Essays" 301].)

The purpose of this bibliography is to list and annotate Corder's more scholarly publications along with his longer pieces of creative nonfiction. While some of these works evoke West Texas geography and history, Corder clearly intended them for both a regional and a national readership.

My coeditor and I chose to exclude Corder's more journalistic writing from this bibliography. Two major reasons guided this decision. First, attempting to include his journalistic output would have extended this compilation for many, many more pages. Second, some of the journalistic pieces address issues specific to TCU and make allusions—for example, to bygone TCU football heroes—that, while familiar to his local readers, would puzzle others. I also include two examples of his poetry.

Baumlin, James S., and Jim W. Corder. "Jackleg Carpentry and the Fall from Freedom into Authority in Writing." *Freshman English News* 18 (Spring 1990): 18–25.

> Uses the vernacular of West Texas while engaging poststructuralist theories of knowledge and authority. States that, upon finishing a job, a "jackleg carpenter" says, "Well, there it is, by God—it ain't much, but it'll hold until we can think of something better." Argues, "Truly authoritative discourse should always [. . .] be in process."

Corder, Jim W. "Academic Jargon and Soul-Searching Drivel." *Rhetoric Review* 9 (Spring 1991): 314–26.

Maintains that scholars should surmount their disdain for personal writing and blend the personal with the academic. Both personal and academic writing "ought to be part of our knowledge and practice" in English studies. Includes two of his own first-person narrative essays.

———. "Against a Mournful Wind." *New Mexico Humanities Review* 4 (Spring 1981): 13–17.

Bemoans the decline in English enrollments and other signs of problems in education. Ends hopefully. Declares, "[. . .] creation is too rich and varied and copious to be comprehended by a single vision." A lyrical essay.

———. "Another Geography Course?" *Perspectives* 19 (1989): 1–7.

Relates a proposal for a course that would explore "landscape and place in the arts" and connect "personal and family movements and dislocations against tribal movements and dislocations." Students would investigate the "ache for home" and "topophilia."

———. "Asking for a Text and Trying to Learn It." *Encountering Student Texts*. Ed. Bruce Lawson, Susan Sterr Ryan, and W. Ross Winterowd. Urbana, IL: NCTE, 1989. 89–98.

Argues for the complexity of students' texts: "I think there is a text that each wanted to write. I think there is a text that each thought he or she wrote. I think there is a text that each did write and turn in. That's three, but not all." Claims more than six "permutations" of each student text. Notes difficulties with grading.

———. "At Last Report I Was Still Here." *The Subject Is Writing: Essays by Teachers and Students*. Ed. Wendy Bishop. Portsmouth, NH: Boynton/Cook, 1993. 261–65.

Wrestles with theories of poststructuralism and reader response. Using the metaphor of a courtroom, concludes that a pragmatic definition of selfhood survives deconstruction. Announces, "If I slander someone in what I write, interpreting readers won't go with me to court and sit beside me as co-defendants. I'll be alone, and I'll be held accountable."

———. "Caught in the Middle." *Liberal Education* 68 (Spring 1982): 69–74.

Argues that college administrators need to view themselves as teachers. Notes that, like their supervisors, faculty can advocate narrow and "reductionist" views that favor their own specific disciplines above all others.

———. *Chronicle of a Small Town.* College Station: Texas A&M UP, 1989.

The narrator, an aging professor, reviews his memory and identity by consulting issues of a local newspaper published during his childhood in West Texas. Discovers that some events happened before or after he recalled them or not at all. The newspaper had headlined other stories that he had entirely forgotten. While memory is basic to selfhood, it is also untrustworthy and problematic.

———. "Collaboration and Autonomy, Owning and Sharecropping." *Freshman English News* 19 (Spring 1991): 11–12.

Interrogates theories of collaborative writing and intertextuality. Observes, ". . . when we write, we're always with someone and alone." Continues, "Today I may be able to manage beautifully by myself, but tomorrow I may need your help."

———. "Corder's Dialogues." *Rhetoric Society Quarterly* 15 (1985): 119–30.

A West Texas version of Platonic dialogue. Offers an indirect, humorous account of why certain people attempt censorship. Observes ways that an ideology can create resistance against another's rhetoric.

———. "Efficient Ethos in *Shane.*" *Communication Quarterly* 25 (Fall 1977): 28–31.

Theorizes a version of *ethos* exemplified by a gunfighter in Jack Schaefer's *Shane,* a novel set in the American West. This figure "is a master of his world" but "is fenced off from the new world." His ethos is "self-completing" but "not self-renewing." Corder returns to this topic in "Varieties of Ethical Argument."

———. "Episodes in the Life of a West Texas Materialist." *New Mexico Humanities Review* 1 (Jan. 1978): 29–34.

A memoir of the Great Depression in West Texas. Tells about Corder's father pawning his watch while convincing his children that it was being repaired. An early expression of Corder's habit of self-correction, in that it recounts the false perceptions of his youth. Creative nonfiction.

————. "Ethical Argument and *Rambler* No. 154." *Quarterly Journal of Speech* 54 (1968): 352–56.

A rhetorical analysis. Argues that Samuel Johnson reverses his argument in the middle of *Rambler* No. 154. "Varieties of Ethical Argument," *Uses of Rhetoric*, and "Hoping for Essays" revisit this specific Johnson essay.

————. "Ethical Argument in Amos." *Cresset* 35 (Jan. 1972): 6–9.

Analyzes the speech of the Biblical prophet Amos, whose persuasiveness stems from his argument from *ethos*, not *logos* or *pathos*. Corder returns to this topic in "Varieties of Ethical Argument."

————. "Evidence that the World Exists." *Concho River Review* 1.2 (Fall 1987): 76.

Reflects on loss, symbolized by a windmill. A poem.

————. "From an Undisclosed Past into an Unknown Future." *Liberal Education* 68 (Spring 1982): 75–78.

Holds that, while professors' work is public and visible to university officials, much administrative work is opaque to the faculty. Prompts administrators to correct this problem by broadcasting their visions and methods through the resources of judicial, epideictic, and legislative rhetoric. Administrative work should include "research and publication before appropriate audiences."

————. "From Rhetoric into Other Studies." *Defining the New Rhetorics*. Ed. Theresa Enos and Stuart C. Brown. Newbury Park, CA: Sage, 1993. 95–108.

Maintains that rhetoric is an architectonic discipline that affords the study of "all forms of discourse." Proposes how rhetoric "might organize literary study, curriculum design, course design, geography, cultural history, and psychoanalytic study." Asserts that "[. . .] any curriculum is a rhetoric."

———. "From Rhetoric to Grace: Propositions 55–81 about Rhetoric, Propositions 1–54 and 82 *et seq.* Being as Yet Unstated; or, Getting from the Classroom to the World." *Rhetoric Society Quarterly* 14 (1984): 15–28.

Highlights the sometimes invisible history that underlies every statement and probes the complexities in pinpointing the reasons for success or failure in communication. Emphasizes the ever-shifting elements of language use, declaring, "Process, not ripeness, is all." Finds that "reaching toward grace" is possible. Like "Argument as Emergence," uses terms of traditional Christianity to undergird an existentialist ethic of communication.

———. "Going Home." *New Mexico Humanities Review* 5 (Summer 1982): 25–33.

Nostalgically contemplates boyhood in dust-caked West Texas. Testifies, "[. . .] I still think God lives on top of the Double Mountains." But acknowledges that that region "was never Eden."

———. "Gulliver in England." *College English* 23 (Oct. 1961): 98–103.

Relates elements in Jonathan Swift's novelistic fantasy *Gulliver's Travels* to events in England during Swift's lifetime.

———. "The Heroes Have Gone from the Grocery Store." *Arete: The Journal of Sports Literature* 5 (1987): 73–78.

Recounts images that appeared on boxes of Wheaties during the narrator's childhood. Relates correspondence with an archivist at General Mills, who replied that such images never adorned Wheaties boxes. Laments, "Apparently, the box I remembered never existed." Reflects on the inaccuracy of memory and the evaporation of sports icons.

———. "Hoping for Essays." *Literary Nonfiction: Theory, Criticism, Pedagogy.* Ed. Chris Anderson. Carbondale: Southern Illinois UP, 1989. 301–14.

Claims that distinctions between creative nonfiction and scholarly prose are dubious. Attacks standard "freshman essay" assignments as pointless. Relates experience of joining first-year students in writing essays to satisfy the assignments that he—the teacher-narrator—gives them.

———. "Humanism Isn't a Dirty Word." In "Voice as Echo of Delivery, Ethos as Transforming Process," by Theresa Enos. *Composition in Context: Essays in Honor of Donald C. Stewart*. Ed. W. Ross Winterowd and Vincent Gillespie. Carbondale: Southern Illinois UP, 1994. 190–92.

Answers attacks on humanism by Christian fundamentalists.

———. *Hunting Lieutenant Chadbourne*. Athens: U of Georgia P, 1993.

Examines the Mexican War in an unorthodox manner that might be called either postmodern or post-postmodern. Largely ignoring such famous figures as Zachary Taylor and Ulysses Grant, the self-correcting narrator provides a thorough and sympathetic biography of an unprepossessing lieutenant who died in 1846, at age 23. The narrator balances his avid curiosity about Lt. Chadbourne against his growing awareness of the ineluctable murkiness of historiography.

———. "I Can't Get Away from Hoppy." *New Mexico Humanities Review* 33 (1990): 107–13.

Narrates images of cowboy masculinity promoted by American popular culture during the Great Depression.

———. "I'll Trade You One Meditation, a Contrary View, and Some Commas for an Electric Coffee Pot and a Video Display Terminal: Or, Some Notes on the Humanities and Technology." *Nebraska Humanist* 3 (Spring–Fall 1981): 29–35.

Offers humorous commentary on the role of technology in the humanities.

———. "Jim W. Corder's Teacakes." *Stirring Prose: Cooking with Texas Authors*. College Station: Texas A&M UP, 1998. 56–58.

Describes his experiments to reproduce, from scratch, teacakes that his mother made.

———. "Learning the Text: Little Notes about Interpretation, Harold Bloom, the *Topoi*, and the *Oratio*." *College English* 48 (Mar. 1986): 243–48.

Explains *topoi* not simply as elements in written texts, but as "places in the mind"—ways the brain conceives and remembers. Declares,

"Invention is not simply a term in a text book; it is a name for some of the living we do." Argues that *narratio* is basic to speech and defines *oratio* as "drama," "sermon," and "dance."

—. "Lessons Learned, Lessons Lost." *Georgia Review* 46 (Spring 1992): 15–28.

Recounts bittersweet memories of childhood. Recalls excitement upon listening to the Lux Theater and other radio dramas and when watching movies that glorified the heroics of British and American fighters during World War II. Explains his later disillusionment upon discovering that British planes had deliberately bombed many civilians in Germany. Ironically remarks, "I didn't make it as far as gallantry."

—. "Losing Out." *Diversity: A Journal of Multicultural Issues* 1 (1993): 97–100.

A reflection on the poststructuralist "death" of the author. Alternately hopeful and melancholy. Asserts, "We all disappear"; then remarks, "We leave tracks." A lyrical essay, gentle sermon, or prose poem.

—. *Lost in West Texas*. College Station: Texas A&M UP, 1988.

Describes a working-class boy's experiences during the economic collapse of the 1930s. A vivid, first-person account of deprivation occasioned by severe poverty. Could be viewed as a prelude to *Chronicle of a Small Town*.

—. "Mickey Mantle, August 10, 1995." *Aethlon* 12 (Spring 1995): 44.

Records death of the baseball great, while acknowledging Mantle's moral failures. An elegiac poem.

—. "Ministry to Mavericks." *New Mexico Humanities Review* 6 (1983): 69–76.

Hails intellectual nonconformity through the Texas metaphor of the maverick. States, "I put uncommon hope in the maverick strain," which "will save us, if we cherish it." Originally a speech given to members of Phi Beta Kappa at TCU.

———. *More than a Century*. Fort Worth: Texas Christian UP, 1973.

Celebrates the one hundredth anniversary of Texas Christian University. Interspersed with photographs by Michael Chesser and Linda Kaye is Corder's unorthodox, meandering essay about the beginnings of a tiny university in sparsely settled, central Texas (where a village named Granbury was "learning" to be a town) and its contemporary incarnation in urban Fort Worth.

———. "Notes on a Rhetoric of Regret." *Composition Studies/Freshman English News* 23 (1995): 94–105.

Weighs the need to narrate the self versus the postmodern conviction that the narrator disappears in her text. All people, including writers, are "still here" but are "drifting into oblivion"; humans are "potentially noble" but "permanently errant."

———. "Occasion and Need in Writing: An Annotated Essay." *Freshman English News* 17 (1988): 3–4, 10.

Explains that students prodded the teacher-narrator to write an essay about "their favorite dull subject," a Cheerio. Includes this putatively serious, actually whimsical essay, while claiming to write by "vamping" and "ooching"—techniques that composition textbooks somehow fail to mention. Calls for essays that are "personal" or "exploratory," rather than thesis-driven.

———. "On Argument, What Some Call 'Self-Writing,' and Trying to See the Back Side of One's Own Eyeballs." *Rhetoric Review* 22 (Spring 2003): 31–39.

Claims that writing, in general, is personal and that narrative is important to argument. Notes that, although understanding the self can be excruciatingly difficult, good writing can involve "continual self-identification." Declares, "An orthodox academic paper, I judge, is only the last half or so of a personal essay."

———. "On Cancer and Freshman Composition, or the Use of Rhetorical Language in the Description of Oncogenetic Behavior." *CEA Critic* 45 (1982): 1–9.

Holds that the rhetorical canons of invention, structure, and style are useful in explaining the operation of not only the mind, but also the body. Claims that cancer results from "crossovers" and "mismatchings" of invention, structure, and style at the cellular level.

———. "On Keeping Posted and Being Nudged: Some Problems in the Continuing Education of Practicing Teachers." *English in Texas* 4 (Winter 1973): 32–34.

Relates the experience of designing a "splendid" series of summer workshops for English teachers, who, unfortunately, did not attend. Still, such workshops can be valuable.

———. "Outhouses, Weather Changes, and the Return to Basics in English Education." *College English* 38 (Jan. 1977): 474–82.

Reports childhood memories of outhouses. Cites shrieking proclamations in *Time* and *Newsweek* that inept teachers are producing a nation of illiterates. Notes journalists' proposed remedy—a nostalgic "return to the basics"—but argues that that solution would be comparable to revisiting the time when people used outhouses and "when all value and culture were presumed to reside in the British Isles."

———. "A Proposal for a New Kind of Liberal Arts Core Curriculum, Conceptual, Not Canonical." *Perspectives* 16 (Winter 1986): 27–31.

Comments that "educational curricula are *always* in disarray." Advocates a curriculum both similar to and different from that proposed in *Uses of Rhetoric.*

———. "The Restoration Way of the World: A Study in Restoration Comedy." Diss. U of Oklahoma, 1958.

Argues that the best of Restoration comedy is neither too artificial nor too immoral, as some critics have alleged. Champions William Congreve's *The Way of the World* as one of the greatest comedies in the English language.

———. "Rhetorical Analysis of Writing." *Teaching Composition: Ten Bibliographical Essays.* Ed. Gary Tate. Fort Worth: Texas Christian UP, 1976. 223–40.

A bibliographic essay on what was, at the time, an emerging subfield of rhetoric/composition. Seeks to blur generic distinctions separating rhetorical from literary analysis. Announces, "I don't know what to exclude [from this essay] because I believe that *all* analysis of writing is rhetorical." But proceeds by noting works by such familiar names in CCCC as James Kinneavy, Edward P. J. Corbett, W. Ross Winterowd, Frank D'Angelo, Richard Larson, and S. Michael Halloran, among others.

———. "Rhetoric and Literary Study." *College Composition and Communication* 32 (Feb. 1981): 13–20.

Protests that critics treat literary texts as "secrets, as holy tablets, the understanding of which is given only to a few priests, who explicate the sacred texts for each other." Argues that literary study should be treated as a subset of rhetorical study. Rhetoric can and should organize an English curriculum.

———. "Rhetoric and Meaning in *Religio Laici*." *PMLA* 82 (May 1967): 245–49. Rpt. in *Rhetorical Analyses of Literary Works*. Ed. Edward P. J. Corbett. New York: Oxford UP, 1969. 73–85.

Rhetorical analysis of a long poem by John Dryden. Explains its structure as a six-part Ciceronian oration—*exordium, narratio, partitio, confirmatio, confutatio,* and *peroratio.* One of Corder's most conventional and impersonal scholarly essays.

———. "Rhetoric and the Structure of the Field of English." *English in Texas* 18 (Winter 1987): 4–7.

Responds to a controversial address at CCCC by Maxine Hairston, chair of the organization. Blasts conservative literary critics. Originally a talk given at CCCC.

———. "The Rock-Kicking Championship of the Whole World, Now and Forevermore." *Arete: The Journal of Sports Literature* 4 (Spring 1987): 1–6.

Wryly elucidates the "sport" of rock-kicking, whose noble history he pretends to elucidate. Spoofs scholarly style by citing Biblical texts to "prove" the longevity and importance of rock-kicking. Gently and self-deprecatingly mocks the reverence for football in American popular culture.

———. "Some of What I Learned at a Rhetoric Conference." *Freshman English News* 15 (Spring 1986): 11–12.

Observes the inventive, structural, and stylistic resources of a bartender who "balanced the interplays of customers, constituents, ingredients, and needs, always moving, [. . .] making drinks, filling orders, chatting a moment, greeting someone, restocking constantly" as he "composed" the bar. Makes an analogy between bartender's abilities and those needed by first-year student writers.

————. "Some Things Change, and Some Things Don't." *New Mexico Humanities Review* 7 (Summer 1984): 19–21.

> Narrates the funeral of his uncle, a taciturn cement mixer who was buried in Jayton, Texas. Claims that the cemetery there "must be the loneliest place on earth."

————. "A Speech about Comanches and Miracles Made to Premedical Students, Who Are Not as Scary as Doctors." *Perspectives in Biology and Medicine* (Winter 1981): 189–94.

> Asks medical students to reconceive the inventive and rhetorical practices of physicians. Patients must be treated as human beings, not simply as sets of body parts. Predicts changes in medical practices and asks students to develop the flexibility needed to adapt.

————. "Stalking the Wild Grade Inflator." *Liberal Education* 69 (1983): 173–77.

> Maintains that, while sometimes illusory and exaggerated, grade inflation does exist. Asserts, "Grades have always been arbitrary" and declares that the inability to accurately measure students' knowledge may underlie certain professors' reluctance to give low grades.

————. "The Time the Cavalry Didn't Come, or the Quest for a Saving Authority in Recent Studies of Higher Education." *Liberal Education* 71 (1985): 305–19.

> Reviews Ernest Boyer's and others' assessment of university education as a failing system. Criticizes Boyer and his allies for assuming that professors can and should agree on what students will learn. Claims, "There is no frame of reference that is self-guaranteeing" and maintains, "[. . .] knowledge is social and indeterminate."

————. "Traditional Lectures Still Have a Place in the Classroom." *Chronicle of Higher Education* 12 June 1991: B2.

> Holds that other approaches have not entirely superseded lectures, especially when those lectures are delivered by enthusiastic and knowledgeable professors whose ability to communicate outstrips any tendency to overspecialize.

————. "Tribal Virtues." *Liberal Education* 69 (Summer 1983): 179–82.

> Notes that academic departments can be "uncommunicative" and "sometimes warlike," each intent on "celebrating its own tribal

virtues." Departmental loyalties can be so intense that they put administrators in the unenviable position of refereeing fractious disputes. But faculty can learn to value other disciplinary perspectives.

———. "Tribes and Displaced Persons: Some Observations on Collaboration." *Theory and Practice in the Teaching of Writing: Rethinking the Discipline.* Ed. Lee Odell. Carbondale: Southern Illinois UP, 1993. 271–88.

Reflects on the seemingly instant and pervasive popularity of collaboration as a form of writing pedagogy. Claims that, although coauthorship can be valuable, the ideology of collaboration has become so widespread as to constitute a kind of "pedagogical monism" and "tribal rhetoric." Hails the "privatized individual" as "the only hope for a continuing critique of the tribe."

———. "Turnings." *Teaching Composition in the Nineties: Sites of Contention.* Ed. Christina Russell and Robert MacDonald. New York: Harper, 1994. 105–17.

Meditates on English classrooms and the "disappearing," postmodernist self. A lyrical essay or prose poem.

———. "The Tyranny of Inattention." *Journal of Higher Education* 64 (Sept./Oct. 1993): 594–99.

Examines the lack of recognition for certain university faculty and administrators. Observes that, while sound governance is sometimes invisible, less-heralded employees generally deserve more attention and less anonymity.

———. *Uses of Rhetoric.* New York: Lippincott, 1971.

Decries 1960s cultural radicalism and offers a neo-Augustinian polemic against youthful egotism. Reverses this conservative direction by advocating visionary proposals for rhetoric as the conceptual basis for all English courses and, for that matter, the entire university curriculum. Heralds today's interest in cultural studies by combining an analysis of eighteenth-century British poetry, contemporary magazine advertisements, and television shows—perhaps the first of such analyses ever published by anyone regularly active in CCCC.

———. "What Lies at the Center." *Contemporary Education* 53 (Summer 1982): 213–16.

Meditates on *ethos*. Relates account of his daughter's playing the violin and becoming a woman.

———. "What to Do with Leftovers." *Bulletin of American Association for Higher Education* 38 (Mar. 1985): 9–12.

Discusses the intellectual and emotional adjustments of academics who move from administrative posts back to the classroom.

———. "When (Do I/Shall I/May I/Must I/Is It Appropriate for Me to) (Say No to/Deny/Resist/Repudiate/Attack/Alter) Any (Poem/Poet/Other/Piece of the World) for My Sake?" *Rhetoric Society Quarterly* 18 (1988): 49–68.

An exploration of the ethics and rhetoric of literary criticism (specifically, the criticism of contemporary poetry). Juxtaposes philosophical antinomies, specifically the need to value the self and the need to transcend self-interest. Notices that criticism of others may violate or displace them. Says, "I want to know how to declare without hurt, how to say No without hurt, without rage, without territoriality, how to hear No said to me without loss of myself." Contends that both self-assertion and self-effacement are often problematic.

———. "Why Deans, Chairmen, and Other Rascals Sometimes Seem (and Maybe Are) Uncreative." *Bulletin of American Association for Higher Education* 39 (Oct. 1986): 8–9.

Half seriously, half playfully examines institutional inertia. Causes include administrators' "Brush Fire Syndrome Activities (BFSA)," which trigger inattention, which in turn promotes "Squelches (Sq)." Frustrated pioneers can develop a "Squelch Factor Tolerance Level (SFTL)" and stop attempting to innovate, which can lead administrators and universities either to seem or to be uncreative.

———. "World War II on Cleckler Street." *Collective Heart: Texans in World War II*. Ed. Joyce Gibson Roach. Austin: Eakin, 1996.

Describes life as a boy in Fort Worth during the early 1940s, especially exposure to comic books, *Life* magazine, *Time* magazine, and Hollywood movies—all of which lionized the exploits of soldiers and pilots during the war. Reports disillusionment upon learning that "heroic" British pilots had intentionally bombed German cities, killing many civilians. Questions the warrior model of masculinity.

———. *Yonder: Life on the Far Side of Change*. Athens: U of Georgia P, 1992.

Confesses unhappiness after returning to the university following personal disasters and psychiatric treatment for severe depression. A nonlinear, but tightly written postmodern or post-postmodern lamentation that plays off apt lines from lesser-known, contemporary American poets.

———. "You Operationalize—I'll Plug Away." *Liberal Education* 66 (Winter 1980): 440–45.

Questions the structures and procedures of administrative authority. Argues that planning in higher education is often reductive because administrators choose to "operationalize" without pausing to reflect on possible outcomes. Decision makers should allow for "a cumulative history of shared thoughts [. . .] where a variety of critical perspectives make it more likely for error to be detected."

Corder, Jim W., ed. *Shakespeare 1964*. Fort Worth: Texas Christian UP, 1965.

Anthologizes a set of scholarly essays about Shakespeare.

Corder, Jim W., and James S. Baumlin. "Lamentations for—and Hopes against—Authority in Education." *Educational Theory* 38 (Winter 1988): 11–26.

Criticizes those who yearn for lost authority and bemoan an alleged loss of coherence, purpose, and unifying principle in higher education. Claims that truth is never "static" or "permanent." Invites readers to rejoice at being "provisional self-makers, provisional world-makers."

———. "Lonesomeness in English Studies." *ADE Bulletin* 85 (Winter 1986): 36–39.

Bemoans the failure of literary theorists and rhetoric/composition specialists to read and cite each other's work. Asks, "Has Paul de Man met James Kinneavy or James Moffett?" Notes that current scholars too often overlook relevant older research.

———. "Opinion Is, of Course, Bad; Research, on the Other Hand, Is Quite Good: The Tyranny(or Is It Myth?) of Methodology." *Journal of Higher Education* 58 (July/Aug. 1987): 463–69.

Observes that the pervasive quest for sound methodology in the humanities is an attempt to replace opinion with certainty. Argues that this effort cannot possibly succeed because the conclusions stemming from any methodology remain, necessarily, tentative and subjective.

Tade, George, Gary Tate, and Jim W. Corder. "For Sale, Lease, or Rent: A Curriculum for an Undergraduate Program in Rhetoric." *College Composition and Communication* 26 (Feb. 1975): 20–24.

Introduces a visionary proposal for an undergraduate major in rhetoric, a proposal that the narrator states was rejected by administrators at TCU. This conception continues to challenge the profession inasmuch as very few universities have ever implemented such a program.

Textbooks (Listed Chronologically)

Corder, Jim W., and Lyle Kendall. *A College Rhetoric*. 1st ed. New York: Random House, 1962. 5th printing, 1966.

Offers current-traditional discussion of diction, sentence style, paragraph style, organization, exposition, and argumentation. Further chapters treat description, narration, and research. Ends with a handbook section. In 1993, referring to one of his collaboratively authored textbooks—probably this one—Corder's autobiographical narrator observed, "I'd rather not ever see it again" ("Tribes" 273).

Corder, Jim W. *Rhetoric: A Text-Reader on Language and Its Uses*. New York: Random House, 1965.

Interlards canonical and contemporary literary works with student essays. Organizes selections into chapters that highlight traditional rhetorical concerns. Includes selections from John Graves's *Goodbye to a River*, a book about rural Texas that Corder favored.

Perrin, Porter, and Jim W. Corder. *Handbook of Current English*. 3rd ed. Glenview, IL: Scott, Foresman. 1968. 4th ed., 1975.

Corder joined Perrin in producing the third edition of this popular, albeit traditional reference. Includes predictable chapters on mechanics and usage, plus others on revision and research writing. (Perrin's first coauthor was George H. Smith.)

Corder, Jim W., ed. *Finding a Voice*. Glenview, IL: Scott, Foresman, 1973.

Collects a large number of canonical and contemporary texts. Among predictable essays and excerpts are less frequently collected works, such as a wonderful letter from Beethoven; a superb selection from John Graves's *Goodbye to a River*; and Robert Heinlein's beautiful short story, "The Green Hills of Earth." Also includes important works by such stellar emerging writers as Marge Piercy, Adrienne Rich, and Joan Didion.

Corder, Jim W. *Handbook of Current English*. 5th ed. Glenview, IL: Scott, Foresman, 1978. 6th ed., 1981.

Evolves into its fifth and sixth editions with Corder as sole author. A comparable work is the second half of Edward P. J. Corbett's *Little Rhetoric and Handbook*. Glenview, IL: Scott, Foresman, 1977. 2nd ed. 1981.

Corder, Jim W. *Contemporary Writing: Process and Practice*. Glenview, IL: Scott, Foresman, 1979. 2nd ed., 1982.

Presents state-of-the-art instruction at a time when the phrase "Teach the process, not the product!" was the prevailing mantra at CCCC. Devotes the first five chapters to invention and audience before explaining the need to develop a thesis. A comparable textbook is W. Ross Winterowd's *Contemporary Writer*. New York: Harcourt, 1975. 2nd ed., 1981.

Corder, Jim W., and John Ruszkiewicz. *Handbook of Current English*. 7th ed. Glenview, IL: Scott, Foresman, 1985. 8th ed., 1989.

Features chapters on invention and revision that did not appear previously. Greatly enlarged and updated.

INDEX

EDITORS

James S. Baumlin is professor of English at Southwest Missouri State University, where he teaches the history of rhetoric, critical theory, and seventeenth-century English poetry. His recent publications include *Rhetoric and Kairos: Essays in History, Theory, and Praxis* (2002), which he coedited with Phillip Sipiora, and *Post-Jungian Criticism: Theory and Practice* (2004), which he coedited with Tita French Baumlin and George H. Jensen.

Keith D. Miller is professor of English and former writing programs administrator at Arizona State University. He is the author of *Voice of Deliverance: The Language of Martin Luther King, Jr., and Its Sources* (1992, 1998). His essays about the rhetoric of King and the civil rights era have appeared in *PMLA, College English, College Composition and Communication, Rhetoric Society Quarterly, Journal of American History,* and numerous scholarly collections. With Theresa Enos, he recently coedited *Beyond Postprocess and Postmodernism: The Spaciousness of Rhetoric* (2003).

This book was typeset in Sabon by Electronic Imaging.
The typefaces used on the cover were Bank Gothic, EnviroD Regular,
and Slimbach.
The book was printed on 50-lb. Accent Opaque Offset paper
by Versa Press.